Globalization

Globalization

A Financial Approach

Nicholas V. Gianaris

PRAEGER
Westport, Connecticut

Library of Congress Cataloging-in-Publication Data

Gianaris, Nicholas V.
    Globalization : a financial approach / Nicholas V. Gianaris
      p. cm.
    Includes bibliographical references and index.
    ISBN 0-275-97076-0 (alk. paper)
      1. International finance. 2. International economic relations. 3. Competi-
tion, International. I. Title.

HG3881 .G487 2001
332′.042—dc21   00-032384

British Library Cataloguing in Publication Data is available.

Library of Congress Catalog Card Number: 00-032384
ISBN: 0-275-97076-0

First published in 2001

Praeger Publishers, 88 Post Road West, Westport, CT 06881
An imprint of Greenwood Publishing Group, Inc.
www.praeger.com

Printed in the United States of America

The paper used in this book complies with the
Permanent Paper Standard issued by the National
Information Standards Organization (Z39.48–1984).

10 9 8 7 6 5 4 3 2 1

To my grandson
Alexander Vasilis Gianaris

Contents

Tables and Figures

TABLES

FIGURES

Preface

The global economy is undergoing dramatic financial changes. The removal of technical, trade, and monetary barriers and the liberalization of the world economies, including those of the transitional economies and emerging nations, create challenges and opportunities from the standpoint of investment and financial transactions.

The privatization of state-owned enterprises and the development of shareholder capitalism acquired great importance in the recent past and constitute a *nova terra* that needs further exploration and research. Private ownership, through titles or stocks, stimulates work incentives and increases productivity, whereas common ownership means common neglect, as Aristotle had predicted some twenty-five centuries ago.

With the drastic reforms in emerging and other nations, the deregulations in industrial countries, the globalization of business, and the growing number of shareholders worldwide, international finance is expected to play a vital role in matters of foreign exchange, cross-border capital flows, joint ventures, and economic growth. Nevertheless, rapid improvement in telecommunications and electronic capital transfers may lead to tremors and remorse in financial markets and make the global economy vulnerable to savage speculation, investors' panic, and economic fluctuations.

This book weaves together a theoretical framework of international finance supported by the latest empirical research and related applications. It provides a comprehensive analysis of traditional and modern theories of international monetary systems, problems of balance of payments, and exchange rates, as well as related adjustment and stabilization policies for industrialized and emerging nations. In addition to a brief historical review, the book deals with advanced theories of international trade and finance, as well as the related real world performance. It examines the strengths and weaknesses of fixed and floating exchange rates, forward exchanges, the spreading of global shareholder capitalism, the problems of emerging markets, the international capital movements and banking activities, market capitalization, and foreign debt, as well as investment movements and cross-border mergers and acquisitions, economic and financial integration, related effects of macroeconomic policies in open economies, and problems of global income inequalities.

From that standpoint, the book is of great theoretical and practical importance to students, scholars, and business leaders with a broad range of interest in international finance and development. The book is also useful to people interested in the growing number of jobs in the field, particularly the young urban professionals. It can be used as a textbook in "International Finance" and as a supplement in "International Economics" and "Economics of Emerging Nations."

Acknowledgments

I want to acknowledge my indebtedness to many professors and former students who provided comments in my previous related publications on regional and global economics, particularly Professors Milica Zarkovic Bookman of Saint John's University in Philadelphia, John Burgess of the University of Newcastle in Australia, George M. Korres of the University of Crete, Pieter W. Moerland of Tilburg University in Netherlands, and G. T. Potter, emeritus, of Ramapo College of New Jersey. I am also grateful to Professors Rocco Andriola, Janis Barry-Figueroa, Ernest Block, Vasilis Bouras, Clive Daniel, Kostas Papoulias, John Roche, Dominick Salvatore, and Shapoor Vali, as well as to financial and legal experts Bill Gianaris, Michael Gianaris, John Giapoutzis, Theresia Kinczier, Susan Kleine, and John Tsapardonis for their stimulating comments. My final debt goes to Laurie Bath, Henry Bryan, Pauline Cusack, Johanna Garcia, Dimitris Karatsis, John Keysor, David Lewis, Maribel Montijo, Anna Meresidis, Catherine O'Connor, Dino Pofanti, Matthew Rawlings, Ricardo S. Vilchez, and Yan Yanovskiy for computer work, copying, and other technical services.

Finally, I welcome comments and criticism from users and readers of the book for further improvement and adjustment to the rapidly evolving field of global finance.

Introduction

GLOBALIZATION OF MARKETS

Growth in foreign trade and primarily rapidly expanding global financial activities have increased dramatically cross-border capital flows and led to closer integration of financial markets around the world. From that standpoint, international finance binds together domestic and global financial transactions in an efficient and competitive way.

Deregulation, privatization, and liberalization in almost all the economies increased the number of foreign banks and brokerage firms, stimulated foreign ownership, and increased the volume of foreign investment significantly. Global computer linkages, the use of the Internet and other innovative financial instruments, such as future contracts, foreign exchange swaps, bonds, and other derivatives, are vital to global financial operations.

Globalization of financial and trade markets is a source of economic growth and prosperity, but it may lead to a growing gap between the incomes of rich and poor nations and the deterioration of the environment. The dramatic growth of international transactions and the rapid capital flows worldwide provide opportunities and risks for direct and portfolio investments, thereby affecting the development and growth of nations, primarily emerging nations.

International trade and finance, which promote specialization, productivity, and living standards for all countries, is one of the biggest industries today, and markets for the exchanges of currencies must exist to facilitate such international transactions. Billions of dollars, euros, yen, and other currencies move instantly between international markets via electronic trading. Production and exchanges in a borderless world present challenges and opportunities for regional and global financial markets.

With the easing of monetary and other restrictions in almost all countries, the capital markets became, to a large extent, global. The internationalization of equity portfolios in the United States and other countries increased the number of investors all over the world. For example, more than 50 million retail investors and about 10,000 institutions in the United States are important constituent groups of the New York Stock Exchange (NYSE), which went through a one-time ownership of non-U.S. equities.

Investors can now invest in a growing number of countries around the globe. At the same time, many enterprises are using equity finance for raising capital, instead of resorting to debt or other expensive measures. More than 300 companies from some fifty countries trade their shares in the NYSE, which are worth about 10 percent of the $11 trillion market value of U.S. equities. Similar trends can be observed in European and other countries.[1]

All over the world, stock markets are going up rapidly, achieving one record after another. For example, in five years (December 1994 to December 1999), the Dow Jones industrials index of the United States (11,383 on December 17, 1999) was up by 205 percent, the Standard and Poor's 500 stock index (1,433) was up by 219 percent, and the technology-heavy Nasdaq composite index (3,753) was up as much as 422 percent, whereas the dramatic changing of directions continues. In the last 25 years, the Dow increased in value 1,727 percent, whereas the Nasdaq increased by 6,174 percent. If the Dow had increased as much as the Nasdaq, it would be around 39,000. On July 8, 1932, the index of the Dow was 41.22; that of the Standard and Poor's 500 Composite was 4.40 on June 1, 1932. More or less the same phenomenon can be observed in other stock markets, during the year 1999, mainly in emerging markets. Thus, in percentages, the Athens Stock Exchange of Greece went up (in dollar terms) by 96 percent, the Bolsa stock index of Mexico 86, the Korea Composite 80, the Bovespa of Brazil 46, the Nikkei of Japan 44, the JSE Industrials of South America 32, the TSE 300 of Canada 30, the Merval index of Argentina 28, the CAC 40 of France 21, the All-Ord of Australia 17, whereas both indexes, the FTSE 100 of Britain and the DAXI of Germany, each went up by 10 percent.[2]

Although stock and bond markets swing and threaten to spread global financial crises, investment banks continue to underwrite new stocks and bonds around the world, reaching about $2 trillion a year. Merrill Lynch & Company; Morgan Stanley Dean Witter & Company;

and Goldman, Sachs & Company dominate the world markets in advice on initial public offerings (IPOs) and other financial transactions, as well as on merger and acquisition (M & A) deals valued at more than $2.5 trillion a year worldwide.

The privatization of state enterprises around the world increased the supply of equity, dramatically. Governments sell assets, worth many billions of dollars every year, by issuing equity. The capitalization of the world's publicly traded equity is more than $20 trillion, compared to $10 trillion in 1990. Large budget deficits, limited internal funds, and the reluctance of banks to accept big credit risks increased equity financing, particularly in emerging nations.[3]

In our computer age, traders and financiers from many countries can share data and exchange information on overseas markets and statistics with flexibility, creativity, and bottom-line advantages. Despite stiff competition in the expanding world markets, many American and other small and large businesses have carved a niche for quality products and sophisticated financial services, thereby creating additional employment and stimulating economic growth. As Aristotle and Thucydides (fifth century B.C.) as well as Adam Smith (1776) and other classical economists advocated, self-interest is always the spirit in such activities.

The connection of the Internet around the world brings together businesses and people with knowledge and information and promotes financial globalization. Countries with advanced networks and bandwidth would tap and use advanced knowledge so that they would be able to compete effectively and invest efficiently. Because the markets become too big and complex, it is difficult to survive without going global and without partners. In this Internet global revolution, similar to the Industrial Revolution but with an incredible pace, countries with innovative prowess and dynamic capitalism would score high on financial and economic performance. Nevertheless, technology is a relentless force that changes economic conditions rapidly to the degree that Schumpeter's description of capitalism as being evolved in a process of "creative destruction" might be apt. Higher efficiency and lower prices lead to consolidation and monopolization. More consolidations and changes take place almost every day, and more are expected to follow, particularly with the use of the Internet, which breaks established rules for almost everything.

The economic conditions of each nation are related to the economies of other nations by complex flows of goods, investments, technologies, and enterprises. Moreover, each nation has its own currency, and international transactions are complicated with the use of multiple currencies. From that standpoint, a price of each currency in terms of other currencies should be determined.

FINANCIAL AND OTHER REFORMS IN EMERGING MARKETS

Reform programs in the emerging markets of developing nations, former communist countries, and even present communist countries continue to advance and try to adjust to economic and financial globalization. Communist China, with a population of 1.3 billion and remarkable success recently, is gradually opening its economy to the free market mechanism. In parts of Africa, Asia, and Latin America enormous disparities in income hinder progress and threaten stability, whereas financial markets are primitive, although serious efforts for improvement are made currently.

The recent agreement of the United States with China will help open the huge Chinese markets to foreign trade and investment, mainly in telecommunications, Internet businesses, banking, cars, and other products and services. Moreover, the expected entrance of China to the World Trade Organization (WTO), with 135 member countries, will expand further international transactions.

All over the world, free markets are replacing bureaucrats and government controls, encouraging foreign investment and globalization. This trend can be observed not only in all the republics of the former Soviet Union and the Eastern European countries but also in the Latin American and other emerging nations. International institutions, such as the International Monetary Fund (IMF) and the World Bank, offer loans and advice to member nations facing debt and poverty problems. However, stringent economic reforms are sometimes required by these institutions, which may lead to high unemployment and even social unrest.

In the former Soviet bloc countries, mainly in Eastern Europe and Russia, the new economic reforms aim at the accession to the European Union (EU) in order to improve their foreign trade and their financial systems. However, difficult conditions exist for the old and the unemployed as a result of the transition from command to market economies, and financial and technological assistance is needed to uplift these emerging nations.[4]

Overoptimism for economic performance and overspeculation in the stock markets around the world may be responsible for the economic crisis in recent times. In spite of the repeated assurances of many government officials and financial gurus, the world economy may be in trouble, as it was in the late 1920s and thereafter when U.S. President Herbert Hoover was giving assurances, in vain, that economic conditions were sound. The Japanese depression, extravagance and corruption in other Asian countries, the Russian economic disaster, and the instability in Latin America, recently, have been painful, particularly for emerging nations. Stock markets may be engaged in "creative destruction," because of overoptimism and overspeculation. Nevertheless, global diversification and the growth of emerging and other markets are expected to continue, although with periodic fluctuations, thereby increasing equity ownership and supporting the theory of "global shareholder capitalism."

In a number of emerging nations, currency is overvalued, and their economies are in trouble. In such cases, wages and prices are rising, in terms of other hard currencies. This means that it is difficult for these countries to compete in international markets, as their exports become more expensive. Moreover, their imports become cheaper, and consumers are expected to prefer foreign, instead of domestic, products, thereby facing deterioration in their balance of trade and eventually accumulation of foreign debt. Furthermore, creditors, anticipating a devaluation, may take their money out of these countries, forcing interest rates to go up in order to stanch the outflow. In reality, though, high interest rates may not stop the outflow of money and instead crumble the economy, as happened with Russia and Brazil during the recent financial crisis.

In order to avoid further economic declines, countries with overvalued currencies should allow their currencies to weaken, in accordance with the differences in inflationary rates, and thereafter reduce interest rates to sustainable levels, so that austerity measures and high unemployment will be avoided. At the same time they should try to achieve an orderly rollover of short-term debt into long-term bonds, through agreements with their creditors and the help of the IMF and the World Bank, which, together with the World Trade Organization (WTO), support the spread of globalization.

EFFECTS OF MERGER TIDINGS

The tidings of mergers and acquisitions, domestically and globally, require financial arrangements, which lead to movements of large sums of dollars and other currencies around the world. Regardless of their bases, many companies operate in many countries and move huge amounts of capital, which affects prices, interest rates, exchange rates, and other economic variables. Although commercial and central banks are directly related to international finance, multinational firms, dealing with world trade and investment, play a crucial role in global financing, as they have to deal with foreign currencies and exchange rates. Such banks include the Bank of America with assets of about $6 trillion (including cross-border assets, fixed income, equities, and eurobonds), Chase Manhattan ($5.6 trillion assets), State Street ($5 trillion), Deutsche Bank ($4 trillion), Citibank ($3 trillion), and Mellon Trust ($2.2 trillion assets). Even domestic mergers have a global outlook.

For example, in the financial sector, Citicorp (with branches in more than 100 countries) merged with Travelers; and National Bank merged with BankAmerica. These banks and many other similar financial institutions, such as J. P. Morgan and Merrill Lynch, are seen as basically American firms but operate in many other countries and finance merger deals and other offshore activities. Moreover, Deutsche Bank, the largest bank of Germany, agreed to buy Bankers Trust, the seventh-largest American bank, after the approval of the regulators and the shareholders on both sides of the Atlantic, in order to move more aggressively into global investment banking. Also, Banc One was merged with First Chicago in a deal worth $30 billion.

Other recent merger deals include Time Warner with America Online ($165 billion); Exxon with Mobil, the two big oil firms ($86.4 billion); SBC Communications with Ameritech ($72.4 billion); Olivetti S.p.A., in competition with Deutsche Telekom, acquired Telecom Italia ($65 billion); AT&T with Tele-Communications Inc. ($55 billion); British Petroleum with Amoco Corporation ($48 billion); Daimler-Benz with Chrysler, two huge car companies ($39 billion); American Home Products with Monsanto ($34 billion); Norwest with Wells Fargo ($34 billion); and Berkshire Hathaway with General Re ($22 billion). Moreover, Vodafone Airtouch P.L.C., the largest mobile phone operator of Britain, plans to acquire Mannesmann A.G. of Germany for $127.7 billion; Warner-Lambert Company, a drug firm, plans a $72 billion merger with American Home Products Corporation, in competition with Pfizer Inc.; whereas Mitsui, Nippon, and Kea, with combined assets of $57.9 billion, plan to merge and form the biggest casualty insurer in Japan; the Monsanto Company, another drug firm, plans to merge with Pharmacia & Upjohn Inc., with a combined market value of around $52 billion; and the Royal Bank of Scotland made a $42.5 billion hostile bid for the National Westminster Bank of Britain. (More details for mergers and acquisitions are presented in later sections).

Free trade and growing financial services in the global economy are expected to improve the standard of living of the participant countries, through specialization and efficient investment allocation, increasing individual skills and encouraging economic growth and democracy. However, the global financial marketplace with its huge force is capable of influencing national policies and even overthrowing governments, and there is no system to control it. Huge flows of money can change direction electronically almost momentarily. Average global trading in financial instruments is around $1 trillion daily.

Global Regulations and Inequalities

As financial transactions become global, periodic crises may be more frequent and deeper, and the haunting memory of the Great Depression remains scary enough. Such crises may force rules and regulations to financial markets on a global scale. Regional volatility may rush foreign lenders out, thereby drying up credit and forcing more external debt.

Lenders and borrowers gamble, mainly on short-term loans, and operate with exuberance when markets are favorable and pull back in panic in cases of market decline. They easily swing from optimism to pessimism, leading to high market volatility. To avoid high speculation and market swings, some type of global guidelines and controls may be needed until the free market finds its own rules for self-discipline.

One way to discourage extensive and risky speculation is to increase reserve requirements for short-term lending. Also, in case of crisis, it is proper to require bondholders to postpone repayment. On the contrary, encouraging long-term productive investment, particularly in developing countries, would reduce unemployment, introduce new technology, and stimulate development.

In order to discourage short-term loans, Chile, for example, introduced a form of taxation on capital inflows, requiring foreign lenders to deposit a certain portion of each loan in an account that gives no interest.

Globalization leads to enrichment and rapid spread of information and the interdependence of human beings all over the world. National restrictions are gradually eliminated, and big corporations are free to move to any country to maximize profits. In this borderless and eventually stateless environment, a homogenous market, a common economic environment, "a global village" is formed. Independent nations are subordinated to big ones, and small enterprises are absorbed by large multinationals.

It seems that the free movement of commodities and capital favors high-income people, but not much low-income people with limited skills, who remain largely theatrical observers in the rapidly changing world, difficult to conceptualize and impossible to follow. Globalization is related more to the protection of big businesses than to the protection of human values. Governmental interventions refer more to the protection of foreign investment and less to the problems of income distribution. It is estimated that only about one fifth of the world population gets the benefits of globalization, and the rest remain in the margin, perpetuating or worsening economic and social inequalities. Ceteris paribus, when someone gains more than the real economic growth, it suggests that somebody else is losing an equivalent amount.

The electronic revolution and the Internet speed up globalization, but the Arcadian utopia of neoliberal theoreticians, like Frederick Von Hayek and Claus Svamp, creates a melting pot of cultural and other differences of the world. This may lead to personal isolation, mechani-

zation of life, elimination of critical thinking, stress, and other psychological problems.

Globalization, Pollution, and Productivity

Global investment and growth increase material wealth and help
eradicate poverty. However, as a result of the recent problems of pollution, resource depletion, and urbanization, some economists question
the desirability and possibility of continued growth. A stationary state
with zero growth, which John Stuart Mill supported more than a century ago and environmentalists suggest now, may be desirable; otherwise doomsday or the end of the world is inevitable, according to such
suggestions. However, it is difficult to ask starving people to give up
their aspirations to improve their economic conditions and remain at
their poverty levels forever. The solution lies in more growth, but
quality growth, that is, growth with environmental protection, resource
preservation, and urban improvement.

With increasing population, industrialization, and urbanization,
the dangers from pollution may become worse unless proper policies,
such as subsidies and tax credits on antipollution investment, in
addition to effluent charges based on cost-benefit analysis, are introduced. Air pollution, primarily in the form of carbon monoxide
produced by automobiles and factories, enters the blood and endan-
gers human health. Also, it is reducing the ozone in the atmosphere,
which protects the planet from ultraviolet sunrays. Industrial and
human waste pollute the surrounding areas of big cities. Such land
pollution breeds organisms that may spread diseases in the overpopulated slums. Large-scale recycling of wastes is technologically not
advanced enough and economically very expensive as of yet. Inadequate sewage in poor cities and industrial and human waste pollute
the waters of streams, rivers, lakes, and seas near industrial centers.
Oil spills and the rapidly growing mining of the seabed also contribute
to sea pollution, destroying marine life in many coastal areas. Noise
pollution at high decibel levels affects the normal functioning of the
nervous and auditory systems and irritates city dwellers. Globalization is rather intensifying such problems, although it helps increase
overall material production.

Class distinction, prejudice, and discrimination may retard economic
growth and social advancement. As a result of gender discrimination,
the economic and social position of women has been inferior in relation
to that of men, particularly in developing countries. However, globalization and economic development have given women great benefits.
Large percentages of women, even in poor countries, have gained
freedom from drudgery and household seclusion and can participate in

many occupations not available to them in the past. Instead of being regarded as beasts of burden, they are gradually gaining respectability and proper social status.

As globalization and development proceed, the gap between rich and poor widens not only between countries but between groups of the same countries. Empirical research reveals that in nonindustrial economies, with small subsistence farms and small factories, income inequality is not high. But in economies at low levels of development, where landlordism, surplus labor, and discrimination among cultural or ethnic groups prevail, economic growth policies increase the inequality of income distribution, mainly between the urban and the rural sectors as well as between skilled and unskilled persons. At high levels of development, growth policies promote income equality.[5]

Globalization and economic progress are associated with division of labor, specialization, mechanization of the production process, and the use of computers, which, in turn, lead to social isolation, nervousness, and psychological disturbances. However, measures to promote development and social welfare may lead to more government, extensive controls, and centralism, which may restrict individual liberties. Central governments, in turn, may use police tactics, bugging devices, and other demons, which modern technology (demonology) provides, to suppress individual freedoms.

GLOBAL INTERDEPENDENCE

In our days, the world economies become slowly but surely interdependent, although, at times, destabilizing factors may lead to turbulence in the form of exchange rate disturbances and financial instability. The main dilemma is how to use countercyclical monetary and fiscal policies to achieve economic stability with high employment and no inflation. The Keynesian economic theory and the dominant theory of monetarism seem to be unable to eliminate instability in trade and financial markets, which have experienced major changes in recent years. From that point of view, the transmission of economic crises across nations may create a volatile global financial environment.

It became obvious that without international cooperation, economic development on a national and global level will stagnate. On the other hand, export subsidies, import restrictions, and other unfair trade practices should be avoided so that fair factor payments and competitive costs prevail. Some of the benefits from unified global markets include healthier competition, professional and corporate mobility, economies of scale, high productivity, and better consumer choices. The transitional and emerging markets are expected to be of great importance to

foreign investment, trade, and finance, and they will affect the redistribution of power in the new millenium.

Global financial competition between the United States, Japan, and
the European Union (EU) is expected to increase, particularly after the
introduction of the euro by the twelve European nations and the expansion of the EU and the North American Free Trade Agreement (NAFTA)
to other countries.

The European Union and the Asian-Pacific Rim, with Japan the dominant economy, are formidable economic competitors of the United
States, selling products to the relatively open American economy, accu-
mulating trade surpluses that undermine the dominance of the United
States as the global largest economy. Nevertheless, they gradually accept greater responsibility and make their markets more open to international trade.

Many rich and poor countries await the outcome of important gestating
common markets, such as the European Union and the North American
Free Trade Agreement with the United States, Canada, and Mexico, as well
as the MERCOSUR (Argentina, Brazil, Paraguay, and Uruguay), with
different economic institutions and sociopolitical traditions. The European
Monetary Union, with a common currency (the euro), an effective central
bank, and a strong European parliament, presents new and complex
problems for the economic and foreign policies of other countries. Such
groups may be considered as the pioneers of globalization.

Risks of protectionism can be avoided, through multilateral agreements, and the economic pooling of many nations may be considered
an opportunity rather than a threat. All over the world, there are calls
for burden-shifting, leadership-sharing, and aggressive trade and investment policies toward cooperation and economic development.
However, some politicians and economists, seeing growing foreign
debts in many countries, ask for more protection.[6]

To liberalize world trade, many countries are moving toward successful compromises on trade disputes and try to eliminate trade-distorting
subsidies in agricultural and other products. Also, the spirit of accom-
modation and compromise in trade and investment relations should
aim to end barriers in financial and other services and to protect trademarks, patents, and copyrights.

Nevertheless, corporate invasions and globalization may homoge-
nize cultures and have detrimental effects on the biodiversity of mother
nature. With economic globalization, sociocultural diversity may gradually disappear. From that standpoint, international institutions, such
as the International Monetary Fund, the World Bank, and the World
Trade Organization, are criticized in that, with their support of globalization, they contribute to the widening gaps between rich and poor
within nations and among nations.

Through globalization, modern nations might be replaced by city-states, which would fight wars not over territories but over trade and cyberspace. There would be "competitive urban regions, a new version of the ancient Greek city-states."[7] National sovereignty would decline, new ideologies and corporate empires would flourish, and high-tech feudalism might prevail in the future, but democratic ideals are expected to endure.

International Monetary System: Financial Institutions

A BRIEF HISTORICAL REVIEW

Hellenic Monetary Units

Historically, any commodity that was generally accepted as a medium of exchange could be used as money. Various objects have been used as money over time, including human skulls, cows, wine, shells, and mainly metals. Even today in the Yap island of the Pacific, large stones (*fei*) are used as money.

Cows were used as money in ancient Greece or Hellas, Egypt, China, Italy, and Britain. In Southern Sudan, even today, people use cattle and goats as a standard of value. Thus, "a reasonably sound wife costs about 40 head of cattle, with perhaps a few goats and chickens thrown in."[1]

From recent discoveries in Dispilio, near Kastoria, Greece, the most ancient signs of written words, fishing and other instruments, and vases were dated back to 5260 B.C. Also, shapes of coins, similar to talents used in ancient Greece and Rome and existing now in the Museum of Heracleion, Crete, were found to belong to the same ancient times (7,260 years ago). Such discoveries put an end to the myths about the Phoenician alphabet and the Indo-European race. Hellenes (Greeks) were living in that area and the rest of Greece at that time. The research continues and is financed by the European Union (LIFE Program), whereas a museum is under construction near the lake of Kastoria where such monuments and tools were found. Moreover, human fossil bones and tools were discovered by French and Greek archeologists in Triglia, Halkidikis (*homo erectus trigliensis*), as ancient as 11–12 million years old, compared to 2.5-million-year-old tools found in Africa.[2]

Lending operations for commodities predates money itself, as for example during the Minoan (Cretan) and Mycenean civilizations (earlier than 3000 B.C.), when values were expressed in terms of cows and oxen. Also, the Code of Hammurabi (about 1800 B.C.) deals with mortgages and debts. However, the use of coins and other monetary units, away from the inefficient barter system, later necessitated the establishment of banks.

In addition to cattle, during the Homeric period (about 1200 B.C.), certain pieces of gold called talents were used as money. Recent research in Mycenae (Greece) discovered a copper ingot 2.5 feet long in a shape of ox-hide, dated around the fourteenth century B.C. Moreover, certain pieces of gold (talents) were in circulation but were expressed mainly in terms of cows. An alternative name to euro, suggested in the European Union (EU), was the talent, used in ancient Greece and classical Rome, which are considered as the common roots of the EU member states. It was considered as a hard currency with a value of 26 kg of silver.

In ancient Sparta, large iron disks were introduced by Lycurgus as money units (ninth century B.C.). The Spartan monetary units had a face value higher than the intrinsic or metal value. This system of debased money is used even today by advanced money societies. Later, gold and silver were deposited by the Lacedaemonians with the Arcadians for safekeeping.[3]

Silver coins (drachmas) replaced previous tortoise-shell currency in Corinth, the island of Aegina, and mainly Athens (seventh–fifth century B.C.). They were stamped to indicate their value on the one side, and with an owl (the wisdom bird of Athens) on the other side. According to Aristotle, commodities have a use value and an exchange value measured in drachmas, which can be used for exchanges and storage of wealth.

Plato proposed, in the *Laws*, that token money be used for domestic transactions and gold and silver for transactions with foreigners. In that way, money was internationalized by the Hellenes at that time.[4] However, Aristophanes noted in "The Frogs" (405 B.C.) that "in our Republic bad citizens are preferred to good, just as bad money circulates while good money disappears." This concept is very near to Gresham's law, after Sir Thomas Gresham, Queen Elizabeth's Chancellor of the Exchequer (A.D. 1559).

As domestic and foreign trade increased, mainly between Athens-Piraeus and Phoenicia, Egypt, Sicily, and other neighboring countries, banking transactions developed. A number of arcades, the most famous called Degma, were used for exhibitions and exchanges of commodities from all the markets of the eastern Mediterranean and beyond. Moreover, regulations similar to our antitrust laws were enacted by the city government.[5]

Other important monetary units used in ancient times were the Pu money, in the shape of a shirt, as well as knives and other metallic instruments, in China around 700 B.C. Also, the first paper or parchment money was issued in China in 140 B.C. In Egypt, the first coinage was established under the Ptolemies at the end of the fourth century B.C.

Roman Period

Money and credit opened new freedoms and opportunities during the period of the Roman Empire. Financiers and profiteers flourished while trade enterprises were growing, and money interest began to play an important role in trade and finance. The Romans used a common currency to help military cooperation and to stimulate free economic transactions with the regions under their domain.[6] Such common currencies were used later by the United States (the dollar) and the European Union (the euro).

Copper bars or ingots were the first monetary units in ancient Rome. Silver coins, called denarii, similar to those previously used in Greece and mostly debased, were introduced after 269 B.C. Furthermore, with the use of gold later, three metals were used together and serious problems of trimetalism or bimetalism appeared as the relative values of the various metals (gold, silver, copper) changed over time.

During the Roman Empire (31 B.C. to A.D. 476), the creation of a new commercial class, the patricians, increased transactions in the cities and necessitated a body of laws that later had a profound influence on legal and economic institutions, including banks and other financial firms. The recognition of juristic or artificial persons by the Roman laws was important for the creation and expansion of the corporate form of modern enterprises. The Romans, with their efficient administration of justice and the security of life and property, created many trading, financial, and shipping centers in their dominion and promoted international transactions.

Nevertheless, Rome suffered at times from too little or too much gold and silver and the frequent debasement of its metal money. The rudimentary banking system was inadequate to deal with price changes in the absence of a paper or check system.

Middle Ages and Later

Moral corruption, slavery, and decline of the silver and gold mines of Spain and Greece were the main reasons for the fall of the Roman Empire.

During the Byzantine Empire (330–1453) and the Middle Ages (476 to about 1500), gold was the main currency used, but there were problems

nessee, and Ohio, with nominal values in labor hours. These labor notes entitled "National Equitable Labour Exchanges," based on the utopian teachings of Charles Fourier of France, were short-lived, primarily because of the difficulties in exchanges.

Nevertheless, bank notes and U.S. Treasury notes were mostly used because they were less costly and more convenient than gold. But, as David Ricardo mentioned, "In issuing paper money . . . it is only necessary that its quantity should be regulated." Moreover, international payments were made in bills of exchange, comparable to postdated checks. Thus, a U.S. exporter would receive gold or more usually bills of exchange from the importers of other countries and sell them for U.S. dollars in New York or other cities.[8]

Because of the Civil War and the increase in prices, payments in gold in the United States were suspended in December 1861. The convertibility of gold for the dollar was restored at $20.67 in January 1879 and remained so until 1933. The pure gold standard system was introduced in 1900 in order to avoid relative price fluctuations in the prevailing bimetalic system of gold and silver. The United States managed to hang onto gold during World War I, but prices increased by more than double from 1914 to 1920, and then by 1932 they fell more than they had risen.

However, new discoveries of gold led to changes in prices and economic instability. Also, when a country had a deficit in the balance of payments, a net outflow of gold would take place, and under a gold standard system, money supply and eventually prices would be reduced, with the possibility of a recession or depression and unemployment. Ceteris paribus, lower prices would lead to more exports and less imports, thereby restoring the balance-of-payments equilibrium. The opposite is expected in countries with surplus in the balance of payments, which would lead to a net inflow of gold, an increase in money supply and prices, less exports and more imports until the balance-of-payments equilibrium is restored.

As mentioned earlier, metals, primarily gold and silver, were used as money mainly in international transactions by different societies. Metals are generally accepted as money because they are homogeneous commodities, easily portable, divisible, storable, and relatively scarce and have a cost to produce and a value in industrial use.

In 1933, the United States abandoned the pure gold standard system, in which anybody could get gold. In its place, the gold reserve system was introduced, in which a certain percentage of the money supply was kept in gold. The price of gold was determined at $35 per ounce in January 1934, but in practice, it was used only for the settlement of international transactions. In March 1973 the price of gold was left to the free market of supply and demand.

The Bank of North America, established by the Continental Congress in 1781, and the Bank of the United States, established by Alexander Hamilton in 1791, were the first U.S. banks. In order to manage money and credit more effectively, the Federal Reserve Bank ("Fed") was established on December 23, 1913, as an institution independent of the federal government.

INTERNATIONAL MONETARY FUND

The most effective international organizations, formed by agreements among a large number of nations, are the International Monetary Fund (IMF), the International Bank for Reconstruction and Development or World Bank, and the General Agreement on Tariffs and Trade (GATT), recently named the World Trade Organization (WTO). The IMF and the World Bank were established by forty-four countries at Bretton Woods, New Hampshire (United States), in July 1944, whereas the GATT was negotiated in Havana, Cuba, and established in Geneva in 1948.

The International Monetary Fund (IMF), which is a pool of central-bank reserves and national currencies, was established at Bretton Woods in 1944 under the auspices of the United Nations, but it actually started operations on March 1, 1947. In order to facilitate international finance and help correct fundamental balance-of-payments disequilibriums, it tied all currencies to gold and hence to each other.

The IMF, with headquarters in Washington, D.C., was created to help finance balance-of-payments deficits and to reform the international monetary system toward mutual cooperation and freely convertible currencies among the member nations. The waves of devaluations in the currencies of a number of countries before World War II, mainly in 1931–1936, as a way to increase exports and reduce imports at the expense of their trading partners (beggar-thy-neighbor policies) was the rationale of the creation of the IMF. These policies resulted in frequent changes in exchange parities, economic instability, and high unemployment.

The IMF makes its own stock of currencies available (gives loans) to the members. It functions as a pool of currencies or an international clearing institution, using the assigned quotas of the member countries to arrange international payments. Also, it provides short-term loans and advice to member countries, primarily emerging nations, with balance-of-payments difficulties. Member nations were committed to keep their currencies within plus or minus 1 percent of parity, although further changes in exchange rates were permitted if needed. From that standpoint, the system can be characterized as an "adjustable peg" exchange rate system. Moreover, because the dollar, being the key currency, was convertible into gold ($\frac{1}{35}$ ounce of gold), every currency had a gold value related to the dollar, which may be considered as a yardstick of value. The Bretton Woods system then may also be characterized as a gold exchange standard system.

Each member nation was responsible to subscribe to the capital of the IMF, paying one fourth in gold and three fourths in its currency (in demand notes), depending mainly on its share of world trade. The member countries were responsible to sell their currencies to the IMF, which could also borrow currencies from its members above their subscribed quotas. Initially the IMF had a total quota of $8.8 billion, but that was increased gradually to about $260 billion (198 billion Special Drawing Rights or SDRs) and 182 members presently.

Immediately after World War II, the United States had about 33 percent of the voting power in the IMF and 35 percent in the World Bank, because of its dominant economic position. Thereafter, the U.S. voting power steadily declined to the current levels of less than 20 percent in the IMF and around 17 percent in the World Bank. As we enter a new millennium, international institutions, mainly the IMF, are expected to play a more important role in regulating financial cooperation and reducing tensions among member nations, particularly between rich and poor nations, which have heavy debts.[10]

Nevertheless, gold is an expensive reserve asset, as human resources are used to dig it in distant areas and bury it in heavily guarded places in central banks or in the IMF in Washington. That is why Professor Robert Triffin of Yale University suggested that central bank deposits with the IMF be denominated in a new international unit of account or a form of paper gold.[11]

A similar system was proposed by John M. Keynes, as an alternative to the U.S. plan for the IMF at Bretton Woods in 1944. Moreover, the use of gold for the determination of money supply may lead to excessive liquidity and global inflationary pressures, when excessive amounts of gold are available, as well as to inadequate liquidity, when not enough gold is available, resulting in recessions or even depressions, as happened with the severe recession of 1907 (rich man's panic) and the Great Depression of the 1930s.

Although the Bretton Woods system performed well in the 1950s, the fact that the United States had large deficits in its balance of payments in the 1960s increased the dollar reserves of other countries and consequently the demand for gold, forcing the United States to apply first voluntary controls (1965) and then mandatory controls (1968) to capital outflows. At the same time, Japan, West Germany, and other European countries with surpluses refused to revalue their currencies, suggesting that the United States eliminate its balance-of-payments deficits.

In an attempt to further discourage European companies from raising capital in the United States, the interest-equalization tax was imposed in the mid-1960s to equalize the cost of raising funds in the United States, where interest rates were lower. Moreover, the U.S. Treasury issued medium-term bonds with an exchange-rate guarantee, known as Roosa bonds, to discourage foreign central banks from cashing their excess dollars for gold. Also, U.S. short-term interest rates were raised to attract foreign funds, but long-term interest rates remained low to encourage domestic investments, a policy known as "operation twist." Nevertheless, the "dollar glut" continued in the 1960s, mainly because of the U.S. trade deficits, in contrast to the "dollar shortage" in the 1950s.

In 1969, a special quota (of $10 billion) was created by the IMF to be used for automatic drawings. They are Special Drawing Rights (SDRs), which are gradually replacing gold as a reserve asset. The acceptance of SDRs is an obligation for members, subject to some limitations. Each member can buy currencies directly from other countries up to the amount allocated by the IMF, without going through the regular Fund operations. In the case of SDRs the IMF acts as an intermediary or guarantor. Although large amounts of SDRs are allocated to developed countries, a growing number of emerging nations receive SDR allocations lately.

The IMF carries on its books $5 billion gold, but at market prices the gold the fund owns is worth more than $30 billion. Therefore, the fund can write off some $8 billion that forty poor countries owe it, but under conditions that would not give them incentives for further borrowing with the expectation of not paying back future loans.

Each member paid one fourth of its quota in gold or in dollars and the rest in its own currency. This pool may be considered as an extension of the central-bank reserves and aimed at stable exchange rates. It was accepted that drawings of member countries could be made on permission, as Harry D. White, the U.S. representative, insisted, and not automatically, as John M. Keynes, the British representative, suggested.

The quotas, which are revised every five years to reflect economic changes of members, determine the number of votes and the borrowing limits of the member countries. As mentioned previously, the United States has almost 20 percent of the total voting power, followed by Germany and Japan with 5.7 percent each, and then Britain and France with 5.1 percent each. These five developed countries with more than 40 percent voting power dominate the IMF, which operates as a central bank for central banks. Member governments select governors, who constitute the highest governing body of the Fund and meet every September in Washington, whereas power is vested in the Board of

Executive Directors (some twenty persons). A member of the Fund can borrow 25 percent of its quota without restrictions (gold tranche) and higher amounts with restrictions (credit tranches), but repayments are normally to be made within three to five years.

Approximately, the quotas (in billions of Special Drawing Rights or SDRs) (one SDR is equal to about $1.3) are: 27 for the United States; 8 each for Germany and Japan; 7 each for Britain and France; 5 for Saudi Arabia; 4 each for Canada, Italy, and Russia; 3 each for Belgium, China, India, and Netherlands; 2 each for Australia and Brazil; and close to 2 each for Mexico, Spain, and Venezuela, and so on. Table 2.1 shows the quotas of all members of the IMF in millions of SDRs.

The U.S. official reserve assets in March 1998 were $69.35 billion, $30.22 billion of which were foreign currencies, $11.05 billion gold, $10.11 billion holdings of IMF SDRs, and $17.98 billion was the reserve position, that is, the U.S. ability to draw foreign currencies from the IMF.

As the cure for sick economies, the IMF usually prescribes tough austerity measures, which lead to deep cuts in public spending, tight credit, high unemployment, sharp currency depreciation, severe stock market decline, and even social unrest. Some of these symptoms occurred in Mexico (1994–1995) and the Southeast Asian countries (mainly Indonesia, Malaysia, South Korea, Thailand) (1997–1998). Some countries blame Washington and other Western capitals for their strong influence on the IMF.

Such austerity measures may result in high unemployment, and many people blame IMF for worsening their misery and for losing their jobs (arguing that IMF stands for I'M Fired?). Moreover, the loans from the IMF are relatively small compared to about $2 trillion traded daily in the international currency market. Although it provided more than $150 billion for the Asian and Mexican bailouts lately, as a lender of last resort, it is criticized that in its effort to save weak economies, it discourages the private sector and the related governments to take the necessary painful fiscal and monetary measures to correct the problems of crony capitalism. That is why the U.S. Congress is skeptical on providing additional financing for the IMF.[12]

THE WORLD BANK AND ITS AFFILIATES

Together with the IMF, the International Bank for Reconstruction and Development (World Bank) was created at Bretton Woods in 1944. The member nations must pay 10 percent of the subscription (1 percent in gold), and the rest is subject to call any time the bank needs it. Its

Table 2.1 IMF Quotas (Millions of SDRs)

MEMBER	QUOTA	MEMBER	QUOTA	MEMBER	QUOTA
Afghanistan, I.S. of	120.4	Cyprus	100.0	Kenya	199.4
Albania	35.3	Czech Republic	589.6	Kiribati	4.0
Algeria	914.4	Denmark	1069.9	Korea	799.6
Angola	207.3	Djibouti	11.5	Kuwait	995.2
Antigua and Barbuda	8.5	Dominica	6.0	Kyrgyz Republic	64.5
Argentina	1537.1	Dominican Republic	158.8	Lao People's Dem. Rep.	39.1
Armenia	67.5	Ecuador	219.2	Latvia	91.5
Australia	2333.2	Egypt	678.4	Lebanon	146.0
Austria	1188.3	El Salvador	125.6	Lesotho	23.9
Azerbaijan	117.0	Equatorial Guinea	24.3	Liberia	71.3
Bahamas, The	94.9	Eritrea	11.5	Libya	817.6
Bahrain	82.8	Estonia	46.5	Lithuania	103.5
Bangladesh	392.5	Ethiopia	98.3	Luxembourg	135.5
Barbados	48.9	Fiji	51.1	Macedonia, FYR	49.6
Belarus	280.4	Finland	861.8	Madagascar	90.4
Belgium	3102.3	France	7414.6	Malawi	50.9
Belize	13.5	Gabon	110.3	Malaysia	832.7
Benin	45.3	Gambia, The	22.9	Maldives	5.5
Bhutan	4.5	Georgia	111.0	Mali	68.9
Bolivia	126.2	Germany	8241.5	Malta	67.5
Bosnia & Herzegovina	121.2	Ghana	274.0	Marshall Islands	2.5
Botswana	36.6	Greece	587.6	Mauritania	47.5
Brazil	2170.8	Grenada	8.5	Mauritius	73.3
Brunei Darussalam	150.0	Guatemala	153.8	Mexico	1753.3
Bulgaria	464.9	Guinea	78.7	Micronesia, Fed. Sts.	3.5
Burkina Faso	44.2	Guinea-Bissau	10.5	Moldova	90.0
Burundi	57.2	Guyana	67.2	Mongolia	37.1
Cambodia	65.0	Haiti	60.7	Morocco	427.7
Cameroon	135.1	Honduras	95.0	Mozambique	84.0
Canada	4320.3	Hungary	754.8	Myanmar	184.9
Cape Verde	7.0	Iceland	85.3	Namibia	99.6
Central African Rep.	41.2	India	3055.5	Nepal	52.0
Chad	41.3	Indonesia	1497.6	Netherlands	3444.2
Chile	621.7	Iran, 1.R. of	1078.5	New Zealand	650.1
China, People's Rep.	3385.2	Iraq	504.0	Nicaragua	96.1
Colombia	561.3	Ireland	525.0	Niger	48.3
Comoros	6.5	Israel	666.2	Nigeria	1281.6
Congo, Dem. Rep. of	291.0	Italy	4590.7	Norway	1104.6
Congo, Rep. of	57.9	Jamaica	200.9	Oman	119.4
Costa Rica	119.0	Japan	8241.5	Pakistan	758.2
Cote d' Ivoire	238.2	Jordan	121.7	Panama	149.6
Croatia	261.6	Kazakhstan	247.5	Papua New Guinea	95.3

MEMBER	QUOTA	MEMBER	QUOTA
Paraguay	72.1	Swaziland	36.5
Peru	466.1	Sweden	1614.0
Philippines	633.4	Switzerland	2470.4
Poland	988.5	Syrian Arab Republic	209.9
Portugal	557.6	Tajikistan	60.0
Qatar	190.5	Tanzania	146.9
Romania	754.1	Thailand	573.9
Russia	4313.1	Togo	54.3
Rwanda	59.5	Tonga	5.0
San Marino	10.0	Trinidad and Tobago	246.8
Saudi Arabia	5130.6	Tunisia	206.0
Senegal	118.9	Turkey	642.0
Seo Tome & Principe	5.5	Turkmenistan	48.0
Seychelles	6.0	Uganda	133.9
Sierra Leone	77.2	Ukraine	997.3
Singapore	357.6	United Arab Emirates	392.1

Table 2.1 Continued

Slovak Republic	257.4	United Kingdom	7414.6
Slovenia	150.5	United States	26526.8
Solomon Islands	7.5	Uruguay	225.3
Somalia	44.2	Uzbekistan	199.5
South Africa	1365.4	Vanuatu	12.5
Spain	1935.4	Venezuela	1951.3
Sri Lanka	303.6	Vietnam	241.6
St. Kitts and Nevis	6.5	Western Samoa	8.5
St. Lucia	11.0	Yemen, Republic of	176.5
St. Vincent & Grens.	6.0	Zambia	363.5
Sudan	169.7	Zimbabwe	261.3
Suriname	67.6		

Source: IMF, *International Financial Statistics Yearbook.*

main source of money, though, is borrowing from the free money market.

The World Bank and its affiliates—the International Finance Corporation (IFC), created in 1956, and the International Development Association (IDA), created in 1960—provide development assistance by extending loans to emerging nations. The IFC specializes mainly in promoting private enterprises through investment in indigenous and foreign sources, whereas the IDA makes long-term loans for housing, sanitation, irrigation, and other projects in poor member nations at subsidized rates. Moreover, within the World Bank Group is a globally operating intergovernmental organization providing investment insurance against political risks, and the International Centre for Settlement of Investment Disputes (ICSID), which provides facilities for arbitration of disputes between foreign investors and governments.

The authorized capital of the World Bank accounts for $171.4 billion, that of IFC for $1.3 billion, and that of MIGA for $1.1 billion. Also, the capital received by IDA in the form of pledged contributions totals $68.6 billion. Borrowing from the World Bank stands at about $12 billion per year and is expected to increase, as external financing remains essential for many emerging nations.[13]

The World Bank, which lends money to emerging nations, issued $4 billion in dollar-denominated global bonds, the largest ever. It was priced to yield 5.703 percent for maturity in 2003, that is, 14 basis points above a similar Treasury security. A basis point is one one-hundredth of a percentage point (0.0001). For this issue, which was the largest of the 14 dollar-denominated bond issues by the World Bank, Europe subscribed for 45 percent, the United States for 35 percent, and Asia for 20 percent.

Some other regional development banks, with limited effectiveness, are the Inter-American Development Bank (IDB) created in 1959 mainly to promote the Alliance for Progress program; the African Development Bank (AFDB), organized in 1964; and the Asian Development Bank (ADB), established in 1966.

GOVERNMENT FINANCIAL INSTITUTIONS

Other institutions dealing with international trade and investment financing, mainly through low-interest loans, are those created by the U.S. federal government to help exporters and investors. They include the Export-Import Bank (EXIMBANK), which was created in 1945 as an independent government institution to aid U.S. exporters and foreign importers through loans, guarantees, counseling, and training. When commercial banks hesitate to give loans to high-risk countries, the EX-IMBANK may guarantee such loans, thereby helping poor nations and U.S. exporters to be able to compete with foreign receiving subsidies.

Moreover, the Commodity Credit Corporation (CCC) was created to support U.S. exports of agricultural products through long-term loans, mainly to poor nations, in competition with other countries providing similar loans.

Finally, the Overseas Private Investment Corporation (OPIC) was created to support U.S. investment in other countries, mainly friendly emerging nations.

Other industrial countries provide export subsidies, mainly Japan and Europe, in many cases disguised, although this is unfair in international economics. For that reason, the United States raises, from time to time, serious complaints against other nations providing such concealed subsidies, which are financed by the governments involved.

BANKING OPERATIONS

Central banks control and regulate commercial banks, primarily through discount rates, reserve requirements, open market operations, and other monetary policy tools. In their efforts to manage money and credit, they influence trade financing, inflation, and exchange rates. They are lenders of the last resort. Also, they intervene in the financial markets in order to reduce volatility or influence exchange rate levels.[14]

Commercial banks are middle-persons or agents of the public. They accept deposits from the entrusting public and lend them back to the public, charging a higher interest rate than they pay to depositors, who are the ultimate lenders. The amount of borrowers' demand for credit depends on the banks' propensity to lend and the rates they charge.

Although they do not create legal-tender money, they create money (or credit) in the form of bank notes.[15] As it is usually said, "Money talks and banks command."

The creation of money depends on the reserve requirement and the money-supply multiplier. For example, if the reserve requirement (RR) on demand deposits (checking accounts) is 10 percent, the money-supply multiplier is 10 (or $1/RR = 1/0.10 = 10$). This means that, assuming no leakage in loans and redeposits, a $100 demand deposit would create $1,000. From that standpoint, bankers are not only middle-persons but also "manufacturers" of money and may affect business cycles. This was the case with the policies of John Law in France in 1720 (the Mississippi Bubble), who was mistaking money for wealth or credit for capital, as well as in other inflationary policies in history that led to serious international financial crises.

In addition to commercial banks, credit unions are engaged in a wide range of banking activities. Thus, in the United States about 70 million people are members of credit unions, which maintain their cooperative structure and their tax-exempt status.

Banks are crucial to domestic and international economies, as they gather savings, make loans, and coordinate financial transactions. In the industrial countries they are the prime providers of financial services, and in the emerging nations they are the heart of the financial markets. However, over the past twenty years, about three fourths of the member countries of the International Monetary Fund have faced problems with bank failures, and many of them considered or adopted measures to protect their financial systems. Thus, in its effort to reform the banking system, the government of Brazil decided to rescue the Banco de Brazil, the largest bank of Latin America, by buying risky bonds worth $3.4 billion. The same policy was used earlier with another bank, run by the federal government, Bovespa. However, sooner or later, both banks would follow the path of privatization implemented currently by Brazil.

Offshore Banking

The volatility of financial markets around the world makes it nearly impossible to discipline them without some form of coordination and regulation. National banking regulations are unable to keep pace with the rapid development of global financial markets. There is no international institution to initiate changes and play the role of an international regulator. Even the International Monetary Fund (IMF) finds it difficult to convince member countries to take measures of exchange rate stabilization and other policies to avoid economic crises. Although more than 100 countries signed an agreement in December 1997 to dismantle national barriers and open their markets to foreign banks, insurance companies, and investment firms, such measures were largely ignored, and the financial turmoil in Asia, Latin America, and other parts of the world continues.

Bermuda is an attractive place for offshore banks and mutual funds. It is considered by affluent international investors as a lightly regulated tax sanctuary. There are around 1,000 funds on the island, with more than \$20 billion net assets, about 30 percent more than from last year. A recent law deals with money laundering and the formalization of mutual funds regulation. It requires approval for any money received, whereas the administrators must prove an acceptable source. Other Caribbean islands are also used for offshore banks and mutual funds as in Bermuda.

On the Cayman islands, which are a British dependency, there are 575 banks with about \$500 billion deposits. More than 20,000 huge and small corporations, including hedge funds, are chartered on the Caymans, where there are financial secrecy laws and no income tax, no inheritance tax, no capital gains tax, no sales or other consumption taxes, and no tax treaties. Other offshore sanctuaries, in addition to Bahamas and the Cayman islands, include the British Virgin Islands, Antigua, the Isle of Jersey, Panama, Liechtenstein, the Netherlands Antilles, Luxembourg, and Switzerland. Although the Group of Seven industrialized nations said that disclosure rules should prevail, it is difficult to implement such rules in practice.[16]

Extensive controls on a global scale may be impossible or ineffective to slow the rapid growth of financial markets and the movement of capital and other banking services from one place to another. Such controls may be difficult to implement in today's advanced technology and may have negative effects on the economies involved, as they may lead to recessions or depressions. Probably the strengthening of the banking system in weak emerging and other economies will promote financial stability and global economic growth. Also, a specialized international institution, possibly under the IMF, may solve the problem.

Intervention by Central Banks and Governments

If a country, say the United States, wants to defend its currency (the dollar) and keep a constant exchange rate with another currency, say the Japanese yen, and the value of the first currency (the dollar) is declining because of higher inflation or other reasons, then the central bank (the Federal Reserve Bank or Fed) would buy some of its currency in order to avoid a reduction in the market value and an expected depreciation. This is what happened in a number of cases when the value of the dollar gradually declined from more than 250 yen to less than 100 yen per dollar.

As Figure 2.1 shows, if the demand for dollars is declining and the demand curve shifts from D to D1, then the Fed, which wants to defend the dollar, would buy ac dollars at a price (say 100 yen per dollar) determined by the equilibrium of supply (S) and demand (D), instead of letting it to drop to a lower price (say 80 yen). The opposite would occur when the price of the dollar is going up and the Fed wants to keep it down to the equilibrium point, in which case the Fed would sell dollars for yen.

In many cases, if commercial banks are in trouble, the government can spend money from the budget to bail them out, thereby avoiding a depreciation in its currency and possible decline in the stock market. Thus, in order to bring stability to its volatile financial system, the Japanese government decided to spend more than $500 billion to bail out banks. Such an action is expected to help dispel pessimism, calm the stock market, and support the currency. As a result, the Nikkei index, which was fluctuating around 17,000 at the beginning of 1999, and the yen, which was quoted at around 120 yen to the dollar at the same time, began to improve. The hope was to help out banks, which had about $620 billion in bad loans, and avoid further credit squeeze and corporate bankruptcies.

Other measures were enacted to guarantee bank deposits and strengthen the Deposit Insurance Corporation (DIC), an institution similar to the U.S. Federal Deposit Insurance Corporation (FDIC). Also, the Japanese government decided to buy preferred shares in banks, as the U.S. government did in the 1930s to pull the country out of the Depres-

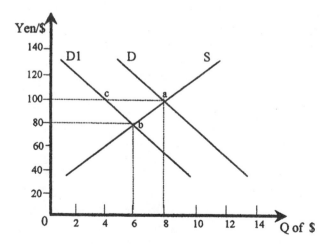

Figure 2.1. Defending a fixed exchange rate by intervention

sion. However, it would be better to allow ailing banks to close down or be merged in order to avoid similar problems in the future. Japanese banks with bad loans include the big banks Daiwa Bank Ltd. and Sumitomo Bank Ltd., as well as Dai-Ichi Kangyo Bank Ltd., Industrial Bank of Japan Ltd., Sakura Bank Ltd., Sanwa Bank Ltd., and Tokai Bank Ltd. After foreign exchange controls were lifted in Japan in April 1998, large amounts of capital are flowing out of the country. Now, more and more Japanese retail and corporate clients are willing to take on foreign exchange risk to enjoy higher returns in stock exchanges. Moreover, the 10-year government bonds in Japan yield only 1.7 percent currently, which is far lower than in other countries.

Hoping to help restore worldwide confidence in the financial system and make it competitive internationally, the Japanese government, which decided to bail out weak banks, tries to imitate the American policy of bailing out banks by the Reconstruction Finance Corporation of the 1930s. However, this is not well accepted by several Japanese banks, which are issuing preferred shares in New York to raise money on their own. In its effort to make the financial system more attractive, the Japanese government is also adopting international accounting standards, relaxing regulations on disclosure, and making the financial system free, fair, and global. Also, it is privatizing the huge Post Deposits with $2 trillion in deposits, which is offering better interest rates than the private sector and better services, as the mailman collects deposits from households every morning.

The once-mighty economy of Japan has been stalled in recent years, and severe fiscal measures are needed to reverse its economic decline and spur the economy, mainly through public works and tax cuts. However, the Organization of Economic Cooperation and Development, a group of twenty-nine industrial countries based in Paris, and other nations in Asia and elsewhere criticized these measures as insufficient to uplift the Japanese economy as well as the other ailing trading partners in Asia. Moreover, the feeling in the United States, which has been urging Japan for years to open its economy to more imports, is that Japan should spend more and save less than some 28 percent of its national income, thereby reducing its huge foreign trade surpluses.

In order to shore up its four gigantic state-owned commercial banks, with some $200 billion in bad loans, China floated a $32 billion bond issue in April 1998 and speeded up economic reforms through streamlining, downsizing, and privatizing public enterprises. This is in addition to the $32 billion the Chinese government pumped into these banks recently, including the Guangdong International Trust and Investment Company, also known as Gitic, for which the government assumed a large part of its $2.4 billion foreign debt after its recent closing.

Although China does not have a convertible currency and it is not immediately affected by the financial turmoil in other countries, it is expected to do that in the near future after privatizing state banks. The Chinese government is in the process of closing many debt-ridden trust and investment companies. Beijing plans to close some 200, out of a total 240, such companies with about $10 billion in foreign debt.

An important measure to counteract an economic downturn as a result of the Asian financial crisis is the plan of the Chinese government to spend $1 trillion in public works projects, thereby hoping to keep the 8 percent growth rate of the $900 billion GDP and avoid high unemployment. The financing of these projects would include domestic and foreign bonds and loans as well as allocations from central and provincial governments. With a relatively small foreign debt of $120 billion and about $140 billion in foreign exchange reserves, China is not expected to face serious problems to find international lenders.

Furthermore, in order to avoid the faltering of private banks, some nations resort to the nationalization of banks, a measure that might create more problems in the future. Thus, the Thai government, which shuttered fifty-six of fifty-eight nonbank finance companies and speculative lenders in the early 1990s, nationalized three large private banks (First Bangkok City Bank, Siam City Bank, and Bangkok Bank of Commerce) in February 1998. This happened after the Thais failed to attract Western banks, such as Citibank (a unit of Citicorp of the United States) and the ING Bank of the Netherlands, to create alliances and bail them out. Nevertheless, purging the financial system is a condition of the IMF's $17 billion bailout of the country. Although Thailand relaxed some strict regulations for foreign ownership, foreign banks cannot hold more than 50.1 percent stake and cannot increase shareholding in Thai banks, many of which are owned by powerful Thai and Thai-Chinese business families.[17]

Another tool the government can use, through the central bank, is to raise interest rates so that private investors would be induced to increase their demand for its currency. The use of the interest rate as a tool of exchange rate stability is extensively used in our day. Recently, it was used by many emerging nations to avoid currency depreciation (devaluation) due to the Asian turmoil.

CONSOLIDATION OF BANKS AND OTHER FINANCIAL INSTITUTIONS

Cross-Atlantic Banking Mergers

Merger mania, which can be observed domestically, is gradually becoming an international phenomenon. The open and competitive world markets require large companies with global reach. Megamergers, such as the Travelers Group, which recently bought Salomon Brothers, intertwined with nine other firms around the world and merging with Citicorp later, are globalizing the financial markets. In competition with other global heavyweights such as Merrill Lynch & Company and Morgan Stanley, Dean Witter, Discover & Company, Salomon also acquired other firms around the world, including most of County NatWest brokerage businesses in Sydney, London, Tokyo, and other cities.

Such acquisitions can exaggerate the volatility in world stock markets and currencies and create economic havoc. Nevertheless, such Goliaths usually introduce new technology, reduce cost, and facilitate capital investment worldwide.

The recent financial deregulations all over the world are allowing banks and other firms to operate internationally and to underwrite securities and distribute stock offerings. However, there are serious concerns regarding the public interest. The ferocious competition of American, European, Japanese, and other financial giants may lead them to speculative trading in risky options and futures contracts. Although powerful financial firms would not be allowed to fall, as governments would shore them up, extensive risky operations may result in international crises. Perhaps this may invite commercial banks and other firms to merge and operate on a global scale.

The cross-border financial services of money management firms, including banks, mutual funds, brokerage firms, and other investment companies, are rapidly growing. Such companies manage huge amounts of savings for pension funds, insurance firms, and ordinary investors in a global scale. Big American financial firms, such as Fidelity Investments, Merrill Lynch and Company, J. P. Morgan and Company, and Citigroup, are accelerating their movements in other countries to become international money managers. Other big money firms eager to expand internationally include Deutsche Bank, the largest German bank, which acquired Bankers Trust, a big U.S. bank; AXA-UAP of France; the Swiss Bank Corporation; and the Zurich Group of Switzerland, which agreed to buy Scudder Stevens and Clark, the American mutual fund company.

Merrill Lynch, based in New York, agreed to acquire Mercury Asset Management Group P.L.C., based in London. Merrill, with $272 billion of funds under management, 5,200 employees, and $22 billion market capitalization plans to finance the acquisition with preferred stock and long-term debt.

The Bank of New York Company agreed to buy trust businesses from the British bank Coutts & Company, a unit of National Westminster Bank P.L.C., for an undisclosed amount. This will add some

$15 billion to the about $400 billion business of the bank outside the United States.

Mercury, with assets of $177 billion under management and nineteen offices around the world, announced that there would be no layoffs among its 1,500 managers and employees. With $4 billion capitalization, it was spun off from S.G. Warburg and Company, a company that was acquired by the Swiss Bank Corporation in 1995. Mercury manages money for about half the companies in the Financial Times–Stock Exchange 100 index and handles funds for half of the largest fifty company pension funds in Japan.

In order for the countries of the world to trade, international financial institutions must exist to facilitate exchanges of different currencies and other transactions. The growing use of the flexible-exchange-rate system, compared to the old gold standard or the fixed-exchange-rate mechanism and the intermediate managed-exchange rate-regime, necessitates the development of sophisticated international banking. As long as there are barriers to cross-border investment, international financial intermediary institutions are needed to deal with different national jurisdictions and investment diversification. From that standpoint, commercial banks play a vital role in dealing with direct and portfolio investment, private debt, different-country risks, and the associated cross-border fees or penalties.

Financial liberalization, diffusion of technology, competition, and trade and capital flows undermine political autonomy and reduce national divergence. Controls over allocation of credit, guided liberalization, and state financing gradually change toward private financing and self-financing on a global scale, as almost all countries try to attract foreign capital.

An important international banking market is the Eurocurrency market. In addition to the European countries, Eurocurrency banking centers include the Bahamas and other Caribbean islands, Canada, Japan, Singapore, Hong Kong, and the United States. The Eurocurrency market, which appeared in the 1950s, grew drastically thereafter to account now for about $4 trillion.

Deutsche Bank A.G., the biggest bank of Germany, agreed to acquire Bankers Trust Corporation, the eighth-largest American bank, for some $9 billion. Deutsche Bank had also acquired Morgan Grenfell of Britain in the early 1990s and lately 10 percent of the Eurobank of the Latsis group, which agreed to acquire the Bank of Athens. Recently, in order to focus more on international banking, Deutsche decided to spin off its industrial assets, worth $24 billion, in such companies as Daimler-Chrysler, a car industry, and Allianz, the biggest insurer of Germany, where it holds large stakes.

Through banks and other financial institutions, large amounts of money from pension funds move to international stock markets. Thus, the U.S. Teachers Insurance and Annuity Association and College Retirement Equities Fund (TIAA-CREF), available to over 6,100 educational and research institutions with 1.8 million participants and more than $250 billion in assets, is moving aggressively to profitable European, emerging, and other well-established world stock markets.

On both sides of the Atlantic, merger fever continues. Recently, the U.S. Federal Reserve Bank approved the merger of the Swiss Bank Corporation, with operations in the United States, and the Union Bank of Switzerland. The new bank, named United Bank of Switzerland, is the biggest bank in the world, after the Bank of Tokyo-Mitsubishi, with some $706 billion assets.

United States Banking Mergers

Recently, many banks follow the general trend of mergers and acquisitions in order to reduce operational costs and be more efficient in the global financial markets. Also, severe competition from brokerage firms, mutual funds, and credit card firms forces them into the creation of mammoth banks with national and international aspirations. Some recent megamergers are described next.

The merger of Citicorp and the Travelers Group in 1998, worth $77.6 billion, formed Citigroup Inc., with a market capitalization of $153.9 billion. This merger created the largest financial service company in the world and deals with banking, securities (stocks and bonds), and insurance activities worldwide. The Citigroup is in fierce competition with Merrill Lynch, American Express, Goldman Sachs, American International Group, and Morgan Stanley, Dean Witter in the field of global investment banking.

The Nationsbank Corporation and the BankAmerica Corporation agreed to merge to create the largest U.S. bank in terms of total branches and deposits and the second bank in total assets. The deal involves a stock-to-stock transaction worth more than $61.6 billion. Furthermore, the Bank One Corporation merged with the First Chicago NBD Corporation, creating the fifth-largest banking company by assets worth $30 billion.

Their combined deposits are more than $340 billion, compared to about $200 billion each for Citicorp and Chase Manhattan and around $170 billion each for BankAmerica and Nationsbank.

Mainly because of the stock market exchange, the Corestates Financial Corporation accepted the merger deal with the First Union Corporation, which it had rejected some time before when the market prices were not favorable. First Union of Charlotte, North Carolina, and

Corestates of Philadelphia (the first U.S. banking capital) have combined assets of about $204 billion and plan to reduce cost primarily by laying off a large number of the 11,000 employees of Corestates.

Wells Fargo & Company agreed with Norwest Corporation in a $31.4 billion merger to create a banking group with $191 billion assets, smaller than Citigroup (with $697 billion assets) and BankAmerica (with $571 billion assets), but bigger than Washington Mutual Inc. (with $144 billion assets). The new group, based in San Francisco, is named Wells Fargo Bank.

Other megamergers in the banking sector, in addition to the First Union's deal with Corestates for $17.1 billion, include the purchase of Barnett Banks by Nationalbank for $15.5 billion and that of the Washington Mutual Inc., a large savings and loans association in Seattle, and the H.F. Ahmanson & Company in Los Angeles, which agreed to merge in a $9.9 billion stock swap and create a new company with $149.2 billion assets, trailing the BankAmerica Corporation but surpassing Wells Fargo & Company.

Merrill Lynch, with some 18,000 retail brokers, is under consideration to be taken over by American International General for $30 billion. Also, Chase Manhattan and Bank of America are in negotiations to buy Merrill Lynch.

The Bank of New York (BoNY) agreed to a friendly takeover of Mellon Bank Corporation for $24 billion, creating a large banking institution. Mellon, which recently acquired a $7.9 billion serving portfolio from the Bankers Trust New York Corporation, expects to sell its commercial mortgage business, including $17 billion of servicing rights, and concentrate on residential mortgages. Moreover, Mellon, parent of the Dreyfus Corporation, agreed recently to buy the Denver-based Founders Funds.

Fleet Financial Group agreed to buy Bank Boston for $16 billion. The new Fleet Boston Corporation, based in Boston, has some $178 billion assets and is about half the size of Citigroup.

Moreover, Fidelity Investments and Lehman Brothers, both big investment companies, announced a broad alliance for distribution channels, research, and other activities.

It is expected that such deals would put pressure on other banks, mutual funds, and financial firms in general to merge so that they can compete internationally. More consolidations are expected after the United States changed, on November 12, 1999, the Glass–Steagel Act of 1993 and the Bank Holding Company Act of 1956, which did not permit banks to get into securities and insurance operations. Other goverments are expected to enact similar banking and other antitrust laws to encourage global competition.

Banking Mergers in Europe

Merger mania in the United States affected Europe as well. Thus, UBS merged with Swiss Banking Corporation, and Dresder Bank of Germany formed alliances with Commerzbank in other European countries.

Moreover, Banque Nationale de Paris increased its hostile takeover offer for Societe Generale and Paribas to $40 billion.

In order to gain approval by the European Union of a $16.6 billion government bailout of Credit Lyonnais, a state-owned bank with heavy losses, France decided to sell a large amount of assets, as well as half of the bank's "commercial presence" in other European countries. Such an action would increase competition in the banking sector of France, as well as among other members of the European Union.

In competition with Fortis, the Belgo-Dutch financial group, ABN Amro, the largest bank of the Netherlands, offered $12.3 billion for Generale de Banque of Belgium so that it can increase its international operations, mainly in Europe, which is expected to achieve a monetary union soon. Such a merger was necessary as other big banks in Belgium and other countries are involved in similar mergers and takeovers. At the same time, Fortis sold 624,000 shares it owns in Munich Re, a large reinsurance company, to Lehman Brothers, which then sold them to European and U.S. investors. Also, Fortis agreed to buy the American Bankers Insurance of Miami for $2.6 billion in cash.

Lloyds TSB P.L.C. acquired Scottish Widows for $11.1 billion to create Britain's biggest bank and insurance group.

Expecting growth in the stock price of Assurances Generales de France S.A. on the Paris Stock Exchange, the Allianz A.G. of Germany agreed to buy 100 percent of the shares of the company, as the French law requires, with $10.4 billion, higher than the $9.5 billion offer by Assicurazioni Generali S.p.A. of Italy. As a result, Allianz shares rose in Frankfurt and Assicurazioni Generali fell in Milan.

The Lend Lease Corporation, with shares in the Sydney and London stock markets, in competition with the Latsis Group and a Portuguese firm, is interested in buying some 350 acres of land in Attica for construction development from the Mesogea A.E. Moreover, Lend Lease recently acquired the Equitable insurance company of the United States.

The government of Poland, which is easing restrictions on foreign banks, sold a 37 percent stake in Bank Przemyslowo-Handlowy S.A. to Bayrische Hypo-und Vereinsbank A.G. of Germany, which is publicly traded for $607 million (1 billion DMs).

Unicredo Italiano, a large bank in Italy, agreed to buy Banca Commerciale Italiana (B.C.I.) for $16 billion, offering eight of its own shares for every five in B.C.I. The Deutsche Bank owns shares in both banks. Also, Unicredito agreed to be acquired by Credito Italiano S.p.A, the largest bank of Italy, for $10.7 billion, thereby creating a financial group with $168 billion in assets and about 3,000 branches. It is expected that the new banking group would be able to compete with other European banks, not only in Italy but in other neighboring countries as well.

Furthermore, the Instituto San Paolo di Torino, the largest commercial bank of Italy, and IMI, a banking group in Rome, plan to merge to create one of the largest EU banks.

The Bankgesellschaft Berlin A.G., which was formed through the merger of three state-owned banks in 1994, agreed to buy the Norddeutsche Landesbank Girozentrale for $3.54 billion in cash and stock. As the EU adopted a common currency, the euro, German states, which operated their own banks for two centuries, plan to keep 60 percent ownership of Bankgesellschaft and trade publicly the rest. As a result of this consolidation, the new bank moved to fourth place behind Dresdner Bank A.G. Moreover, the Deutsche Bank A.G., with global investment banking business in North America and other places, plans to concentrate in Europe in order to be able to face the expected stiff competition into the European Union.

Expecting that the monetary union of Europe will shake out the banking sector, Banco Bilbao Vizcaya (BBZ) and Banco Santander, both in Spain, plan to cooperate and eventually to merge because banking concentration became inevitable in a wider Europe. Already, the group has cemented a partnership with the Royal Bank of Scotland, raised to 100 percent its stake in CC Bank of Germany, and is moving aggressively into Latin America, mainly Brazil and Chile.

To make the banking sector more competitive with other international banks, mergers are sometimes encouraged. Thus, Spain approved the merging of Banco Espanol de Credito and Banco Central to create the biggest commercial bank in Spain and the twentieth in the world in capital and reserves. The combined profits of the two banks are more than 60 billion pesetas (120 pesetas to the U.S. dollar) per year. Their total assets are more than 7 trillion pesetas, deposits about 5.5 trillion, and equity 530 billion pesetas.

In competition with the Piraeus Bank S.A., the European Financial Group (EFG) owned by the Latsis family, which owns already a 15.6 percent stake in Ergo plus 5 percent owned by its parent Deutsche Bank, agreed to buy Ergo Bank S.A. for $5.2 billion. The new bank, with its subsidiaries, Hiosbank A.E. and Macedonia-Thrace Bank A.E., would have more than 250 branches. Such mergers are needed so that the Greek banks would be able to survive strong competition from EU banks before the adoption of the euro in 2001.

In the process of privatization and reorganization of state enterprises, the National Bank of Greece announced its merger with the National Mortgage Bank of Greece through the exchange of 1.9 shares of National Mortgage Bank for each share of the National Bank. The new financial institution, with more than 12.5 trillion drachmas assets and some 10 trillion drachmas deposits, has 605 branches in Greece and more than 100 branches abroad. Moreover, the Bank of Piraeus acquired 37 percent of the Bank of Macedonea-Thrace and 51 percent of the Marathon Bank, which is based in New York and has a number of branches. Other banks privatized or under privatization include Ionian Bank, Cretabank, Central Bank of Greece, and Commercial Bank of Greece.

UBS merged with Swiss Banking Corporation, and Dresdner Bank of Germany formed alliances with Commerzbank in other European Countries.

Other Banking Mergers

Consolidation and restructuring eliminate banks in almost all countries through acquisitions, mergers, and joint ventures. The rapid consolidation of banks became a worldwide phenomenon.

In Canada, the Royal Bank of Canada and the Bank of Montreal announced their merger in early 1998 to create the largest bank of Canada with some $333 billion assets. About three months later, the Canadian Imperial Bank of Commerce and the Toronto-Dominion Bank announced their merger to create the second-largest bank in Canada and the tenth in North America with assets of about $320 billion (United States) and 2,300 branches all over Canada. The market capitalization of the new bank, named ICBC, is estimated at $30 billion. Moreover, there are expectations that the two remaining large banks that is, the Bank of Nova Scotia and the National Bank of Canada, with a market capitalization of about $18 billion, may merge in the near future.

In contrast to the U.S. unit-banking system, Canada has the branch-banking system, which is highly concentrated in four large banks, after these mergers, creating problems for government regulators and consumers regarding competition stifling. Such deals would also affect financial services in the United States, where Toronto-Dominion owns Waterhouse Securities and Waterhouse Bank, whereas Canadian Imperial owns CIBC Openheimer, a securities firm.[18]

Under the $58 billion IMF rescue program, Korea decided to sell two large banks to foreign investors. Thus, Newbridge Capital of the United States agreed to acquire Korea First Bank. Also, HSBC Holding, a British financial group, agreed to buy SeoulBank.

Barclays, an international bank, and Standard Chartered, which covers Africa, Asia, and the Middle East, are discussing the creation of a $60 billion international banking group.

Salomon Smith Barney, which is an investment banking arm of the Travelers group of the United States, agreed to buy the National Westminster's Australian and New Zealand banking firm, which makes sizable profits from flotation and privatization. This is the first international acquisition of Solomon since its merger with the Travelers group in November 1997, worth $9 billion, whereas plans exist for expansion in the Asian Pacific area. As a result of the relaxation of Australia's resistance to takeovers by foreign investment banks, other investment firms, such as Morgan Stanley, Goldman Sachs, and Credit Suisse First Boston, plan to move into Australia.

Garantia S.A., a big investment bank in Brazil, was purchased by Credit Suisse First Boston, a Swiss-American investment banking group, for $675 million in cash and stock. In competition with Merrill Lynch, which won a mandate to underwrite the $6 billion privatization of Petrobras, Brazil's national oil company, Credit Suisse Group, which paid $10 billion to buy the Winterthur Insurance Company of Switzerland in 1997, is making serious efforts to expand in Asia, Europe, and other areas.

Citibank, a unit of Citigroup, agreed to take over the Banca Confia SA of Mexico, after the government pays $1 billion for the bailout of the bank.

Banco Bilbao Vizcaya S.A. reached an agreement to acquire, for $450 million, a 55 percent stake in Banco Excel Economico, which is based in São Paulo.

World Trade, Balance of Payments, and Currency Adjustment

GAINS FROM INTERNATIONAL TRADE

Absolute and Comparative Advantage

More and more, we live in an interdependent world in which countries are not self-sufficient, but they trade with each other according to their comparative advantage. Exports and imports of goods and services and financial transactions have increased drastically since World War II.

The direct or indirect benefits of international trade and finance come primarily from the enlargement of the market and the specialization and more efficient employment of productive resources, as well as technological advances.

Each country has certain advantages, compared to other countries, that can be better exploited through foreign trade. When a country is able to supply another country with a cheaper commodity, it would be better for the latter country to import this commodity and concentrate instead on the production of other commodities in which it has some advantage. In this case, the first country has what is called an absolute cost advantage over the second country. This might be due to better climatic conditions, more advantageous soil and subsoil resources, cheaper labor or other factors of production, or better technology.

What matters most, though, is not the absolute but the relative cost. One country that may be able to produce two commodities, say jute and wheat, more cheaply than another country has an absolute advantage in both commodities. But if the production of jute is comparatively cheaper than wheatmore the first country can still benefit from trade by specializing in the production of jute and exchange some of it for the other country's wheat. And the second country will be better off by specializing in the production of wheat and exchanging some of it for jute. In this case, the first country has a comparative advantage in jute over wheat and an absolute advantage in both jute and wheat. Likewise, the opportunity cost of jute is equal to the amount of wheat to be given up to release resources for the production of a unit of jute.[1]

The Multiplier Effect and Absorption

Additional investment (dI) in the economy would increase income (dY) by a multiple amount and the multiplier ($k = dY/dI$) depends on the marginal propensity to consume (MPC), that is,

$$k = 1/1 - MPC = 1/MPS$$

where MPS stands for the marginal propensity to save.

For example, if MPC is 0.8 or the MPS 0.2, then $k = 1/0.2 = 5$, that is, each additional $1.00 invested would increase national income by $5.00, assuming no leakage in the spending rounds. In an open economy, the leakage of spending outside the economy into imports (M) is making the multiplier smaller depending on the marginal propensity to import (MPM). That is,

$$k = 1/(MPS + MPM)$$

Thus, assuming MPM = 0.2 and using the above example, we have,

$$k = 1/(0.2 + 0.2) = 1/0.4 = 2.5,$$

which is smaller than that without imports. The same thing would occur from additional government spending or exports, which increase the multiplier.

National production (or gross domestic product, GDP) may be different than national expenditures for consumption (C), investment (I), and government spending (G). That is, total domestic output, or what an economy produces, may be different than total domestic expenditures (demand), or what it absorbs (A). The difference is net exports, that is, exports of goods and services (X) minus imports of goods and services (M). Then, total output is equal to total expenditures, or

$$GDP = C + I + G + (X - M)$$

As absorption, A, is equal to C + I + G, then GDP = A + X − M and

$$GDP - A = X - M$$

If absorption or total domestic spending exceeds total domestic production, then the difference will be covered by imports. Depending on the elasticity of exports, a devaluation, ceteris paribus, is expected to increase exports if there is unemployment in the economy; but if there is full employment, the result would be inflation.

The Use of Geometry

Figure 3.1 shows the gains from foreign trade. Before international trade, country 1 produces and consumes at point A, where the indifference or consumers' preference curve meets the production possibility curve. After trade with other countries, production moves to point B as the country specializes in the production of commodity X for which it has a comparative advantage, that is, a comparative cost advantage. A straight line tangent to the production possibility curve at point B and the shift of the indifference curve I to indifference curve II indicate the gains of society from foreign trade from A to D. As a result, the country exports BC of commodity X and imports CD of Y.

Likewise, country 2 with a comparative advantage in the production of commodity Y would specialize in the production of commodity Y, exporting B' C' of Y and importing C' D' of X. In a broad sense, a country has a comparative advantage in the production of a commodity if the exports of this country's commodity, as a percentage of total exports, is higher than its imports of this commodity. For example, the U.S. chemical exports are 12 percent of total exports and imports are 6 percent of

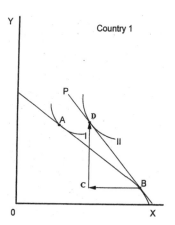
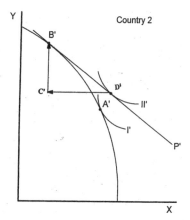

Figure 3.1 Gains from foreign trade

total imports, the United States has a comparative advantage in chemicals, whereas Japan has a comparative advantage in cars with exports of more than 20 percent of total and imports of only 3 percent of total, respectively.

Figure 3.2 shows two countries with identical production possibility curves but different indifference curves (tastes). Before foreign trade, country 1 produces and consumes at point A and country 2 at point A'. With foreign trade, the first country specializes in the production of commodity Y, where it has a comparative advantage, producing at point B, whereas country 2 specializes in the production of commodity X, producing also at point B. A straight line tangent to the production possibility curve at point B shows the higher consumption levels through the shift of the indifference curves from I to II for country 1 and from I' to II' for country 2. Both countries enjoy higher consumption at points D and D', respectively, because of trade between them. Country 1 exports BC of Y and imports CD of X, whereas country 2 exports BC' of X and imports C'D' of Y.

Figure 3.3 shows two countries with the same taste, as the common indifference curve I indicates. The tangency of this curve on the production possibility curves at points A and B shows production and consumption of countries 1 and 2, respectively, before foreign trade. After

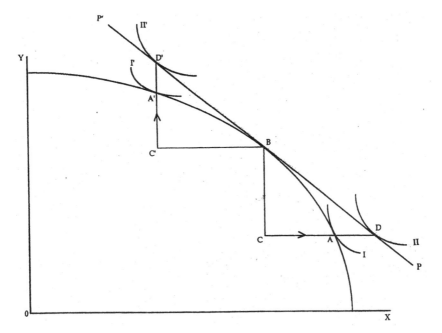

Figure 3.2. Trade of two nations with different tastes

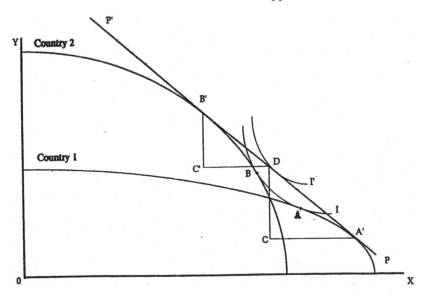

Figure 3.3. Trade of two nations with equal tastes

trade, country 1 specializes in the production of commodity X, producing at point A', whereas country 2 specializes in the production of commodity Y, producing at point B', which are determined by a straight line tangent to the production possibility curves of country 1 and country 2, respectively. Both countries consume at point D on a higher indifference curve I', and country 1 exports A'C of X and imports CD of Y, whereas country 2 exports C'B' of Y and imports C'D of X. (Figures 3.2 and 3.3 explain the Heckscher-Ohlin model).

Figure 3.4 indicates the gains from free trade. With foreign trade, the quantity of supply increases from Q2, determined by the equilibrium of domestic demand and supply, to Q3. Domestic demand is Q1, total supply is Q3, and the difference Q1 – Q3 is absorbed by exports, whereas additional production due to free trade is Q2 – Q3.

TERMS OF TRADE AND CURRENCY DEVALUATION

In general terms, the ratio of export prices to import prices is called the terms of trade. A distinction can be made between commodity or net-barter terms of trade, measured by the ratio of the export price index to import price index $(Px/Pm)100$; gross barter terms of trade, measured by the ratio of physical quantity index of exports to that of imports or $(Qx/Qm)100$; and income terms of trade, which can be derived by

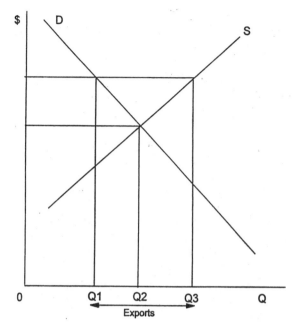

Figure 3.4. Gains from free trade

multiplying the price index of exports by the quantity index of exports and dividing by the price index of imports or $(Px \cdot Qx)/Pm$. Finally, by multiplying net-barter by gross-barter terms of trade, the current-account terms of trade is derived or $(Px \cdot Qx)/(Pm \cdot Qm) \times 100$. The last expression is important because it incorporates both prices and quantities of exports and imports and, therefore, indicates whether a country has a deficit or a surplus in its trade balance. Thus, if the index of a current-account terms of trade is lower than 100, this means that total export proceeds are less than total import payments. Inversely, if it is higher than 100, the country is better off; at 100 there are no net gains or losses for the country from foreign trade. When productivity of exports (Rx) is also considered, we can measure the single factorial terms of trade $(Px/Pm)Rx$. When the productivity of both exports and imports (Rx/Rm) is considered, we have the double factorial terms of trade, that is $(Px/Pm)(Rx/Rm) \times 100$.

The reciprocal demands between two countries establish the terms of trade, which are affected by domestic costs. This principle can be explained with the help of what Alfred Marshall called the reciprocal demand curves, or offer curves, which are presented in Figure 3.5. Thus, the offer curve of country X (say the United States) indicates how much steel the country demands from another country Y (say Japan) in ex-

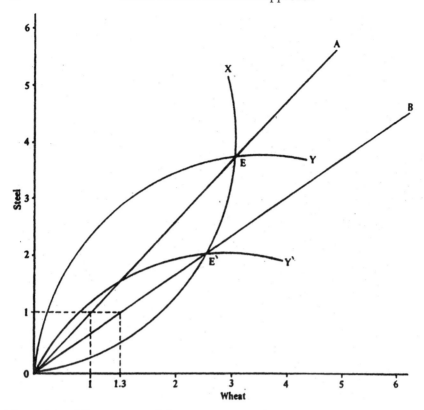

Figure 3.5. Offer curves and changes in terms of trade

change for wheat at different prevailing prices and vice versa for country Y. Such offer curves can be used also for bundles of exportable goods in exchange for bundles of importable goods. After successive trade transactions between the two countries, the two offer curves meet at the equilibrium point E, where the amounts of wheat offered and steel demanded by country X equal the amounts of steel offered and wheat demanded by country Y; that is, where the reciprocal demands of the two countries are equal.

The price ratio, which is measured by the slope of the ray 0A, shows the terms of trade. A change in the supply or demand against country X and in favor of country Y is reflected by the shift in Y's offer curve to a new position (Y'), establishing a new price ratio, 0B; that is, new terms of trade more favorable for Y and less favorable for X. Thus, at the price ratio 0A, one ton of steel was exchanged with one ton of wheat, whereas at 0B, the same one ton of steel is exchanged with more wheat (1.3 tons). This means that X's terms of trade deteriorated by 30 percent in favor of Y.

Exports and imports react to exchange rate changes. Net exports, that is, exports minus imports, are expected to rise when the currency of a country depreciates and to fall when it appreciates, after a time lag. As the price of a currency, in terms of other currencies, rises, export prices increase and prices of imports fall. As a result, the volume of exports declines and that of imports rises, or the gross-barter (quantity) terms of trade decline. Ceteris paribus, this has a contractionary effect on domestic output and employment. This is so, because with a currency depreciation (devaluation) exports rise and imports fall, thereby improving the balance of trade and the economy of the country in question, and vice versa with a currency appreciation.

An appreciation of the currency of country Y (Japanese yen) would shift its offer curve to Y' and the slope 0A to 0B, in which one ton of steel would be exchanged with 1.3 tons of wheat. Therefore, through the currency appreciation, the gross-barter or quantity terms of trade improves for country Y and deteriorates for country X, which is exchanging more of its product (wheat) for the same amount of steel.

The opposite is expected to occur with currency depreciation, as the prices of exports would be lower for other countries, without an equivalent currency depreciation, and foreign demand for exportable goods would increase. This would lead to deterioration of the net-barter or price terms of trade, but to the improvement of the gross-barter or quantity terms of trade. Therefore, the net effect on the balance of trade would depend on which index, the price index or the quantity index, would be higher, and this would be shown by the current-account terms of trade.[2]

The exchange rate depreciation (devaluation) is affected by the price elasticity of imports and exports. In order to pay for imports, foreign exchange is needed, which can be obtained by exports. The size of the devaluation of a currency depends on the price elasticity of demand for imports (Epm), which is determined by the percentage change in the quantity (Q) of imports (m) demanded over the percentage change in price (P) of imports, or,

$$Epm = (dQm/Qm)/(dPm/Pm)$$

Likewise, price elasticity of exports is equal to the percentage change in the quantity of supplied exports over the percentage change in price.

In the case of devaluation of a currency, expectations are that the balance of trade would improve, depending on the international demand elasticity. Thus, if the price elasticity of demand for imports is 1.2, $Epm = \frac{(dQ/Q)m}{(dP/P)m} = 1.2$, and that for exports is 0.7, $Epx = \frac{(dQ/Q)x}{(dP/P)x} = 0.7$, then a devaluation of the currency of the country by 20 percent would improve the balance of trade by 38 percent [(0.20 × 1.2) + (0.20 x 0.7) = 0.24 + 0.14 = 0.38)].

If the summation of the elasticities of imports and exports is higher than 1, ceteris paribus, there would be improvement in the balance of trade. In our example, Epm + Epx = 1.2 + 0.7 = 1.9. If this summation is equal to 1, there would be no change, but if it is less than 1, there would be deterioration in the balance of trade. For example, if the elasticity of imports is 0.4 and that of exports 0.5, then Epm + Epx = 0.4 + 0.5 = 0.9, and the balance of trade would be worse off.

Usually, the summation of the international demand elasticities is higher than 1, thereby ensuring improvement in the balance of trade following a devaluation or depreciation of a currency (Marshall-Lerner condition). This is so because a devaluation or depreciation of a currency means higher prices for imports and lower prices for exports, and therefore less imports and more exports, thereby improving the balance of trade of the country.

Moreover, the income elasticity of imports (Eym) is determined by the percentage change in the quantity of imports demanded over the percentage change in national income (Y), or,

$$Eym = (dQm/Qm)/(dY/Y)$$

Also, income elasticity of exports is equal to the percentage change in the quantity of supplied exports over the percentage change in national income.

DETERMINATION OF EXCHANGE RATES

Exchange rates, that is, prices of a currency in terms of other currencies, may be fixed or flexible. In the case of a fixed exchange rate, the central bank of a country determines the price of its currency versus the currencies of other countries. With flexible exchange rates, the price of a currency in terms of other currencies is determined by free market supply and demand.

Figure 3.6 shows the price of the dollar in terms of euros, the new currency introduced by the European Union. The equilibrium point (E), where the familiar downsloping demand (D) curve meets the upsloping supply (S) curve, indicates the price of the dollar in euros and the quantity of dollars demanded and offered at this price. If the price is higher than the equilibrium price, there would be more dollars supplied than demanded; that is a surplus of dollars. When the price is lower than the equilibrium price, there would be a shortage of dollars. Ceteris paribus, in the case of surplus, there would be a pressure for lower

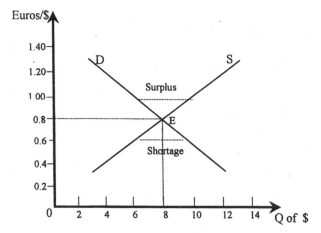

Figure 3.6. Supply and demand diagram

prices, whereas in the case of shortage, there would be a pressure for higher prices, back to the equilibrium point.

Globalization driven mainly by information technology and impressive financial development is revolutionizing production, constantly expanding markets, changing social conditions, and intensifying the interdependence of nations. In this type of globocracy and internetocracy, globocapitalism is subordinating politics and resulting in what Marx and Engels predicted more than a century ago, withering the state away, but voluntarily, not through the dictatorship of the proletariat. With the liberalization of capital in a growing borderless world, huge amounts of money circle the planet instantly, replacing the use of letters of credit and other previous financial instruments.[3]

Nevertheless, there are arguments, mainly by Professor John Gray, that globalization, based on laissez-faire capitalism and Thatcherism, is a utopian idea, an Enlightenment thinking, which erodes social cohesion and imposes cultural imperialism that vests on British-American power. It is an unstable, inequitable, and immoral neoliberal system, destroying the welfare state, traditional societies in emerging nations, and families everywhere. Varieties of capitalism and national variations, with state spending to avoid stagflation and high inequality, which prevails largely in Latin America and even in the United States, should be the economic goal, according to these arguments, because, in an analogy to Aristophanes and Gresham's law, under globalization, "bad capitalism drives out good."[4]

It seems that, in spite of the disadvantages of globalization and neoliberalism, global-capitalism would prevail in the twenty-first century, because welfarism and state intervention lead to inefficiency and laziness.

The rise in the middle class and the spread of ownership in shares, as many countries follow the U.S. system in which over 50 percent of Americans have investments in stocks, supports the argument of Joseph Schumpeter of the trend toward the system of people's capitalism or in practical terms "shareholder capitalism."

The evolution of the international monetary system went through a number of stages, from the use of different goods as money to the gold standard period, the interwar instability, and the Bretton Woods fixed exchange rates. The postwar trade deficits in many countries led to the dollar shortage up to the late 1950s, but severe competition from abroad turned the United States from a surplus to a deficit country and to a substantial gold drain from the U.S. reserves resulting in the post-1973 floating exchange rates.

The growing capital mobility made pegging exchange rates, that is, the price of a currency following the value of another hard currency, such as the dollar, difficult to maintain. The implication is that floating rates are expanding all over the world.

Through arbitrage, equalization of spot and forward exchange rates can take place almost instantly, whereas foreign exchange options are rapidly growing worldwide.

Although international trade is, in principle, no different from domestic trade, the use of different currencies and different laws and regulations distinguish global from domestic trade and finances and require separate analysis. Some important international currency symbols are shown below.

Country	Currency	Symbol
Brazil	Real	R1
Australia	Dollar	A$
Canada	Dollar	C$
European Union	Euro	€
France	Franc	FF
Germany	Mark	DM
Greece	Drachma	Dr
India	Rupee	Rs
Japan	Yen	Y
Mexico	Peso	Ps
Saudi Arabia	Riyal	SR
Singapore	Dollar	S$
South Africa	Rand	R

Switzerland	Franc	SF
United Kingdom	Pound	£
United States	Dollar	$

Figure 3.7 shows the equilibrium (E1) of supply of and demand for dollars ($), in terms of yen, at a price of 80 yen per dollar and quantity 6 (say billion dollars). In case of shift in the demand curve from D1 to D2, the new exchange rate would be 100 yen per dollar and the quantity $8 (billion). This would be the result of an increase in the price of the dollar, through a depreciation of the yen. If the U.S. Federal Reserve Bank (Fed) decided to reduce the price of the dollar, it can supply dollars to the market, thereby restoring the initial price.

Changes in exchange rates affect foreign trade. Thus, as a result of the rising exchange rate (appreciation) of the dollar, above the rate of inflation, in the early 1980s, net exports (exports minus imports) fell sharply. The opposite occurred when the dollar began to fall after 1985 and net exports began to improve, but with a time lag of more than a year.

BALANCE OF PAYMENTS AND FOREIGN EXCHANGE

Table 3.1 presents the U.S. balance of payments, that is, an accounting statement showing the transactions of the United States with all the other countries for a period of time, here for the year 1997. Positive figures (credit) show items that bring gains in foreign exchange. Negative figures (debit) indicate items that bring losses in foreign exchange.

The U.S. balance of trade, that is, exports minus imports of merchandise, was negative since 1975, reaching a record deficit of $168.8 billion

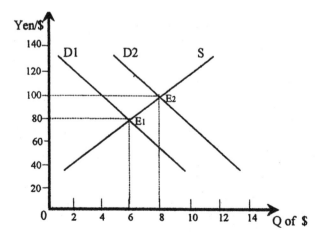

Figure 3.7. Exchange rates of the dollar in terms of yen

Table 3.1 U.S. International Transactions (millions of dollars)

Line	(Credits +; debits -)	1997
1.	Exports of goods, services, and income	1,179,380
2.	Goods, adjusted, excluding military	679,325
3.	Services	258,268
4.	Transfers under U.S. military agency sales contracts	18,269
5.	Travel	73,268
6.	Passenger fares	20,895
7.	Other Transportation	26,911
8.	Royalties and license fees	33,676
9.	Other private services	84,465
10.	U.S Government miscellaneous services	784
11.	Income receipts on U.S. assets abroad	241,787
12.	Direct investment receipts	109,407
13.	Other private receipts	128,845
14.	U.S. Government receipts	3,535
15.	Imports of goods, services, and income	-1,294,904
16.	Goods, adjusted, excluding military	-877,279
17.	Services	-170,520
18.	Direct defense expenditures	-11,488
19.	Travel	-51,220
20.	Passenger fares	-18,235
21.	Other transportation	-28,949
22.	Royalties and license fees	-9,411
23.	Other private services	-48,421
24.	U.S. Government miscellaneous services	-2,796
25.	Income Payments on foreign assets in the United States	-247,105
26.	Direct Investment payments	-45,674
27.	Other private payments	-113,959
28.	U.S. Government Payments	-87,472
29.	Unilateral transfers, net	-39,691
30.	U.S. Government Grants	-12,090
31.	U.S. Government pensions and other transfers	-4,193
32.	Private remittances and other transfers	-23,408
33.	U.S. assets abroad, net (increase/capital outflow (-))	-478,502
34.	U.S. official reserve assets, net	-1,010
35.	Gold	....
36.	Special drawing rights	-350
37.	Reserve position in the International Monetary Fund	-3,575
38.	Foreign currencies	2,915
39.	U.S. Government Assets, other than official reserve Assets, net	174
40.	U.S. credits and other long-term assets	-5,302
41.	Repayment on U.S. credits and other long-term assets.	5,504
42.	U.S. foreign currency holdings and U.S. short-term assets, net	-28
43.	U.S. private assets, net	-477,666
44.	Direct investment	-121,843
45.	Foreign securities	-87,981

Table 3.1 Continued

46.	U.S. claims on unaffiliated foreigners reported by U.S. nonbanking concerns	-120,403
47.	U.S. claims reported by U.S. banks, not included elsewhere	-147,439
48.	Foreign assets in the United States, net (increase/capital Inflow (+))	733,441
49.	Foreign official assets in the United States, net	15,817
50.	U.S. Government securities	-2,936
51.	U.S. Treasury securities	-7,270
52.	Other	4,334
53.	Other U.S. Government liabilities	-2,521
54.	U.S. liabilities reported by U.S. banks, not included elsewhere	21,928
55.	Other foreign official assets	-654
56.	Other foreign assets in the United States, net	717,624
57.	Direct investment	93,449
58.	U.S. Treasury securities	146,710
59.	U.S. currency	24,782
60.	U.S. securities other than U.S. Treasury securities	196,845
61.	U.S. liabilities to unaffiliated foreigners reported by U.S. nonbanking concerns	107,779
62.	U.S. liabilities reported by U.S. banks, not included elsewhere	148,059
63.	Allocations of Special drawing rights	....
64.	Statistical discrepancy	-99,724
	Memoranda:	
65.	Balance on goods (lines 2 and 16)	-197,954
66.	Balance on services (lines 3 and 17)	87,748
67.	Balance on goods and services (lines 65 and 66)	-110,206
68.	Balance on investment income (lines 11 and 25)	-5,318
69.	Balance on goods, services, and income (lines 1 and 15 or lines 67 and 68)	-115,524
70.	Unilateral transfers, net (line 29)	-39,691
71.	Balance on current account (lines 1, 15, and 29 or lines 69 and 70)	-155,215

Source: Survey of Current Business, November 1998, D52.

in 1998, some $64 billion with Japan and $ 56.9 billion with China. The balance of current accounts, which includes the balance of goods, services and investment income as well as unilateral transfers, reached a record deficit of $233 U.S. billion dollars in 1998. The previous record deficit was that in 1987 of $168 billion. Even higher current account deficits are predicted in the near future.

Ceteris paribus, under flexible exchange rates, the depreciation of a country's currency restores the trade equilibrium and eventually the balance of payments of the country in question. Countries with fixed exchange rates will face problems of excess supply and overvaluation of their currencies, then running balance-of-trade deficits. Once their reserves of foreign exchanges are depleted, their currencies, sooner or later, would be depreciated to correct the trade imbalance.

The main reason of depreciation of a currency is inflation, which may be due to excess demand over supply, which may be the result of an increase in spending and in money supply (demand-pull inflation), or to higher costs due to an increase in wages and other costs (cost-push inflation). Figure 3.8 shows demand-pull and cost-push inflation as a result of the shifts in the demand and supply curves, respectively. Moreover, inflation may be the result of structural rigidities and inflexibility in production, imports and income distribution (structural inflation), mainly in emerging nations.

Figure 3.9 shows the effects of a devaluation or depreciation upon the balance of trade of a country. As a result, the prices of imports of the country in question increase and those of exports decline. With inelastic demands, quantity for imports changes little, as does quantity for exports. Therefore, the balance of trade deficit and the demand for foreign currencies could increase for some time, as a result of the devaluation or depreciation, before improving later through long-run increases in the elasticity, as the J-curve shows.

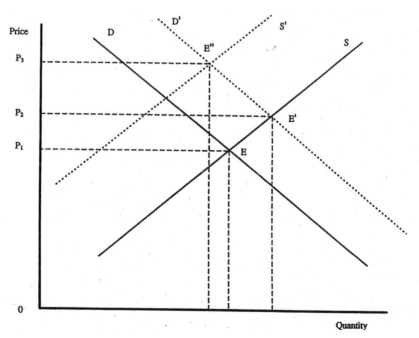

Figure 3.8. Demand-pull and cost-push inflation

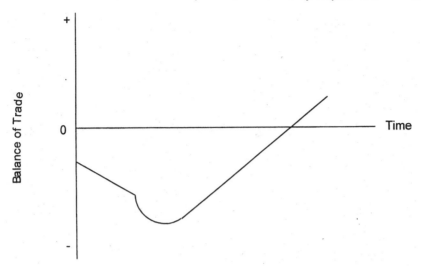

Figure 3.9. Devaluation and the J-curve

Figure 3.10 indicates the equilibrium price after trade. Country 1 exports commodity Y and country 2 imports Y until the equilibrium price is reached in the middle graph. Figure 3.11 shows the relationship of foreign trade and national income. Investments (I) and exports (X) act as injections in the economy, increasing national income (Y), whereas savings (S) and imports (M) are considered as leakages. When S + M = I + X, then we have the equilibrium level of income. An increase in exports (X') leads to a new equilibrium of income (Y").

Figure 3.12 shows the relationship of balance of payments and foreign exchange. Suppose that U.S. buyers demand more European products. Ceteris paribus, this would lead to a deficit in the U.S. trade balance and a lower price of the dollar in terms of euros, from 1.2 to 1.0, as the

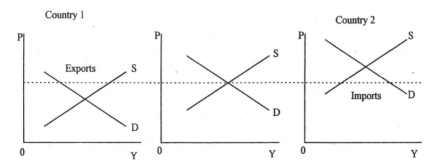

Figure 3.10. Equilibrium price after trade

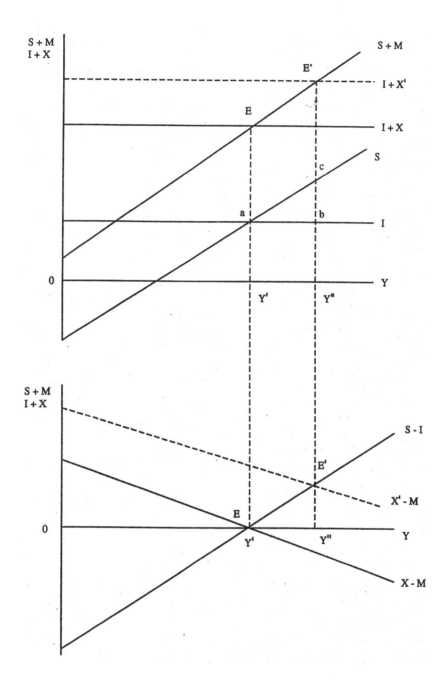

Figure 3.11. Relationship of foreign trade and national income

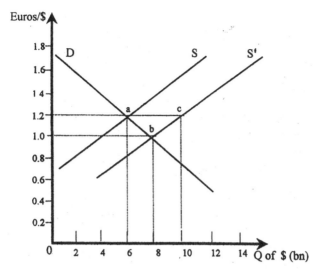

Figure 3.12. Effects of the balance of payments on foreign exchange

supply curve would shift to S'. Assuming the same demand curve, the new equilibrium would be at point b at a price 1.0 and quantity 8, that is, a lower amount of euros per dollar and more dollars offered than at the previous equilibrium. Therefore, under flexible exchange rates, the depreciation of the dollar restores equilibrium to the foreign exchange market at point b.

PROBLEMS OF PROTECTIONISM AND THE WORLD TRADE ORGANIZATION

From time to time, protectionist measures, in the form of quotas, tariffs, or capital movements, are imposed by a number of governments around the world, which inhibit free trade and investment. Restrictions on imports of steel, cars, textiles, dairy products, fruits, and a host of other products, as well as on financial instruments and multinational companies, were and still are imposed by a number of developed and developing countries.

For example, the United States wants to limit annual steel imports, mainly from Japan, Brazil, South Korea, India, Italy, France, Indonesia, and Russia, to about 29 million tons because unfairly they sell in the United States market at prices less than the cost.

It is argued that protection may be needed for infant industries, mainly in developing countries. Alexander Hamilton, the first Secretary of the Treasury of the United States (1791), and Frederick List, a German political refugee in the United States, urged the use of tariffs to foster growth in U.S. manufacturing. Via internal economies of scale and cost reduction, as well as external economies, through backward and forward linkages with other industries, industrialization would improve. Moreover, through industrial protection, diversification in the domestic economy would be achieved, and overspecialization in agricultural or mining products in poor countries, which are easily exposed to cyclical fluctuations, would be avoided. However, it is doubtful if protection would be removed when the "infants" become "adults" able to compete in open markets.

Policymakers can move closer to the competitive ideal and maximize social welfare, reaching Pareto's optimum, by removing distortions to this ideal, thereby achieving the first-best solution. However, this may be difficult in practice because of the eventual side effects of such a policy. For example, removal or reduction of a tax on gasoline may increase the satisfaction of one group but reduce the welfare of society as a whole by increasing air pollution. If the adverse side effects of the first-best solution are excessive, then the second-best policy may be applicable through the introduction of another distortion to reduce or offset the effects of existing distortions, as for example, the shift from a gasoline tax reduction to an income tax reduction, as long as expected gains are greater than losses to society.[5] Similar evaluations of second-best policies can be made in the formations of common markets, regarding inner group benefits versus the rest of the world.

In order to reduce protectionism and encourage free international trade, the General Agreement on Tariffs and Trade (GATT) came into existence in Geneva on January 1, 1948. Its main functions were to organize conferences for nondiscriminatory tariff reduction, enforce international agreements regarding prohibitive barriers (quotas, export subsidies, and the like), and to help improve the position of the poor member nations.

Under the auspices of GATT, extensive negotiations for tariff reduction produced good results during the Kennedy Round (1962–1967) for industrial countries, but limited results for developing countries. Such reductions were sizable (up to 50 percent), mainly for raw material and manufacturing goods. The Trade Expansion Act, which the U.S. Congress passed in 1961, authorizing the President to make across the board tariff cuts, influenced, to a large extent, the negotiations of the Kennedy Round.

Because poor countries received little attention in their appeal for more trade and no aid, by the GATT, which was considered as the "rich countries' club," they supported the creation of the United Nations Conference for Trade and Development (UNCTAD). The main conferences of UNCTAD in Geneva in 1964 (attended by 122 countries), in New Delhi in 1968, in Nairobi in 1976, and so on, made suggestions to help poor nations improve exchange reserves and increase imports of capital goods.

In order to end unfair trade practices mainly by Japan and to meet the European complaints as well as to reduce the pressure for import quotas by Congress, mainly in textiles, steel and agricultural products, the Nixon administration called for a new round of GATT negotiations. As a result, the Tokyo Round (1973–1979) produced results similar to the Kennedy Round, cutting tariffs on manufacturing products by 36 percent, on the average.

The meeting of GATT members at Punda del Este, Uruguay, in 1986–1993, known as the Uruguay Round, produced new measures for trade liberalization through cuts in tariffs and subsidies, as well as for protection in intellectual property and elimination of dumping. Particular attention was given to the interests of the developing countries, mainly Brazil and India, and the encouragement of foreign investment. In 1993, it was agreed by all member nations to reduce the subsidized agricultural exports by 21 percent over six years, whereas restrictions on rice imports in South Korea and Japan were eliminated. The United States, Australia, and Canada, as large exporters of farm products, want to liberalize trade of such products and they object to the EU Common Agricultural Policy (CAP).

The World Trade Organization (WTO), which replaced GATT in 1995, extended its authority to agricultural products and services, whereas a vote of two thirds of members was enough to settle trade disputes rather than a unanimous vote as under GATT. In the meeting of the member nations in Seattle, United States, in November 1999 (Millennium Round), and in Washington in April 2000, developing countries complained against the industrialized countries that rich nations get benefits from the trade rules at their expense. They proposed to reintroduce subsidies that are needed to protect their native industries and to weaken antidumping measures that protect mainly U.S. producers from cheap imports. Also, they proposed to delay the enforcement of intellectual property rights (copyrights, patents, trademarks), to shorten the ten-year restriction on imports by rich countries, and to avoid policies that harm the environment. Furthermore, it is argued that infant industries need protection until they become competitive through economies of scale and experience.

Representatives of developing countries, environmentalists, and labor unionists argue that globalization and the WTO ignore core labor issues and environmental standards. As the argument goes, by reducing tariffs and supporting greater openness, the WTO encourages investment in countries with low wages, without the protection of the environment. Such problems would have more importance after China's membership in the WTO.

Because of the rebellion by developing nations, the riots, and the infighting among the 135 member countries, the WTO conference in Seattle (November 29 to December 3, 1999) collapsed. The argument of poor nations, mainly Brazil, India, and Egypt, was that Washington had tried to benefit the United Steelworkers, Boeing, Amazon.com, and other industries in this conference at their expense, whereas Europe and Japan emphasized their disputes over agriculture and steel.[6]

Nevertheless, open global markets foster the movement of capital, products, and people around the world. Moreover, free trade spurs competition, lowers prices, increases average wages, and improves the quality of life. However, globalization may increase inequality, which is poisoning democracy. As Aristotle mentions (fifth century B.C.) and Adam Smith later (1776), democracy cannot function if there are extremes of wealth.

Some countries unfairly subsidize exports to infiltrate and increase their shares in foreign markets. Japan did that for exports of steel and other products in the United States. Such policy forced the U.S. government not to allow the sale of Japanese steel at a lower price than that of American steel ("trigger price mechanism") and to establish quotas for the number of imported Japanese cars. Lately, the U.S. Department of Commerce complained that NEC and Fujitsu, both Japanese supercomputer makers, sold their products on the American markets at prices well below fair values, thereby harming Silicon Graphics, a U.S. competitor. For that reason, and as a result of the International Trade Commission ruling, the United States imposed duties to compensate for the related damage.

EFFECTS OF CUSTOMS DUTIES

Although tariffs and other restrictions are in the domain of international economics, their growing importance for domestic fiscal and financial policies requires a brief review here. In taxed imports, through tariffs or customs duties, foreign suppliers have to sell their products at lower net prices, affecting domestic policies on subsidies, employment, and bankruptcies. The burden of product taxes is thus shifted to foreigners. Such a shifting runs counter to the international equity principle, according to which each country should pay its own taxes. However, other countries whose products are taxed use the principle of retaliation and impose their own taxes on products they import. The results of such protectionist policies are higher prices and lower quantities of products exchanged.[7]

Similar changes in prices may take place through taxes on exports, which burden foreign consumers. Countries that enjoy monopolies or

oligopolies in natural resources or products and dominate export markets may impose export taxes, thereby increasing the cost of exports.
Again, the foreign consumers will pay more, free trade will be re-
stricted, and conflicts among countries may arise, unless such policies
are in harmony through mutual understanding or international agreements among the governments concerned.

The government can use customs duties to collect revenue and, at the
same time, to protect domestic production and employment, especially
in infant industries. The amount of revenue from tariffs and the degree
of protection depend on the elasticities of supply and demand for the
commodity imported. The higher the elasticity of demand for imports,
the more the decrease in the quantity of imports and the less the revenue
from custom duties. The same holds true for the elasticity of supply.

Figure 3.13 shows the supply and demand for a commodity that is
partly produced domestically and partly imported (AG) to cover total
demand. When a tariff per unit is introduced, total demand would be
reduced, domestic production would be increased, and imports would
be reduced to EF. The government would collect total revenue BCFE
(revenue effect), that is, (EB) × (EF). The triangle ABE measures the
benefits of tariffs to the producers (protective effect); the triangle CGF
measures the sacrifice to the consumers (consumer effect) because of
higher prices due to tariffs. Domestic producers produce more output
by AB, and consumers demand less output by CG as a result of tariffs.
The result is a payment of subsidies to domestic producers, which can
be considered as an income transfer from the consumers to the producers of the import-competing good considered.

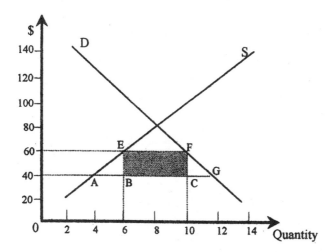

Figure 3.13. Effects of custom duties

Some governments provide budget subsidies for certain products that can be unloaded to other countries at prices below the cost of production (dumping). To retaliate, other nations use antidumping and countervailing duty measures. Such subsidies and antidumping policies restrict free and fair trade among nations and increase the possibilities of protectionism, in addition to budgetary expenditure needed to pay for subsidiaries.[8] Among the products subsidized are textiles, electronics, and primarily steel. Steelmakers in the United States complain against Japan and the EU and ask for quota restrictions; the Japanese complain against South Korea; EU steelmakers complain against Romania and Brazil; and those in developing countries, against industrial countries, accusing them of trying to keep the "new boys"—the Third World producers—off the world markets.

To avoid protectionism and trade wars, many steelmakers and other producers ask for multilateral agreements among interested nations similar to that of cotton textiles in the 1960s, which allow developed countries to restrict textile imports from developing countries. However, steel users and primarily automakers and construction industries object to such agreements, which protect inefficient domestic manufacturers and push up prices. For the government, though, such agreements lead to less unemployment and more tax revenue.

An unwise policy of protectionism in the 1930s exacerbated the Great Depression of that period. Throughout the 1920s, U.S. exports increased, as did private loans to finance such exports to other countries. After the crash of 1929, average tariffs were raised to 40 percent (Smoot-Hawley Law of 1930). Foreign firms could not sell their products to the United States and could not collect dollars to pay their loans. The tariffs of the 1930s walled out competition and walled in inefficiency. They cut back imports, but they reduced exports as well. The result of the beggar-thy-neighbor policy of protectionism reduced world industrial production by about 30 percent and increased unemployment by more than 25 percent, whereas world trade in manufactured goods declined by more than 40 percent and overall government revenue from tariffs was reduced.

For some commodities, effective tariffs are relatively high in the United States, mainly for clothing, fabrics, milk, cheese, butter, cigars, cigarettes, plant, vegetables, olive oil, and other primarily agricultural products. Similar and even higher tariffs prevail in Japan and the EU countries. Tariff reductions and improvements in trade with the poor nations would also allow reduction in U.S. aid, which is a burden on the budget, and stop the cry of the poor nations for "trade, no aid."

Recently, the United States and the European Union had a "banana war" because the Europeans refused to open their markets to bananas produced mainly in central American countries and shipped by Chiquita Brands International and Dole Food, two American companies. In retaliation, the United States announced 100 percent tariffs on some European products, such as cashmere sweaters, Mont Blanc pens, tapered candles, and bath products. The Europeans argue that the companies are American and influence politicians through generous contributions to both Democrats and Republicans, but the bananas are produced elsewhere. However, the World Trade Organization ruled that Europe has to abide and negotiate a settlement in order to avoid retaliation.[9]

LETTERS OF CREDIT AND BANKERS' ACCEPTANCES

In order to reduce foreign trade risks, exporters want assurances that they will receive payment for the products they sell. Normally, an importer applies to a commercial bank for a letter of credit (LOC) in which the bank guarantees payment to the exporter, at a specific time, with the presentation of required documents, mainly the bill of lading.

The LOC may be revocable, that is, it can be changed by the parties or, usually, irrevocable, in which case it cannot be changed without the consent of the parties. Also, the LOC may be revolving, when it is used for many shipments for a period of time, or may be a standby LOC, when the bank, with a fee by the exporter, promises to pay the exporter in case the importer defaults.

To facilitate trade financing and minimize currency risks, banks or other firms may buy invoices from exporters at a discount, collecting the invoices from the importers (factoring). Moreover, the exporters can sell the promissory notes, endorsed by importers' banks, to forfeiting banks with a discount. These financial (forfeiting) devices are used by banks and other institutions to finance exports to emerging nations. Also, barter trade or counter trade can take place among traders of different countries to conserve foreign exchange and avoid tariffs and other restrictions.[10]

Bankers' acceptance is a time draft an exporter draws and presents, together with the shipment documents, to a bank for acceptance. The bank that accepts the draft usually pays the exporter before maturity at a discount and may rediscount it with the Federal Reserve Bank at the prevailing discount rate. At maturity, the bank will pay the holder of the draft the face value of the draft received from the importer a day earlier. Bankers' acceptances are used mainly for large amounts of trade between different countries, for which the importer pays a fee, usually 1.5 percent of the draft value.

For example, a U.S. importer of coffee from Brazil requests a sum in LOC from a U.S. bank for payment. The exporter ships the coffee and gives to a bank in Brazil the draft and the needed shipping documents. The Brazilian bank, in turn, sends them, together with the letter of credit, to the U.S. bank that is issuing a bankers' acceptance (BA). The exporter may discount the BA, and the U.S. bank gives the documents to the importer, who takes possession of the coffee.

Nevertheless, modern technology with rapid telecommunications, advanced computers, and the Internet improved global trade financing and reduced the cost of transactions. Moreover, large commercial banks, such as Citigroup, have established special units to transmit automatically electronic letters of credit and other financial instruments worldwide.

Foreign Exchange and Securities Markets

PURCHASING POWER PARITY THEORY AND EXCHANGE RATES

Purchasing Power Parity

The theory of purchasing power parity (PPP) suggests that exchange rates between two countries will adjust to reflect changes in the price levels of the two countries. In its absolute form, the ratio of the price levels of the two countries (Px/Py), in a free exchange rates system, determines the equilibrium exchange rate (Rxy). That is,

$$Rxy = Px/Py \text{ and } Px = RxyPy$$

For example, if the price of a skirt in the United States (country x) is $10 and in France (country y) is FF50 and the $/FF exchange rate is $0.20 or 20 cents per French franc, then,

$$Px = RxyPy = (0.20)(50) = 10$$

Therefore, the price of a skirt in France is the same as in the United States, once we use the exchange rate to convert the price in French francs into dollars and compare prices in a common currency. That is, identical products have the same price in the two countries in terms of the same currency (law of one price). However, the absolute PPP is not reliable because of different weights across countries for each individual good. Moreover, there are nontraded goods and services internationally, and the absolute PPP does not express the relationship of exchange rates and price differentials in a proper way, particularly in the long run. Many services, such as those of family physicians, mechanics, and the like, have systematically higher prices in rich than in poor countries.

An alternative to the absolute PPP is the relative PPP, measured in percentages. According to the relative PPP, the percentage change in the rate of inflation of two countries determines the percentage change in the exchange rate. Thus, the percentage change in the exchange rate (R') of a country (x), as related to another country (y), would be equal to the percentage change in the price levels (P') of the two countries, that is:

$$R' = P'x - P'y$$

For example, if the rate of inflation in a country (x) is 10 percent and that of another country (y) is 4 percent, then the percentage change in the exchange rate is equal to 6 percent. In money terms, the exchange rate for a current period (1), compared to that of a base period (0), would be:

$$Rxy1 = (Px1/Py1)Rxy0$$

Thus, assuming a price index for France $(Px1)$ 106 and that for the United States $(Py1)$ 100 (no inflation) and the exchange rate of the base period $(Rxy0)$ equal to 6 French francs (FF) per dollar ($), then the exchange rate in period 1 would be FF6.36/$, that is:

$$Rxy1 = (106/100)6 = 1.06 \times 6 = 6.36$$

A higher inflation rate in a country tends to change the equilibrium exchange rate and to lead to a depreciation of its currency in relation to the currency of another country with a lower inflation rate. Although exchange rates may diverge from their PPP level, in the long run the PPP theory is a useful guide to exchange rate determination.

The law of one price states that the price of a product in free markets must be the same in all markets, after tariffs and transportation costs are considered. Exchange rates should conform to PPP, which holds when money is neutral. If an identical basket of goods, for example, has a price of $100 in the United States and 500 French francs, ceteris paribus, the exchange rate should be $1 = FF5. If the same basket of goods has a price of FF400 and the exchange ratio is $1 for FF5, then U.S. imports from France and the demand for French francs would increase until the price of the basket again reaches FF500.

The use of PPP exchange rates is preferable to the use of market exchange rates because a large part of output comes in nontraded services, particularly in low-income countries in which output is understated. Although empirical evidence in many countries is not conclusive, it seems that the PPP theory holds in the long run but not so much in the short run, mainly because financial and goods markets are not perfect, as there exist different controls, taxes, transactions costs, and tastes in different countries. However, technological improvement in communications and freely floating markets tend to reduce such differences and move the world economies toward what Plato postulated, an ideal or perfect condition, regarding the law of one price in all the markets.[1]

Arbitrage

Arbitrage is the buying of a currency in a place with a lower price for resale immediately in another place with a higher price, for profit. Such a two-point arbitrage and also a three-point or triangular arbitrage (where three places are involved) tend to equalize exchange rates through the mechanism of demand and supply. Because communications among the financial centers of the world are virtually instantaneous, exchange rates tend to be equal, but when they are not, arbitrage would take place to profit from the differences and make them equal. The same can be said for other assets, such as sugar or cocoa. Such transactions occur immediately (spot transactions) at a spot price.

For example, if the dollar price in Paris is 6 French francs and in New York FF5.6, an arbitrageur would buy francs in Paris and sell them immediately in New York, making a FF0.4 profit. This is known as two-point arbitrage. Furthermore, if the dollar price is 2 German marks (Deutsche marks, DM) in Frankfurt and a DM is equal to FF3.5 in Paris, then it is profitable to buy DM2 with a dollar and sell them in Paris for FF7 and resell them in New York for $1.25, making $0.25 profit. This is known as triangular or three-point arbitrage. This process would continue, triggering large flows of funds, until the opportunity for profit is eliminated.

Figure 4.1 shows the price of the dollar in terms of euros. At equilibrium (E), where supply (S) is equal to demand (D), the price is 1.2 euros per dollar and quantity 6 (billions of dollars, for example). If there is an increase in the demand of dollars and the demand curve shifts to D1, the new equilibrium is at E1, with a price 1.4 and quantity 8. However, if there is an increase in the supply of dollars and the supply curve shifts to S1, then there is a new equilibrium at E2 with a price back to 1.2 euros per dollar, but a higher amount of dollars offered, that is 10 (billion dollars).

Effects of Interest Rates and Inflation

Exchange rates are closely related to interest rates. Profit-seeking arbitrage (covered interest arbitrage) leads to interest rate parity, through the forward premium adjustment. For example, if the spot exchange rate (S) is 6 French francs per dollar, the French interest rate (*iff*) for a year is 10 percent and the U.S. interest rate (*i$*) is 5 percent, the forward exchange rate (F) is expected to be 6.30 in a year. That is:

$$1 + iff = (1 + i\$)F/S \text{ or } (1 + iff)/(1 + i\$) = F/S$$

By subtracting 1 from both sides, we have the interest parity equation:

$$(iff - i\$)/(1 + i\$) = (F - S)/S$$

Which is approximately (and it is known as the interest parity condition):

$$iff - i\$ = (F - S)/S$$

or $0.10 - 0.05 = (F - 6)/6$ or $0.05 = (F - 6)/6$ and $F = 6.30$.

The forward premium for a year would then be equal to the 0.05 interest differential. The nominal interest rate (*i*) tends to incorporate

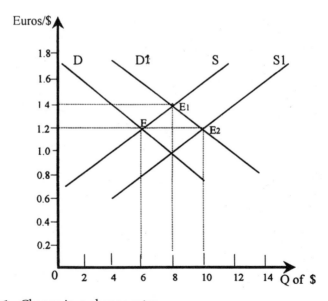

Figure 4.1. Change in exchange rates

the rate of inflation (P'), so that the real rate of return of money lent (r) is equal to the nominal interest rate minus the rate of inflation, that is,

$$r = i - p'$$

In this equation (from the pioneering work of the American economist Irving Fisher in the 1930s), an increase in inflation tends to increase the interest rate. Thus, using the interest parity condition and assuming the same real rate of interest in France and in the United States, that is:

$$Rff = r\$$$

and

$$iff - i\$ = P'ff - P'\$ = (F - S)/S$$

or $(6.30 - 6)/6 = 0.30/6 = 0.05$. That is, the interest differential is also equal to the interest discount.

In addition to expected inflation, higher future taxes on holders of bonds and other domestic assets would lead foreign investors to require higher yield to hold the riskier domestic bonds; otherwise they would switch to foreign bonds or other international assets. Likewise, expected depreciation or devaluation of a currency, under a floating system, would lead to the increase in nominal short-term interest rates, which act as shock absorbers, to avoid the sale of bonds and other assets in domestic currency and the outflow of foreign currencies.

For example, if a foreign investor has $1 million in Brazilian bonds, worth 1 million reals ($1 = one real), and it is expected that the real would be devalued to 2 reals per dollar, then the bonds would be sold as soon as possible, and the Brazilian currency would be exchanged with dollars before devaluation. But, Brazil would increase interest rates in order to avoid massive sales of bonds and other assets and the outflow of dollars and other hard currencies. Actually, this is what happened, not only in Brazil, but in Russia and other countries as well during the last financial crisis. Nevertheless, the Bovespa stock index of Brazil fell 5.1 percent to 6,954.17 on January 7, 1999, mainly because a large state, Minas Gerais, announced the postponement of payments due to the central government. Thereafter, the floating real depreciated but the Bovespa stock index improved.

An interest rate swap is an agreement to transform a fixed-rate debt or deposit to a floating-rate instrument, or vice versa. Usually large banks, which have access to low-cost Fed funds, enter interest rate swap markets. Such markets have grown to more than $3 trillion in securities since their beginning in the 1970s. Normally, swaps have maturity of up to five to ten years. However, some swaps have maturity of up to thirty years, that is, far beyond forward or options markets. A swaption call is a contract that gives the right to receive payments on a fixed interest rate, but to pay a floating interest rate, that is, the right to go short; whereas a swaption put payment is in fixed rate but the receipt is in floating rate (going long). Swaptions are used primarily by American and European financial institutions to hedge an exposure or to manage risks in option portfolios.

STOCK MARKET CONCENTRATIONS AND GYRATIONS

The movements of shares of different companies to big stock markets may create problems of financial concentration and monopolization or oligopolization of financial activities. This trend makes emerging stock markets weak and largely affected by the gyrations of the big markets, such as the New York Stock Exchange (NYSE), which is 207 years old, with around $11 trillion market value of more than 3,000 listed companies and an average daily trading volume of more than 620 million shares. Also, the Nasdaq in New York, which was born a quarter century ago and which its parent, the National Association of Securities Dealers (with some 6,000 brokerage firms that make up the association), agreed to merge with the American Stock Exchange (AMEX), has a combined $2 trillion ($0.2 trillion in AMEX) market value of 6,270 listed companies (783 in AMEX) and an average trading volume of 676 million shares (28 million in AMEX).

The number of shares traded in all American exchanges reached 400 billion shares in 1998, compared to about 100 billion in 1992, whereas trades made on-line reached 14 percent of all trading, compared to 7 percent in 1996.

Investors all over the world gallop into stock markets seeking short-term riches or retirement income. Because of high demand for shares, prices tend to go up and volume to rise significantly. As a result, new firms want to share part of the growing stock exchanges pie. Thus, Island Electronic Communication Networks, or Island ECN, a computerized stock-trading service, applied to the Securities and Exchange Commission to become a new stock exchange in the United States. With its software, it matches automatically orders from buyers and sellers and expects to compete effectively with NYSE and Nasdaq, which plan to use lower fees and longer trading hours. However, the cost of getting through the SEC's regulatory labyrinth is estimated at $10 million.

Listing of Companies in Foreign Exchange Markets

Among the important companies listed in foreign stock exchange markets is the Aglo American Corporation of South Africa, mentioned earlier, the financial services units of which were acquired recently by the RMB Holdings Ltd. for $9.2 billion (46 billion rand). As a result, the American depository receipts of the Aglo American Corporation jumped to $44 in Nasdaq, an increase of nearly 10 percent. The main reason for this merger was to counter an anticipated merger of two other competitors, the Liberty Life Group and the Standard Bank group, both in South Africa, worth $7 billion.

To increase liquidity in its shares, Amvescap, a London fund management group, tries to achieve a full listing in New York, in addition to that of London. At present, the group's shares are traded in NYSE as American Depository Receipts (ADRs), that is; paper traded in lieu of underlying shares, because U.S. regulations do not permit a full listing of foreign stocks. However, Amvescap, with assets more than $190 billion, trades close to 100,000 shares in New York, compared to about 3 million shares in London. The group is based in Atlanta and has half of its shareholders in the United States, but is listed in Britain.[2]

In order to attract new companies and halt the drift of old companies to New York and other overseas markets, some stock markets introduce favorable rules. Thus, the newly privatized stock exchange of Milan reduced the cost of trading and simplified regulations. After 1990, a number of Italian firms have been or are set off for NYSE. They include Gucci, the Florentine fashion house; Luxottica, the producer of spectacle frames; Fila, the sportswear company; Natuzzi, the sofa maker; and others. Gucci decided to list also on the Amsterdam Stock Exchange, whereas the shares of Luxxotica, Fila, and Natuzzi are traded in NYSE as ADRs. Under the new regulations, companies do not have to show profits for the last three years to be listed in the bourse of Milan; instead, they have to show the last balance sheet audited, a capitalization of $5.9 million, and that their activities can generate profits. Moreover, at least 25 percent of the company's capital is to be floated on the Milan market.[3]

Telecoms and other firms in Europe and other continents are doing very well in selling shares in the American stock markets. For example, France Telecom sold in the United States in October 1997 shares at a price of $32, which later went up to more than $60 or about 100 percent.

Stet Hellas Telecommunications SA, a Greek mobile telecommunications firm in which Telecom Italia SpA holds a 60 percent stake and Nynex Network Systems (a unit of Bell Atlantic Corporation) maintains 20 percent, raised $297 million through a successful U.S. (Nasdaq) initial public offering (IPO). The sale was made through J.P. Morgan

Securities of 11 million American depository receipts (ADRs) at the offering price of $27 and a close price $32.75 (a 20 percent premium). The capitalization of Stet Hellas is estimated at $2.4 billion.

Gyrations of the Stock Markets

Historically, the Dow Jones Industrial Average (DJIA) had a number of drastic ups and downs. On December 18, 1899, it dropped 8.72 percent (or 5.57 points), on March 14, 1907, 8.29 percent (6.89 points), on October 28, 1929, 12.82 percent (38.99 points), and the next day, October 29, 1929, it dropped again by 30.57 points. On October 30, 1929, the DJIA was up 12.34 percent, closing at 258.47, and a few days later, November 6, 1929, it dropped 9.29 percent (25.55 points). On August 12, 1932, it dropped again 8.40 percent (5.79 points).

On October 19, 1987, the DJIA dropped 22.61 percent (508 points). On October 21, 1987, it raised 10.15 percent (186.84 points), closing at 2,027.85 points, and on October 26, 1987, it dropped 8.04 percent (158.83 points). Some ten years later, October 27, 1997, the Dow industrials dropped 7.18 percent (554.26 points) from 7,615.41. However, the next day, October 28, 1997, it increased by 337.17 points (4.7 percent) whereby the volume of shares exchanged reached 1,202.55 million that day, the highest ever. On November 23, 1998, the DJIA reached a record of 9,374.27 and on July 27, 1999, a new record of 11,209.84. On July 27, 1999, the Nasdaq reached a record of 2,864.48, whereas the Standard and Poor's (S & P) 500 reached a record of 1,418.78 on the same date. Later, new records were achieved, whereas large global gyrations continued.

From December 8, 1994, to December 8, 1998—that is, in four years—the Dow Jones Industrials increased by 139.89 percent (although historically the Index has doubled every seventeen years), the Standard & Poor's 500 stocks by 161.54 percent, and the Nasdaq Composite by 180.34 percent On July 2, 1999, these indexes increased, from December 8, 1994, by 202.23 percent for Dow Jones Industrials, 212.32 percent for Standard and Poor's 500, and 281.16 percent for Nasdaq Composite. This is a phenomenon of "irrational exuberance," as Alan Greenspan, the Chairman of the Federal Reserve Bank, said.

It seems that the stock prices are largely inflated, thereby generating wealth for individual investors that may decline later. The Standard & Poor's 500, for example, increased since the end of 1994 to the end of 1998 by more than 150 percent, creating about $5 trillion for investors. This bonanza addicted the consumers to spend more (0.2 percent) than what they earn and save less (negative saving). This is a dangerous policy, and the bubble may burst leading to a severe recession or depression when spending declines, particularly on appliances, furniture, cars, and other durable goods. This phenomenon can be observed not only with the Americans, who are spending themselves to oblivion, but with peoples of other industrial countries as well.

In order to cool off transactions when there is a sizable decline in the stock market, one- and two-hour breakers were introduced for 350 and 550 point declines, respectively.

Effects of Market Gyration on Mergers

As the stock exchange markets soar, the buying power of stock increases and companies are able to bid and buy more easily other domestic or foreign companies. Ceteris paribus, when markets soar, mergers and acquisitions, which involve stocks, increase and vice versa.

Thus, about half of the about $800 billion in U.S. mergers in 1997 involved stock and affected huge bids such as that of Worldcom Inc. for MCI Communications for $36.5 billion in stock and cash, in competition with GTE all-cash ($28 billion) and British Telecommunications ($19 billion). Also, Starwood Longing Trust, a hotel and casino company, acquired ITT for $10.2 billion in competition with Hilton Hotels for $9.3 billion, half in cash and half in stock. Likewise, Bell Atlantic acquired NYNEX, the New York telephone company, for $24 billion. Moreover, Travelers Group acquired Salomon Brothers, a large investment firm, for $9 billion, financed mainly by large investment banks, whereas Travelers merged with Citicorp in a deal worth $70 billion. However, offers in cash are not seriously affected by stock market gyrations because banks, not stock markets, finance primarily such offers.

Stock trading activities are growing rapidly with the Internet, through which one out of seven shares are changing hands now and far more are expected in the future. Charles Schwab, E* Trade, Waterhouse, DLI Direct, and many other companies became on-line traders, rapidly expanding Internet brokerage activities. This trend is expected to revolutionize stock exchanges and supports the theory of shareholder capitalism, but it incorporates the risk of worldwide market gyrations.

Similar gyrations can be observed in European and other countries. Thus, the FTSE 100 in London rotates around 6,000 points, the DAX index of Frankfurt around 5,000, the CAC-40 index of Paris around 4,000, the Madrid index around 10,000, the Milan index around 35,000, the Amsterdam index around 500, the Swiss index around 7,000, and index of Athens around 4,000.

Nevertheless, alliance and cooperation among exchange markets reduce competition and gyrations, as, for example, the alliance of the Chicago Board of Trade with Eurex, whose management is controlled by Deutsche Borse A.G., which are the biggest trans-Atlantic derivative exchanges. Moreover, the London Stock Exchange plans to merge with the Deutsche Börse A.G. of Germany (Frankfurt) to create the world's largest derivatives market.

GLOBALIZATION OF FINANCIAL MARKETS

The rapid expansion of financial transactions is reducing the power of political leaders to control market forces. Not only politicians but labor unions and business executives gradually are losing their ability to interfere in the economy on matters of social safety net, Social Security, wage inequalities, mergers and acquisitions of banks, brokerage and other firms on a global scale. With the significant spread of communications through the Internet and other electronic means, it would be difficult for politicians to blame mysterious global forces for their national or regional woes.

The globalization of financial markets leads to the reduction or elimination of national restrictions regarding banking transactions on stocks and bonds. Thus, the Glass-Steagall Act, introduced in the United States in 1933 as a result of the stock market crash of 1929 and the subsequent Great Depression, was repealed in 1999, allowing banks to underwrite stocks and corporate bonds. But, through court cases and liberal rulings by the Federal Reserve, banks could provide investment and merger advice and perform virtually all the functions of stockbrokers, especially after the 1984 Supreme Court case that allowed the Bank America Corporation to buy Charles Schwab and Company, a discount brokerage firm. Moreover, the Bankers Trust New York Corporation agreed to buy Alex Brown & Sons, Inc., the oldest stock brokerage firm in the United States, for about $1.7 billion in stocks, whereas Bankers Trust itself was acquired by Deutsche Bank of Germany. Similar acquisitions are expected by banks of other nations and vice versa.

A Eurocurrency deposit is a deposit in a bank outside of the country. Thus, a Eurofranc is a French franc deposit outside France, and a Eurodollar is a dollar deposit outside the United States. An offshore banking market refers to the deals of the banks in one country in currencies of other countries.

An important international banking market is the Eurocurrency market. In addition to the European countries, Eurocurrency banking centers include the Bahamas and other Caribbean islands, Canada, Japan, Singapore, Hong Kong, and the United States. The Eurocurrency market appeared in the 1950s and grew drastically thereafter to account now for about $4 trillion.

Likewise, Euronotes or Eurocredits (medium-term securities) and Eurobonds (long-term securities) are sold to other countries by banks, corporations, and governments in order to borrow funds in other currencies, in fixed rates or floating rates (refixed periodically, say every three or six months).

There are 8,000 stock and bond funds in the United States markets, 6,425 of which are stock funds. Also, there are more than 50 funds of funds, also known as multifunds, compared to only 18 in 1990. Many of these stock and bond funds and 5 of the multifunds also dabble in overseas stocks. Overseas stock markets, in many cases, outperform the American market. This is so especially in emerging markets mainly in Eastern Europe and Latin America. Diversification in domestic and international stocks and bonds, primarily under the umbrella funds or multifunds, improves performance and reduces volatility through the growing number of shareholders. The number of Americans who own shares in mutual funds increased to 63 million, a growth of neophyte fund investors by a third in the last two years.[4]

As long as the global economy is stable and improving, long-term holders of financial assets continue to invest, mainly through retirement plans. However, there are fears about the side effects of economic globalization, the erosion of national decorum, and the uninhibited pursuit of laissez-faire ideology. A serious question is how to tame the oligarchy who can move huge amounts of financial assets and cause instability in global markets, thereby threatening the social safety net in many parts of the world. Such unwise speculation by a few managers of hedge funds and other managers led to an average loss of some 77 percent of the emerging stock-market stock funds in 1998.

As a result of the rapidly growing electronic trading, there is a sharp decline in the prices of seats on many financial exchanges. For example, a seat at the New York Stock Exchange was sold for $1.35 million in June 1998, down from a record $2 million a few months ago, despite the large growth in stock trading. Likewise a membership seat at the Chicago Board of Trade, the biggest futures exchange of the world, was sold for $495,000 recently, compared to a record $857,500 at the beginning of 1998, a decline of 42 percent. Similar declines in seat prices can be observed at the New York Mercantile Exchange, the American Stock Exchange, the Pacific Stock Exchange in San Francisco, and the Chicago Board Options Exchange.[5]

The same phenomenon can be observed not only in the United States but also in Europe and in other places where stock markets use electronic trading, replacing traditional floor trading. Such replacements occurred, for example, in the Matif, the French Futures Exchange, and the Deutsche Terminborse (DTB) of Germany, which captured market share from Liffe, the London International Financial Futures and Options Exchange, a large auction market.

In addition to electronic trading, introduced in the 1970s by the Nasdaq stock market, the sharp decline in the cost of membership on many financial exchanges is also due to the consolidation among financial exchanges and the global nature of securities markets. Such consolidations include the recent mergers of the American Stock Exchange with the National Association of Securities Dealers, which operates the Nasdaq stock market, and the Philadelphia Stock Exchange. Also, the Board of Trade of New York, which was created by the merger of the Coffee, Sugar and Cocoa Exchange with the New York Cotton Exchange, agreed with Cantor Fitzgerald to form the Cantor Financial Futures Exchange.

In order to link financial markets together globally, the Nasdaq stock market, which recently acquired the American Stock Exchange, is pursuing affiliations with other stock markets around the world, including those of Frankfurt, Paris, Tokyo, Hong Kong, Singapore, and Mexico City. Such global market ties, amid competition for company listings, would let firms trade their shares internationally and reduce transaction costs.

Table 4.1 shows foreign transactions in stocks, as well as in bonds, and the areas and countries involved. Most of the transactions are with Europe, mainly Britain, Latin America, and Asia, primarily Japan.

Foreign purchases are higher than foreign sales of both U.S. corporate stocks and primarily bonds, including state and local government bonds, as well as those of U.S. government agencies. Overall, foreigners buy more securities from the United States than they sell. Europe (mainly U.K., Germany, France, and Switzerland), Latin American and Caribbean countries, and Japan are the main partners in buying and selling foreign securities.

DEPOSITORY RECEIPTS

Non-U.S. equities are traded in the New York Stock Exchange (NYSE) through American Depository Receipts (ADRs), quoted and settled in dollars. ADRs are receipts for the shares of foreign-based corporations held by U.S. banks, which entitle the holders to all capital gains and dividends. A requirement for companies that want to tap the huge American pool of capital and to be on the U.S. list is to adjust their financial statements to U.S. Generally Accepted Accounting Principles (GAAP). However, global investors, as well as financial and technological progress, demand ordinary shares to be quoted and settled in the issuers home currencies and eventually in currencies of many countries.

A growing number of countries and an increasing number of non-U.S. companies joined the NYSE, which became a truly global market. From that standpoint, young urban professionals ("yuppies") and other persons providing financial services should be trained to be familiar with

Table 4.1 Foreign Transactions in Securities (millions of dollars)

Transaction and area or country	1996	1997
U.S. CORPORATE SECURITIES		
Stocks		
Foreign purchases	590,714	1,097,958
Foreign sales	578,203	1,028,361
Net purchases, or sales (-)	12,511	69,597
Europe	5,367	62,688
France	-2,402	6,641
Germany	1,104	9,059
Netherlands	1,415	3,831
Switzerland	2,715	7,848
United Kingdom	4,478	22,478
Canada	2,226	-1,406
Latin America and Caribbean	5,816	5,203
Middle East	-1,600	383
Other Asia	918	2,072
Japan	-372	4,787
Africa	-85	472
Other Countries	-57	342
Bonds[1]		
Foreign purchases	393,953	610,116
Foreign sales	268,487	475,958
Net purchases, or sales (-)	125,466	134,158
Foreign countries	125,295	133,595
Europe	77,570	71,631
France	4,460	3,300
Germany	4,439	2,742
Netherlands	2,107	3,576
Switzerland	1,170	187
United Kingdom	60,509	54,134
Canada	4,486	6,264
Latin America and Caribbean	17,737	34,733
Middle East	1,679	2,155
Other Asia	23,762	16,996
Japan	14,173	9,357
Africa	624	1,005
Other countries	-563	811
FOREIGN SECURITIES		
Stocks, net purchases, or sales (-)	-59,568	-40,942
Foreign purchases	450,365	756,015
Foreign sales	509,633	796,957
Bonds, net purchases, or sales (-)	-51,369	-48,171
Foreign purchases	1,114,035	1,451,704
Foreign sales	1,165,404	1,499,875
Net purchases, or sales (-), of stocks and bonds	-110,637	-89,113
Europe	-57,139	-29,874
Canada	-7,685	-3,085
Latin America and Caribbean	-11,507	-25,258
Asia	-27,831	-25,123
Japan	-5,887	-10,001
Africa	-1,517	-3,293
Other countries	-4,087	-2,288

Source: *Federal Reserve Bulletin*, November 1998, A60.

[1]Includes state and local government securities and securities of U.S. government agencies and corporations. Also includes issues of new debt securities sold abroad by U.S. corporations organized to finance direct investments abroad.

the new global changes, including the principles produced by the International Accounting Standards Committee (IASC). The Securities and Exchange Commission (SEC) and the Financial Accounting Standards Board (FASB) in the United States, as well as the global accounting authorities, should agree to use common accounting standards, regardless of the country of origin.

Some foreign companies that recently entered the New York Stock Exchange (NYSE), sponsored by the Bank of New York, include: Asia Pulp & Paper Company (PAP) of Singapore, with a ratio of four ordinary shares for one American Depository Receipt (ADR); Saatchi & Saatchi PLC (SSA), an advertisement company of Britain, with a ratio of five ordinary shares for one ADR. Also, VA Technologies AG (VATXY), an engineering firm of Austria, entered the Over the Counter (OTC) stock market, sponsored again by the Bank of New York, with a ratio of one ordinary share for ten ADRs, as well as Niugini Mining Limited (NGIMY), a mining company of New Guinea, with a ratio of one ordinary share for one ADR. Many more foreign firms join the American stock markets every month, particularly when the economy is stable and the prices of stocks are rising.

Already scores of enterprises, not only from developed countries but from emerging nations as well, have joined the American stock exchanges, mainly the NYSE and the OTC markets. They include, for example: Banco Frances, Metrogas, Telecom Argentina, and Telefon Argentina of Argentina; Elecrobras, Itaubanco, Petrobras, and Telebras of Brazil; Cervezas, Electricidad, Enersis, and Telecom Chile of Chile; Huaneng Power International, Shanghai Hai Xing Shipping, Shenzhen S.E.Z. Real Estate, and Yizheng Chemical Fibre of China; Boutari & Son (wine), Credit Bank, Telecom (OTE) and National Bank (expected) of Greece; Century Textiles, East India Hotels, Great Eastern Shipping, and Indian Aluminium of India; Grupo Elektra, Grupo Financiero Ser, Grupo Televisa, and Telefon Mexico L of Mexico; Lukoil, Minfin, Seversky Tube Works, and Sun Brewing of Russia; Aglo-American Coal, Beatrix Mines, Ocean Diamond Mining, and Sub Niger Gold Mining of South Africa; Banco Provincal, Ceramica, Elec Caracas, and Telef Venezuela in Venezuela; and Mhangura Copper mines in Zimbabwe.[6]

The globalization of capital markets is also indicated by the growing holdings of non-U.S. equity by U.S. investors, primarily U.S. institutions, such as pension funds and mutual funds. From the more than $9 trillion portfolio of the United States, about 6 percent or more than $500 billion is non-U.S. equity and is rapidly growing, particularly as a result of the privatized state-owned enterprises worldwide. Aggregate trading of non-U.S. stocks (by NYSE, Amex, and Nasdaq) accounts for more than $1 trillion a year. Britain and Canada represent the largest national concentration of non-U.S. stocks, followed by Mexico, the Telefonos de Mexico of which trades a large number of shares (about 1 billion a year). The non-U.S. companies listed on the NYSE, where the average daily volume is running at about 520 million shares (and in a recent single day 1.2 billion), increased from 23 in 1956 to 38 in 1980, 96 in 1990, and as high as 290 in 1996 and far more thereafter.[7]

It seems that the ADRs will continue to be used, mainly by the U.S. retail investors, because of the difficulties of accepting other currencies when non-U.S. shares are sold or dividends are received. However, institutional investors have the capacity to deal with local currencies and are ready to tap the home markets of non-U.S. issuers. Nevertheless, a creation of a pan-European stock market, supported by the common currency (the euro), as well as an eventual stability in emerging markets would mitigate the introduction of growing foreign shares into the U.S. stock markets, where large numbers of global investors are buying and selling shares every day.

The rapidly growing use of the internet for cross-border trading by investors worldwide, is revolutionizing transactions and quickly speeds shareholder capitalism. Investment firms, such as E*trade, Charles Schwab, Ameritrade, Consors, Paribas, and many other competing on-line brokerage firms and their subsidiaries, started allowing their clients to use the Internet in their global trading.[8]

BOND MARKETS

Bond markets play an equally or a more important role than stock markets for portfolio diversification. It is estimated that the capitalization of the bond markets is about 20 percent more than that of the stock markets. In addition to high liquidity of the bond markets, returns to bond investors may include coupon interest, appreciation in value when interest rates decline, and currency gains. On the other hand, currency risks can be neutralized through hedging in currency forwards, futures, and options.

Instead of pension funds and insurance companies being the usual customers of bond markets, more and more other traders, foreign investors, and aggressive speculators use these huge and globalized markets for twenty-four hours a day. The 30-year Treasury-bonds, or T-bonds, are the most actively traded around the world, because they are backed by the U.S. government and are therefore default-free. Prices of corporate and other bonds react to the prices of such T-bonds, which are traded by investment houses all over the world. About 70 million T-bond futures are traded by more than 600 traders each day, mainly in the Chicago Board of Trade (CBOT).[9]

The amount of domestic debt securities of the countries of the Organization for Economic Cooperation and Development plus major emerging markets was $25.8 trillion in 1996, $16.2 trillion of which was with the public sector and $9.6 trillion with the private sector. The amount of outstanding international debt securities, during the same period, was $3.2 trillion, $2.4 trillion of which was in bonds and the rest mainly in notes.[10]

Some 55 million Americans own savings bonds. Investors hold more than $6 billion in bonds that no longer earn interest, mainly because they have already been matured and the investors or their heirs forgot to sell them. Mostly, they were bought through payroll withholdings or gifts for newborns or graduates.

The low yield of bonds in mature markets enhances the interest of international investors for higher yields on emerging debt markets. Moreover, the reduced credit risks and the increased liquidity of such markets improve the ability of international investors to diversify and hedge their exposure regarding debt instruments and derivatives in these markets. However, expected declines in emerging and mature market spreads would reduce investor interest and the attractiveness of such debt instruments in the future, thereby diminishing the benefits of diversification.

When stock prices decline, investors seek security in bonds. In such cases, investors try to exit stocks altogether, or to cut their holdings in equities, taking refuge in bonds. Such bonds include treasury bonds, municipalities, mortgage-backed securities, corporate bonds, junk bonds, and emerging-markets bonds.

Many companies issued high-yield debt (junk) bonds, particularly after 1985. However, only a few remain solvent of some twenty-five firms that issued $1 billion or more such bonds related to buyouts.

Capitalizing on booming stock markets, corporate managers swap bonds for shares. Thus, taking advantage of Europe's stock market euphoria, Swiss Life/Rentenanstalt, a large life insurance company, sold bonds worth $2 billion. The bonds, which are denominated in Swiss francs, dollars, and euros, can be exchanged for shares in six European multinational companies, including Graxo Wellcome PLC, a drug firm of Britain; Novartis AG, a drug firm of Switzerland; Unilever NV, a large Anglo-Dutch food and household products company; Mannesmann AG, a German engineering company; Royal Dutch Petroleum Co.; UBS, a bank that resulted from the merger of the Swiss Bank Corporation and the Union Bank of Switzerland.

Furthermore, Bell Atlantic also issued bonds recently, worth $2.4 billion, exchangeable into shares of Telecom Corporation of New Zealand. Moreover, Allianz, a German insurance company, sold bonds worth $1.09 billion exchangeable into shares of Deutsche Bank AG.

The Latin American Brady bonds are among the most important and most liquid debt instruments in emerging markets, transactions of which increased from $1.0 trillion in 1993 to $2.7 trillion in 1996. The total turnover of the debt instruments in emerging markets was $5.3 trillion in 1996, $4.3 trillion of which were in the emerging markets of the Western Hemisphere. Nevertheless, higher credit risk and lower liquidity in other emerging debt markets are responsible for more volatile returns. Thus, emerging-markets bonds showed big losses in 1998 (more than 30 percent), mainly in Latin America.

Because of the instability in their economies, Latin American governments offer high yields for their bonds. Although all or part of repayment of the principal (not interest) of these dollar-denominated bonds is guaranteed by the U.S. Treasury (Brady bonds), they are traded at a low price. Thus, some Brazilian par bonds due in 2024 traded at 7 cents on the dollar recently, yielding about 11 percent, which is more than 5 percent higher yield than similar U.S. Treasury bonds. Likewise, similar Mexican bonds traded at 77 cents, yielding around 9 percent, and so on. Nevertheless, the low partial guarantee, 28 cents on the dollar on Brazilian pars, and the big denominations of Brady, more than $250,000, keep many investors out of the market.

As part of investment in stocks, when Argentina government bonds were only worth 11 cents on the dollar, Citibank Argentina decided to trade them in for stock in state-run companies. This was a magnificent deal because the state did not object to take back the bonds and the value of the stocks increased significantly, whereas Citibank raised approximately $4.5 billion profit.

Confidence is high for Latin American countries, and investors continue to finance investment projects by buying bonds. Thus, Argentina plans to sell $1 billion of bonds, Panama $500 million, and Brazil has sold $3 billion worth in international markets, whereas Venezuela will reduce its debt by retiring $4 billion of Brady bonds in exchange for issuing new Securities and Exchange–registered global bonds for the same amount. This will allow Venezuela to retire U.S. Treasury debt by $1.3 billion, retire government debt to the central bank and reduce outstanding debt.

FORWARD EXCHANGES

Foreign exchange futures are forward contracts between two parties, individuals or banks, to buy or sell foreign currencies delivered at a future date at a predetermined price. They were introduced in 1972 by the International Money Market (IMM) of the Chicago Mercantile Exchange and later, in 1982, by the London International Financial

Futures and Options Exchange. Such currency futures are also used by the Commodities Exchange (COMEX) in New York and the American Board of Trade. In addition to spot exchange rates, forward rates are presented in daily publications for 30 days, 90 days, and 180 days for a number of countries (Britain, Canada, France, Germany, Japan, Switzerland).

According to the Modigliani-Miller theorem, not only managers can hedge corporate exchange exposure but investors as well by engaging in forward contracts and hedging strategies in accordance with their share in the corporation. However, individual shareholders do not have detailed knowledge of markets and technology, as well as quality information, as operating managers of corporations have, in making decisions with precision, less risk, and lower cost.

Among the important international financial transactions between the United States and the European or other countries are the spot exchanges, which normally involve two business days for arrangement, and the forward exchanges, which typically involve one month, mostly three months, or six months. The spot exchange rate (S) of a currency related to another currency is the present exchange rate, for example, 120 Japanese yen per dollar or 5 French francs per dollar. The forward exchange rate (F) is the case of buying or selling a foreign currency at a future date at a rate agreed upon at present.

When the forward rate is higher than the present spot rate, the foreign currency is at a forward premium (FP), and when it is lower, the foreign currency is at a forward discount (FD). For example, if the spot rate of a dollar is FF5 and the forward rate a year later is 6FF, then the forward premium would be:

$$FP = (F - S)/S$$

or $(6 - 5)/5 = 1/5 = 0.20$, or 20 percent.

If the spot rate is the same (FF5) and the forward rate is FF4, then the forward discount would be: $FD = (4-5)/5 = -1/5 = -0.20$, or -20 percent. When the forward rate is for one month, then we multiply by 12 to express the FP(+) or FD(−) on an annual basis. If it is for three months, we multiply by 4, and so forth. Thus, if the spot rate of a dollar is 5FF and the forward rate for three months is FF4.8, the forward discount on an annual basis would be:

$$FD = (F - S)/S \times 4$$

that is, $(4.8 - 5)5 \times 4 = -0.2/5 \times 4 = -0.04 \times 4 = -0.16$ or -16 percent.

In more detail, suppose the spot rate is FF/$ = FF5 and the six-month forward rate is FF/$ = FF5.20. The premium is FF0.20 or 2,000 basis points (a basis point is 1/100 percent, or 0.0001). This means that the FF0.20 premium is equivalent to a swap rate of 2,000 points, and this is what matters for the swap parties and not the actual spot or forward rate. If the swap or premium (discount) rate of 20 percent is divided by the spot rate, the six-month rate becomes 4 percent (0.20/FF5 = 0.04) and the yield at this swap is 8 percent per annum (0.04 x 2), for the two six-month periods.

Intermediary banks can arrange borrowing domestic currencies for the participant firms in two or more countries and then swap them for foreign currencies, at a lower cost than the firms can by borrowing and obtaining foreign funds directly. Such swaps are avoiding foreign exchange risk by borrowing foreign currencies and lending domestic currencies, which are repaid at predetermined future exchange rates, thereby hedging related risk. Also banks may use a broker who often achieves better prices among many banks with a commission at less than 0.01 percent of the selling price split by the buyer and the seller. Nevertheless, more and more trades are facilitated electronically through computer networks. It seems that the majority of foreign exchange transactions are forwards, followed by spot transactions (about 40 percent) and a limited amount (about 5 percent) of options and futures.[11]

A futures contract is an obligation to buy or sell an asset, whereas an option is a right to buy or sell an asset. Futures contracts were used many years ago mainly for agricultural commodities, such as corn, wheat, coffee, cattle, orange juice, and other items, as well as gold, silver, platinum, and other metals and energy products such as crude oil. A speculator who thinks the price of corn will go up in the next six months would buy futures contracts at a fixed price per bushel from farmers who want to know now the price they will get in six months and hedge their own risks. Likewise, a speculator who thinks the price of corn will decline would sell futures contracts, a process similar to the short sale of a stock. Such futures contracts are used domestically and internationally, particularly on foreign currencies. Stock exchanges in other countries move rapidly into modern futures and options exchanges, as, for example, the Montreal Exchange did recently.

It is expected that the European Monetary Union (EMU) and the common currency in the EU, the euro, would consolidate derivative transactions in the sixteen European futures and options exchanges. However, the big three exchanges in Europe, that is, the London International Financial Futures and Options Exchanges, the Deutsche Terminborse (DTB), and the Marche a Terme International de France (MATIF), are expected to use more electronic trading and other innovations to achieve technological prominence and compete with American and other exchanges on an international level.

Other markets that deal with the growing trade of futures include New York Futures Exchange (NYFE), Sydney Futures Exchange (SFE), and the Tokyo International Financial Futures Exchange (TIFFE). In addition to currency futures, more than $50 billion annually, they deal with stock market index futures, about $200 billion a year, and interest rate futures of more than $6 trillion (primarily three-month Eurodollar and Euroyen). North America accounts for about half of all these transactions, Europe 30 percent, and the Asian-Pacific region for around 20 percent.

Moreover, developing and transitional countries gradually become integrated into the global financial system, introducing new instruments and policies used in developed countries that give traders and speculators the flexibility to take spot and forward positions in foreign exchanges and other transactions. Such instruments and policies increase competition and make the global allocation of savings and investment more efficient, thereby stimulating economic development in those emerging nations.

OPTIONS

Options are contracts that give the right to buy or sell foreign currencies and other underlying assets at or before stated dates. Such rights to buy (call options) or to sell (put options) can be used by individuals, companies, or banks, but there is no obligation to exercise such options. The purchasers pay the sellers a premium, usually from 1 to 5 percent of the contract's value, as a price for the privilege to exercise the option or not.

Options on stocks were first traded in an organized fashion in 1973 and increased drastically thereafter. Huge volumes of options are traded globally not only on stocks but on other underlying assets including foreign currencies, stock indices, futures contracts, debt instruments, and commodities.

A buyer (caller) can exercise the option to buy or not to buy a stock or any other asset into a specified period, usually 30, 90, or 180 days. A seller (putter) can exercise the option to sell or not sell a stock or any other asset into a specified period of time, normally 1 month, 3 months, or 6 months. Likewise, a similar premium is paid for not exercising the option to sell. In about 85 percent of the transactions, the future price falls within 5 percent of the predetermined (striking or exercise) price.

The date in an option's contract is called the exercise date, expiration date, or maturity. European options can be exercised on the expiration date, whereas American options, which are more usual, can be exercised at any time until the expiration date, regardless of the location of the exchange (in Europe, in America, or elsewhere). An option gives the right to buy or sell an underlying asset with a cost, but in forwards and futures the holder is obligated to buy or sell such an asset without a cost.

For example, suppose that an investor buys 100 European call options on Motorola stock at a strike price of $60 and the current stock price is $57, the expiration date of the option is in three months, and the cost of the option is $2 per share or $200 total. If the price of the stock on this date is less than $60, the investor will not exercise the option, losing the initial investment of $200 (100 × $2), but if the price of the stock is above $60, say $66, the option will be exercised and a profit will be realized from the difference in price (considering also the cost of the option). Thus, there will be a gain of $4 (66–60–2) per share or $400 total (minus of course the brokerage commission).

In addition to options on actual stocks, stock index options provide the right to buy or sell just an abstraction, a number derived from averaging the prices of actual stocks, the most popular of which is the Standard & Poor's 500 Stock Index. If you buy an option to buy the index at a certain average price and the market goes up, you gain. If the market goes down, you lose.[12] It can be considered as gambling similar to the roulette game and the stock market a sophisticated casino.

A call spread is the simultaneous purchase of a call option and the sale of a higher strike call option. Buying a call is used to profit from, or achieve protection against, an increase in the price of an asset, whereas buying a put is used to profit from a price decline.

Options are among the most important and rapidly growing derivative financial instruments. Interest rate options (calls plus puts) increased from $600 billion in 1990 to around $4 trillion recently, stock market index options increased from $94 billion in 1990 to about $400 billion currently, whereas currency options remained the same around $60 billion a year, mostly in North America.

The Philadelphia Stock Exchange started offering option markets since 1982 for different currencies in large amounts at spot and strike prices for different months, as well as call and put premiums. The currencies include those of Australia (A$50,000), Canada (C$50,000), Germany (DM 62,500), France (FF250,000), Japan (¥ 6,250,000), and Switzerland (SF62,500).

THE BLACK-SCHOLES OPTIONS FORMULA

In order to determine the value of options and other derivatives, the following Black-Scholes formula is used by investors and traders throughout the world for protection against future price changes of stocks, bonds, commodities, and other assets.

$$C = SN(d) - Le^{-rt} N(d - \sigma\sqrt{t})$$

Today's value of a call option (C) depends on the difference between the expected share value or the price of the underlying asset and the expected cost of exercising the option. In more detail, C depends on today's share price (S), the strike or agreed sale price of the option (L), the volatility of movements of the stock price as related to the movements of the option's value (d), the interest rate offered with a secure bond (r), and the time of expiration of the option (t). N is the normal distribution function, or the price's standard deviation, and e the base of natural logarithms (a constant, that is, $e = 1/0! + 1/1! + 1/2! +1/3! + \ldots = 2.71828$).

In practical terms, the formula, which was developed together with the late Fisher Black by Robert C. Merton of Harvard University and Myron S. Scholes of Stanford University, the Nobel Prize winners in economics in 1997, is used in derivatives trading, estimated at about $55 trillion a year. Banks and thousands of traders and investors use the Black-Scholes formula, as their hedging technology, to value stock options and to reduce their risk exposure in financial markets. The formula became known in 1973 when the Chicago Board Options Exchange introduced trading in options. Like stocks, bonds, currencies, or interest rate swaps, options are forms of financial derivatives, which derive their value from the value of other underlying assets.

Thousands of traders and businesses around the world use the formula to hedge risks, which affect many people with a stake in financial markets, including those under Employee Stock Ownership Plans (about 11 million employees in the United States alone). Farmers and grain dealers want to lock in prices and avoid unfavorable future changes, as do investors and mutual funds, using the Black-Scholes model to reduce the cost of options in the rapidly growing global financial markets. However, although Myron Scholes and Robert Merton made possible more efficient risk management in society, their advice to the Long Term Capital Management hedge fund, with huge and highly risky bets, proved to be inappropriate and dangerous. Sometimes, brilliant persons may fall into the Icarus complex, flying high, close to the sun, without proper wings.[13]

By punching S, N, L, r, and t in a pocket calculator, investors can determine the value of, say, an option to borrow 300 million DMs at 8 percent by the end of next month or the value of the right to buy 1,000 shares of Motorola at $60 each before next October.

SWAP ARRANGEMENTS

Swap or exchange arrangements are frequently used to facilitate corporate and other financial services. They include primarily currency swaps, interest rate swaps, and debt-to-equity swaps. Central banks can trade in the foreign exchange market as they do in open market operations in the domestic market. In order to discourage large money flows, central banks may agree to exchange against each other's currency, using the forward exchange against the domestic currency, in order to sterilize capital inflows, and buy it back at a specified date and a predetermined exchange rate. Vice versa, a central bank can use a swap contract to buy foreign exchange, thereby reducing the domestic currency fluctuations. Although such swaps have short-term maturity, they can be rolled over, allowing foreign exchange adjustments and encouraging economic stability. Moreover, debt-to-equity swaps are used by firms with heavy debt, issuing shares to pay for part or all of their debt.

Also, commercial banks can enter into swap agreements instead of using forward exchange contracts for interbank trading. For example, an American bank that wants French francs can trade dollars ($) for French francs (FF) now and FFs for dollars in six months, instead of borrowing FFs and arranging payment in six months. The premiums or discounts that prevail in the forward exchange market would determine the terms of the arrangement or the swap rates.

Figure 4.2 shows that if speculators expect that the spot exchange rate of euro, or other currency, will be equal to forward rate (F), then they will not buy or sell forward euros. If the forward rate is F1>F, then the speculators will sell forward euros. Vice versa, if the forward rate is F2, then the speculators will buy 0b forward. For example, if the spot exchange rate, 90 days from now, is expected to be $1.2 per euro and the forward rate (F) at that time $1.4 (F1>F or 1.4>1.2), then speculators will sell euros forward. Likewise, if the spot exchange rate 30 days from now is expected to be $1.6 per British pound and the forward rate at that time $1.8 per pound (F1>F or 1.8>1.6), then speculators will sell pounds forward, gaining the difference $0.2.

HEDGING OPERATIONS

Hedging refers to buying or selling future or option contracts in order to reduce the risk of price movements of an asset or any other legitimate commercial activity. It is a financial device, mainly used in foreign currencies to cover an open position or a foreign exchange risk, that has acquired great international importance, and it is used in order to protect a buyer or a seller against unfavorable price changes in physical markets.

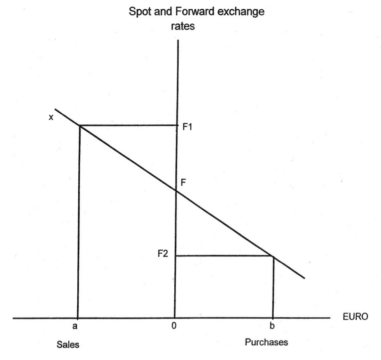

Figure 4.2. Foreign exchange arbitrage

Hedge funds, basically, buy securities that seem to be cheap while they sell other equivalent securities that seem to be relatively overvalued. However, the term "hedge funds" is misleading, as such funds are not actually hedged. Thus, if Brazilian bonds yielded more than Argentine bonds, the hedge fund might buy Brazilian bonds and sell short Argentine bonds of the same maturity. Nevertheless, losses could mount on both sides of the trades in such two-way bets, and the hedge funds might be in serious trouble, thereby being considered the barbarians at the gates of global capitalism.[14]

Operations of such high-flying funds may include speculations on interest rates, foreign currencies, and other derivatives. For example, an importer of French wine (boziole) can borrow FF100,000 at a spot price rate now of FF5/$1, leaving the money on deposits in a bank account for six months, when payment is made, thereby avoiding the risk of paying a higher rate six months from now. At that time, the importer will pay $20,000, the equivalent of FF100,000. The cost of such an insurance against the foreign risk is the small difference between the interest rate that the importer receives on the deposit of the same amount (FF100,000). For example, if the importer pays 10 percent annually for the money borrowed and the deposit rate is 5 percent, then the difference is 5 percent or, for six months, FF2,500 (100,000 x 0.05 : 2), that is, $500. However, instead of tying up money, the importer or any investor can use hedging in the forward market, buying French francs forward for delivery in six months at today's six-month forward rate. Assuming that the six-month premium is 2 percent a year, the importer (the hedger), would pay $200 (1 percent of $20,000 for the six months) as hedging cost.

Likewise, the exporter, expecting to receive FF100,000 for his exports of wine, could sell French francs forward for delivery in six months at the present six-month forward rate. If the six-month forward discount rate for French francs is 1 percent, the exporter would receive now $19,800 for the FF100,000 or $20,000 delivered in six months, but if the French franc forward premium for buying dollars is 1 percent, the exporter will get $20,200 in six months by hedging.

Open or share operations are uncovered sales. In this case, shares are borrowed and sold but not yet covered by repurchase agreements. If the price of shares fall, the investor can buy the shares and replace the borrowed ones, making a profit, but if they rise, the seller faces losses.

The open position can be avoided and the foreign exchange risk of our importer can be hedged also by buying an option to purchase FF100,000 in six months at FF5/$1 and paying now the premium of 1 percent, for example, or $200 on $20,000 option. If in six months the spot rate is FF5.2/$1, the importer could not exercise the option and get the FF100,000 with only $19,230 (100,000 : 5.2), saving $570, that is $20,000 − $19,230 = $770 − $200 (the premium) = $570.

Hedgers in financial futures can be either buyers (long hedgers) or sellers (short hedgers) of futures contracts. They greatly facilitate international trade and investments of multinational corporations and banks. Hedge-fund managers who borrow money for currency bets watch like wolves for anomalies and profit opportunities. The ambitious project of the European Monetary Union (EMU), with a single currency (euro) and a superbank, presents good opportunities for hedge-fund managers. EU countries with no sufficient fiscal discipline and weak currencies, like Finland, Greece, Italy and Spain, would generate speculation in favor of stronger currencies, like the German mark, and against their currencies.

There are some 4,000 hedge funds that handle trillions of dollars of derivatives, whose values rise and fall with the prices of underlying stocks, bonds, currencies, and interest rates. Even financial gurus, such as Merton H. Miller, a Nobel Prize winner in economics, are not clear about their operations. One may say that derivatives will destroy society; a second, that derivatives makes the world safer. Pension funds, foundations, endowments, and investment managers invest heavily in hedge funds. They accounted for only 5 percent of the hedge funds' assets in 1993, but now they account for about 80 percent.

Sizable losses from derivative gambling on risky financial contracts were incurred, for example, in 1994 by Orange County in California when it lost $1.6 billion and declared bankruptcy, as well as by Procter and Gamble when it lost $150 million on derivatives it bought from Bankers Trust. Also, in 1995 Barings Bank, the British bank, faced similar problems, whereas in 1997 Yamaichi Securities of Japan lost $2 billion mainly because of its off-balance sheet trades.

Moreover, the bets in July 1997 that the Asian currencies would not be devalued and the bets in July 1998 that the emerging markets bonds would recover were the main reasons for the huge losses of Long Term Capital Management (LTCM) in September 1998 and losses by other hedge funds later. More than 80 percent of the funds, such as LTCM, use borrowings to leverage their returns. It is estimated that about 5 percent of the hedge funds have assets of more than $500 million, a quarter of them have less than $10 million and 30 percent from $50 million to $500 million. The total investors' capital of the hedge funds, which are among the most risky and least regulated of investment, increased from $50 billion in 1990 to some $300 billion at the end of 1997 and far more later.

From the derivative international transactions, representing $1.25 trillion of underlying securities, the LTCM hedge fund had at least $4 billion in losses, mainly from bets on Russian, Brazilian, and other securities and currencies. The fund, the manager of which is John Meriwether (a former vice president of Salomon Brothers, with an M.B.A. from the University of Chicago), used $2.2 billion in capital from investors as collateral to borrow from different sources and buy $125 billion in securities (some $50 for every $1 investment), which in turn were used as collateral for the $1.25 trillion transactions. It accepted participants with more than $10 million realizing up to 40 percent investment returns, whereas its partners enjoyed 25 percent of any profits realized.

In order to avoid bankruptcy and perhaps a global financial crisis, a consortium of fourteen financial firms, many of which have financial stakes in LTCM, as well as many managers of these firms, contributed $3.6 billion to rescue the ailing hedge fund, in exchange for 90 percent ownership. The financial firms that contributed $300 million each are: Barclays, Bankers Trust, Chase Manhattan, Credit Suisse First Boston, Deutsche Bank, Goldman Sachs, J.P. Morgan, Merrill Lynch, Morgan Stanley, Dean Witter, Salomon Smith Barney, and UBS (a Swiss large bank); Lehman Brothers, Paribas, and Societe Generale contributed $100 million each. The Federal Reserve Bank of New York coordinated this bailout. Sometimes, the government and politicians in general are bailing out large corporations, such as Chrysler and Lockheed, to save jobs, but to protect losers in a free market economy will attract losers galore.

Other hedge funds with heavy losses include Tiger Management L.L.C. and the BankAmerica Corporation, mainly because of their investment in emerging nations, particularly in Asia, Russia, and Latin America. Tiger Management, based in New York, with assets of $22 billion, had $600 million in losses from Russian ruble-denominated debt in August 1998. Likewise, BankAmerica lost more than $330 million in the third quarter of 1998.

Because of periodic financial crises such as those of Asia, Russia, and Latin America, there are arguments that the global capitalist system faces the greatest problems in decades and may come apart. An important reason for such a dismal prediction is the use of derivative securities for buying and selling, risks regarding currency moves, interest rate changes, stock market indexes, and a host of other speculative activities and big bets by using leverage, or borrowing money, to cover such risks (hedge funds). As a result, some countries with serious financial problems, such as Malaysia, Russia, Brazil, and other South American countries, took measures to protect their markets from the detrimental effects of the casino-style speculative global capitalism.

Nevertheless, the risks of making big bets sometimes backfire and put hedge funds and other derivative operations, with virtually no regulatory oversight, in jeopardy. Hedge funds, which are designed to hedge risks for individual participants, create risks to themselves and the system as a whole by using capital and securities of investors as collateral, tending to create a form of global capitalism with oligopolistic gambling. However, Alan Greenspan, the Chairman of the Federal Reserve, suggested that derivatives, investments with values connected to other assets, could operate better with less regulation. The success of the over-the-counter or privately negotiated financial derivatives without regulation supports the argument for reduction in federal control on derivative markets, related to the Commodity Exchange Act. About 25 percent of the contracts of the derivatives market, estimated at $80 trillion a year, are held by U.S. commercial banks and 15 percent by securities firms.

Because many hedge funds operate offshore, it is difficult for any country to regulate their hugely leveraged investment portfolios. However, governments can regulate banks, brokerage firms, and other deposit institutions, under their jurisdiction, concerning hedge-fund lending and full disclosure of related risks.

It seems that an international regulator and lender of the last resort for financial institutions, perhaps a stronger IMF, is needed. At the same time, the international conferences of the Group of Seven industrial countries (G7) should be enlarged to fifteen (G15) or more to include emerging nations as well.

In many cases, reduction in the U.S. interest rates is not enough to deter the flood of money into the U.S. Treasuries from the fragile financial markets, particularly in emerging nations. Moreover, bond prices do not always rise and fall together, as for example, in the recent financial crisis prices of U.S. bonds increased, as investors preferred them for safety, but prices of many other bonds with high risk declined.

REPURCHASE AGREEMENTS

Repurchase agreements (repos) are contracts for collateralized loans, with the agreement to repay the loans (repurchase the collateral) by a specified time (normally less than a week). There is a growing displacement of traditional interbank credit by repos in cross-border banking.

The United States, where repos were first used, plays an important role in integrating domestic with international repo markets. Other countries, where repo markets were opened recently as a result of deregulation, are, for example, Britain (1996) and Germany (1997). International overnight and term (mostly one week) repos increased to around $1 trillion, primarily in the United States, whereas the annual turnover is estimated at $50 trillion or about 10 percent of gross international bank lending and is growing at a rate of more than 20 percent a year. This is due mainly to less risk and cheaper short-term funds provided by repos, compared to noncollateralized funds and the growing integration of securities and banking markets. Reverse repos is a purchase with an agreement to resell at a determined price and date.

Global Shareholding, Market Capitalization, and External Debt

GLOBAL SHARE OWNERSHIP

There is a growing number of people in almost all countries who acquire shares through direct investment in the stock market or through managed funds. The global trend for privatization promotes share ownership in the place of state ownership. From Europe to Asia (even China), Africa, Latin America, and other regions, governments sell shares of state enterprises to individuals and investment institutions, thereby spreading an equity culture on a worldwide scale. This form of shareholder capitalism encourages a wider share of ownership as more and more individual investors participate in the stock markets. Such a trend encourages saving and investment and promotes economic stability and growth.

Financial exchanges around the world are rising rapidly via electronic trading. In the United States, Britain, France, Germany, Japan, and many other places, installed electronic systems speed up transactions in stocks, bonds, and other financial instruments all over the world. Such a revolution in financial services is globalizing shareholder capitalism to the degree that investors from all corners of the planet will be able to acquire shares and other financial instruments instantly from a number of stock markets.

Already, in New York, Chicago, Philadelphia, London, Paris, Frankfurt, and other places the old-fashioned auction markets on the floor, with hand signals and wads of paper, are rapidly being replaced by electronic trading. Electronic commerce networks around the globe can match a buyer and a seller independently with such services as "Instinet" and "Island." The introduction of new technology, growing global competition, and the consolidation of stock markets, such as the Nasdaq with the American Stock Exchange and the Philadelphia Stock Exchange, intensify the use of the Internet and similar devices.

Democratic capitalism is based on freedom and openness, that is, on the combination of a free political society and an open economic system. It should not be based on economic combines and cliques of governments, business, and banks, as can be observed in Japan and other Asian countries, as well as in fascist, terrorist, and militarist regimes that result in nepotism, corruption, and oppression.

Nevertheless, in its effort to modernize its markets, Japan is urging individuals to invest more of their savings in securities. They have only about 7 percent investment in stocks, 2 percent in bonds, 35 percent in trusts and insurance and as much as 56 percent of their saving is kept in deposits with banks, including deposits with mailmen every morning. The Japanese are known for their high percentage of saving, being around 28 percent, compared to about 18 percent for the Europeans and as low as 2–4 percent or even negative for the Americans. It is expected that Japanese investment in stocks and bonds would increase as the government is restructuring the financial system. Already the government, from time to time, buys large amounts of stocks to help prop up the stock market. There is skepticism, though, that some individuals would invest in U.S. stocks and bonds, where the yield is higher than that in Japan. Other countries in Asia and other parts of the world follow the example in Japan in reforming and opening their economies to global shareholder capitalism.

Large privatizations, particularly in telecommunications, airlines, and energy, foster the people's appetite for equity ownership and strengthen the system of what Joseph Schumpeter called people's capitalism. In Europe, Deutsche Telecom, France Telecom, Greek Telecom (OTE), Telecom Italia, Portugal Telecom, and Telefonica of Spain, along with Air France, Lufthansa of Germany, Olympic Airlines of Greece, Eni (the oil and gas group of Italy), Endessa (a Spanish energy group), and many other state enterprises offered shares to the public recently and induced people to buy more shares from private companies, thereby popularizing share ownership.

The United States, with more than 70 percent government ownership in postal services and 25 percent in electricity and railways, has a very small public sector, compared to other countries. However, the question of privatization versus public operations troubles many states and cities, including New York. Subways, public hospitals, posts, and other natural monopolies can raise prices as long as there is no competition or price controls by state and city commissions to protect the consumers. The dilemma of government inefficiency and private monopoly, which bothered Adam Smith and other classical economists, still remains and demands further research and reliable socioeconomic answers.

A number of big enterprises introduced schemes of employee ownership. For example, in order to succeed in its effort of privatization and reduce overheads, Air France allowed its pilots to acquire shares in the airline in return for wage cuts. The main offer is for the pilots to forgo 2–3 percent of their wages throughout their careers in exchange for an equivalent value of shares. The government will hold 53 percent of the airline, which is valued up to $4.2 billion, 15 percent will be reserved for the employees, and the rest will be offered to other investors.

Moreover, Lufthansa, the German state airline, introduced a program according to which employees can have a stake in the company. In place of a pay raise, they can choose cash payment or an equivalent amount of stock. Moreover, employees can buy additional stock with interest-free loans from the company, and after two years they can sell the shares. If the price of shares at that time is lower, Lufthansa buys them back at no loss to the employees.

In Italy, small investors are buying most of the stocks of privatized state enterprises. Some 2 million Italians signed up to buy shares in Telecom Italia S.p.A. No one was permitted to buy more than 1,000 shares. However, employees of Telecom Italia could buy as many shares as they wanted.

Finland also decided to privatize Sonera, the state telecom, offering 100 million shares to Finnish and international investors, worth up to $1.4 billion (FM7 billion), in a similar way to Swisscom and the Greek OTE. Sonera employees would get 2 million shares and Finnish investors 26 million, whereas the government would keep 80 percent ownership. The global offering is directed by Merrill Lynch.

The Greek government transferred 49 percent ownership of Skaramaga Shipyards to the employees and 51 percent to the National Bank of Industrial Development (ETBA), but with management by a British company. The Greek Shipyards of Aspropyrgos were sold to shareholders, whereas the shipyards of Elefsina and Neorion Syrou were privatized earlier. Moreover, shares of the state-owned telecom (OTE) are sold in the New York Stock Market.

Although the economic role of the government was expanded during the last half of the twentieth century, many state-run enterprises have been sold or are in the process of partial or total liquidation to domestic or foreign investors through the sale of shares. However, in order to preserve managerial competence with strong motivation and control, widely dispersed ownership may be forgone, although at the sacrifice of short-term distributional considerations. A large number of stockholders, in privatized public enterprises, with relatively small numbers of shares for each individual may be uninformed, ignorant, or apathetic. They may not have good knowledge of the position or operation of the enterprise and be unqualified to vote for efficient management, particularly during the early stages of transformation from the public to the private sector.

From the standpoint of efficient privatization, it is better to start with the liquidation or sale of small public enterprises and proceed with more complex large state-owned firms, as Mexico did in the 1980s.[1] Sales in cash are always preferable to accepting debt because of the liquidity provided to settle liabilities of the state firm under privatization and to buy new machines and other technological instruments to modernize the firm. Moreover, it may be difficult for banks and other financial institutions to provide the needed funds.[2]

France plans to sell shares of the France Telecom S.A., the biggest initial public offering ever, and to put on the market at least part of the company that will result from the expected merger of Aerospatiale S.A. and Dassault Aviation S.A.[3] Moreover, Alitalia, the Italian state carrier, is in the process of privatization. A similar phenomenon can be observed with the Greek Olympic Airlines.

Macroeconomic, anti-inflationary, and other stabilization measures taken before privatization would have positive effects on prices and demand for shares of the privatized firms and other state assets.

SPREAD OF EMPLOYEE OWNERSHIP

In the United States, there are about 10,000 companies, compared to only 200 in 1974, that are partially or totally owned by more than 11 million employees through employee stock ownership plans (ESOPs). The decline of the labor unions from 33 percent of the labor force to around 14 percent seems to encourage the growth of ESOPs. About 500 ESOP companies are 100 percent owned and 1,500 are majority-owned by the employees. Approximately 1,000 ESOPs, or 10 percent, are in publicly traded firms, which employ more than half of the U.S. employee-owners. Around 4 percent of ESOP companies are unionized. Many companies created ESOPs for better performance or tax shelter.

Some large firms announced stock-ownership requirements for their executives. Also, shares may be held in a trust that the executives may not have bought (indirect ownership), whereas stocks may be held in retirement savings plans under the U.S. tax regulation 401(k).

Included among some important firms that established an ESOP are Publix Supermarkets, Parson Corporation, Morgan Stanley Company, Thermon Electron Corporation, Bell Atlantic, Charles Schwab Corporation, Houston Industries, Avondale Shipyards, Amsted Industries,

Southwestern Bell, Todd Products Corporation, New York Times Company, PPG Industries Inc., Austin Industries, and Weirton Steel Corporation. Also, American Airlines, in which employees own 55 percent of the company's equity, created an ESOP in exchange for wage concessions. It is expected that this arrangement, which expires in 2000, would be renewed and the rule that restricts employees from making other investments or to cash in their stock until retirement would be changed. Other airlines with ESOPs include United Airlines, TWA, Delta Airlines, Western, Republic, and Eastern Airlines.

More than half of the adult Americans own stock, either directly or through mutual funds, compared to about one fourth of the British, one sixth of the French, and about one tenth each of the Italians and the Germans. The proportions of shareholders of private firms are growing rapidly all over the world. American companies, such as Lehman Brothers, Salomon Brothers, and others, help promote the flotation of such firms.[4]

In more details, about 100 million Americans own stocks (78.7 million at the beginning of 1999). About half of them are baby boomers (born from 1946 to 1963). Most of the shareholders are married and college graduates. Some 48 percent of American households owned stocks in 1999, directly or through mutual funds, mainly for retirement and other financial goals. Although only about 10 percent of stock trades are over the Internet presently, the numbers are expected to grow rapidly as electronic investing is easier and cheaper.

However, there is a significant concentration of stock ownership in the United States. About half of the stock is owned by the richest 5 percent of American households, those in the bottom 50 percent own less than 5 percent, whereas the bottom 75 percent of households own less than 20 percent. Stocks held through pension plans are included in these figures.

In order to expand at home and abroad, some companies, under partnership or other forms of ownership, may decide to go public, through issuing stocks and selling them in the stock market. Although a large number of international investors are expected to become shareholders of such companies, there is a danger that they may become acquisition targets in the present rush to consolidate. For example, Goldman, Sachs & Company, which advised clients such as BankAmerica and NationsBank as well as Daimler A.G. and the Chrysler Corporation to merge, plans to issue stocks and to go public, although there are fears of losing its independence by being a target of acquisition.

Some 20 percent of U.S. firms have programs that allow their employees to buy stocks at a discount of 15 percent or more. Sometimes the discount is more than 20 percent when the firms apply it to the lower stock price of a certain period. However, there are proposals to limit the discounts in new issues of stock options to a lesser amount. Such discounts are popular with corporate executives but expensive for the issuing companies.

As automation is growing and machines and computers replace labor, a good alternative to unemployment or underemployment is share ownership, through which former and present employees become partial owners of companies and directly or indirectly they become employers of themselves. The reduction of work hours per week, all over the world, and possibly reduction in wages, because of growing international competition, suggest the introduction and expansion of shareholder capitalism. The dividends and profits of employees and other small stockholders would keep overall demand for goods and services at satisfactory levels, thereby reducing the danger of severe recessions or depressions.

There is a growing trend of granting stock options to a broad range of employees by the companies in which they work, all over the world. According to a recent survey of 350 large U.S. firms, companies that have provided for broad-based option grants amounted to 30 percent; more than 11 percent of them made grants to most employees, particularly in high technology, compared to less than 6 percent in 1993. At least 1 in 10 of the companies offer stock options, typically in addition to salary and bonus, at a discount, not only to top executives as before but now to about 50 percent of midlevel managers, as well as to the lower-level employees.[5]

Stock options give the employees the right to buy shares at a predetermined price after a specific date. It is estimated that 8 million Americans have such options, compared to only 1 million in 1992. Such options can be negotiated along with salaries and may be used for protection against hostile takeovers and against a falling stock price. Usually they can be converted into stock in three to five years and are popular with initial public offerings (IPOs).

An attractive form of options is that of the incentive stock options (ISO), often reserved for top executives. If the stock is sold, one year after the option is exercised, at a higher price, the tax to be paid is 20 percent (and Congress voted to reduce it to 15 percent, recently) on the profit (on long-run capital gain). This is usual with the options-rich tech sector for which people are optimistic currently. However, a falling stock renders options worthless. That is why it is better to ask for stock instead of options, unless the firm cuts the exercise price. Moreover, if the stock is sold into a year after the option is exercised, then full taxes would be paid on the profit (nonqualified tax).[6]

The proliferation of stock options to employees is reducing the polarization between the executives and the lower-level employees, as employees with options feel more like owners, have high work incentives, and increase their wealth when the Dow Jones rises, as it did over the last decade (from 1,000 in the early 1980s to more than 11,000 currently). In this Corporate America lottery, in which 28 percent of U.S. wealth is tied up in stocks, giant mergers, such as that of Citicorp-Travelers Group, lead to stock-price jumps and high profits for the executives in charge.[7] The same trend can be observed in other countries as well.

For that reason, the Securities and Exchange Commission allows companies that list their stock on the New York Stock Exchange to add new stock option plans as long as more than 20 percent of employees are eligible for options and at least half of them are below the level of company officer. In such cases, there is no need for shareholder approval for issuing stock options to top executives by many of the 3,046 companies on the Big Board.

Columbia Falls Aluminum reduced wages by 15 percent in return for profit-sharing for its employees. After one year from the related agreement with the workers (1986), the company started making profits. In recent years, however, the two executives of the company awarded $231 million to themselves and only $84 million to the employees, cutting them off from future profits. Nevertheless, with union membership declining and real wages stagnant, workers care more about job security and share ownership than profit-sharing.

Support of Shareholding

Under a U.S. law introduced by Senator Russell Long in 1983, business owners who sell at least 30 percent of their companies to an Employee Stock Ownership Plan (ESOP) can defer capital gains if they invest the proceeds in bonds, stocks, or in a new company within a year. In this case, no capital gains taxes are paid when the new holdings are sold. A number of companies were sold to bigger competitors in exchange for shares of the acquiring firm, and no capital gains taxes are due from the sale of the new shares.

In order to increase international employee stock ownership, the Procter and Gamble Company, based in Cincinnati, announced that its 106,000 employees worldwide can buy up to 100 shares five years from the grant date of May 15, 1998, up to 10 years from and at the price of that grant date. Some 75 percent of the employees already own stocks of the company from previous years.

Polaroid, with headquarters in Cambridge, Massachusetts, is one of the thousands of U.S. companies with an ESOP. Every full-time employee of the company is a shareholder. In order to avoid a hostile takeover by Shamrock Holdings and preserve the jobs of the workers,

Polaroid took a loan to buy 16 percent of its shares for its employees, which can be cashed after leaving the company. The employees accepted a cut of 5 percent of their salary for the payment of the loan and feel that the ESOP is a form of their pension plan, or forced savings, in addition to the power of the partial ownership and management they enjoy. Additional shares are distributed each year, and employees can buy shares on their own, especially when they expect that the prices of such shares will go up in the stock market.[8]

The Eastman Kodak Company announced a program to give 90,000 nonmanagement employees the option to buy 100 shares in a period of two years. Although employees are not making Polyanna's predictions, they feel optimistic about the performance of the company. At the same time, the pay of the chief executive, George Fisher, was cut in half, to $2 million, compared to the previous years. Some 20 percent of Kodak's work force was eliminated because of recent disappointing performance in world markets, where the Fuji Photo Film Company grabbed customers with lower prices. However, Fisher received options and shares worth about $64 million in place of a bonus.

Goldman, Sachs Company decided to go public at a value around $24 billion and give its 13,000 employees a stake of 20 percent in shares.

The Aramark Corporation, a managed-services company based in Philadelphia, plans to buy back all shares held by outsiders, worth $440 million, and become 100 percent employee-owned. This is a process the company started in 1984 when the management bought it for $1.2 billion. Employee-owners of the Trade Winds and the Sandpiper resorts in St. Pete Beach, Florida, agreed to sell them to South Seas Resorts for an undecided amount. The employees bought the properties through an ESOP in 1995 and plan to roll the profits over to an individual retirement account (IRA).

However, Kiwi International Airlines, with 550 employees, once successful under employee ownership, is in trouble again under the private ownership of Charles Edwards.

Some insurance companies, which are organized as mutual insurers and are owned by the policyholders, move toward changing their legal nature to become for-profit companies, in which the policyholders would be shareholders. In that way they would be able to sell stocks in the stock markets, domestically and internationally. Such companies are able to sell bonds and have lots of cash but they like to issue stocks as well and be able to compete long term and raise capital in the future. From the biggest life insurers in the United States only Teachers Insurance and Annuity, Connecticut General Life, and Equitable Life Assurance have the form of stock ownership. Many others, including Prudential, Metropolitan Life, New York Life, and others have the mutual status, and they want to issue and sell stocks. Some fifteen U.S. states allow such insurance firms to form holding companies and sell stock equal to 49 percent of the company's stake but without compensation to policyholders.

The Prudential Insurance Company of America, the nation's largest with some $260 billion assets, plans to convert policyholders to shareholders and distribute some $12 billion accumulated profits in stocks, instead of entirely in cash, to policyholders. However, there are complaints that the transformation of such companies to regular publicly traded companies would enrich management, enabling executives to collect lucrative stock options.[9] Similar companies in other countries are expected to follow this measure of converting policyholders to shareholders and investors around the world to buy shares from different stock markets, thereby spreading the system of shareholder capitalism.

INITIAL PUBLIC OFFERING

Although there are cases in which companies buy back stock, reducing the number of shares outstanding, the new shares of companies entering the stock markets and the new issues of shares by the existing publicly traded companies are expanding rapidly worldwide. Among the recent buy-back cases is that of Bank of America Corporation, the largest American bank, which decided to buy back up to 130 million shares, or 7.5 percent of its stock, worth about $9.3 billion. Also, Morgan Stanley, Dean Witter, Discover and Company decided to buy back up to $3 billion of its stock. They completed their $11 billion merger in 1997, retiring some 8.2 percent of the 594.7 million shares outstanding. Likewise, Thermo Electron Corporation, founded in 1956 by its present chairman George Hatsopoulos, a Greek immigrant, is in the process of restructuring its twenty-three publicly traded subsidiaries dealing with energy, recycling, biochemical, and other technologies (including production of patriot rockets), as well as in an aggressive share-repurchasing program. Moreover, the May Department Stores Company plans to buy back up to $650 million, the third purchase plan in two years. Furthermore, Waste Management Inc., the largest U.S. trash hauler, decided to sell some assets in order to buy back shares to increase the value of its depressed stock.

A growing number of companies worldwide enter the stock market through sales of stocks for the first time. Such initial public offerings (IPOs) are promoted by specialized IPO underwriters, as Morgan Stanley, Dean Witter, Merrill Lynch, Goldman Sachs, Credit Suisse First

Boston, J.P. Morgan Securities, Salomon Smith Barney, and other major securities firms all over the world.

Although there is a risk in buying IPO stocks early, prices of such stocks increased dramatically in recent years, particularly for Internet companies. Such companies include RSL Communications Ltd., which is registered in Bermuda and decided to sell stocks for its Delta 3 subsidiary, IDT Corporation of New Jersey for its Netz Phone subsidiary, MarketWatch.com, Muktex.com, and many smaller firms. Even the London Stock Exchange, almost two centuries old, the New York Stock Exchange, and the Nasdaq Stock Market decided to end mutual ownership system and issue tradeable shares to their members.

When the stock market goes up, IPOs trade above their offering price. That is why some 70 percent of 3,200 hot IPOs since 1994 traded at higher prices than their offering price. Some shareholders realized very high returns in a short period of time, particularly with Internet-related stocks. Such IPO boomers include Healtheon (HLTH), which had an IPO on February 10, 1999, with $8 and the current price is $67 per share, which is a 738 percent return. Likewise, Theoglobe.com had 606 percent, Priceline.com had an IPO return of 550 percent, Foundy Networks 525 percent, Marketwatch 474 percent, Sycamore Networks 386 percent, Ask Jeeves 364 percent, and VerticalNet 300 percent. Twelve other companies had returns varying from 150 to 280 percent. Moreover, in a big IPO, the United Parcel Service (UPS) offered 109.4 million shares, on November 9, 1999, at $50 a share, and by the end of the day the price jumped to $68.125 a share.

Nevertheless, some cold IPOs, such as Aerospatiale (AERL) and Comps.com (CDOT), had some 50 percent loss each into one month. Some ten other companies had lower losses, varying from 28 to 48 percent, mostly in a period of two months. Moreover, Planet Hollywood gained 49 percent on the first day (4/19/1996), from $18 to $25.40, but by May 1999 it dropped to less than $1.[10]

Therefore, domestic and international investors should be careful with IPOs, especially the noninstitutional investors, because the short-term performance, particularly in the first day of trading, is, in a number of cases, unreasonably high.

A number of companies sell shares to collect money to pay their debt or to cover expanding and other expenditures. For such initial public offering or additional equity offering to the public, they need the approval of the Securities and Exchange Commission (SEC) in the United States or similar institutions in other countries. Because many pension funds request more disclosure, some insurance firms are considering converting their operations from mutual to stock companies through IPOs.

In addition to Prudential Insurance Co. of America, mutual ownership firms that are in the process of converting to public trading companies in order to tap into the equity market include: Allmerica, with a value of about $230 million; Trigon Healthcare, with a value of more than $200 million; AmerUs Life, with a value of $77 million; Farm Family, with a value of $40 million, and many others that are announced almost every week. With the walls between financial services firms coming down, mutuals redefine themselves and move into some form of public ownership to stay competitive.

The partners of Goldman, Sachs & Company voted to sell shares of the worldwide known underwriter, which provides investment banking services to large firms and other rich clients. With this initial public offering, Goldman, which is worth more than $28 billion, expects to compete more effectively with Merrill Lynch & Company, Morgan Stanley, Dean Witter (which went public in 1986), and Salomon Smith Barney, which are using their stock to expand internationally, particularly through financing big mergers and acquisitions. By going public, the Goldman partners will be able to cash in by selling shares.

In addition to so many domestic IPOs, from time to time, foreign companies enter into IPOs, mainly in the United States, through American Depository Receipts (ADRs). For example, from the 9.4 million ADRs of Celumovil S.A. of Colombia, each ADR representing two common shares, 5.6 million were offered in the United States and Canada, with Salomon Smith Barney as underwriter. Also, 32.8 million ADRs were offered by Corporation Bancaria de Espana S.A., each ADR representing half of a share. Moreover, Genesis Microchip Inc., Ontario, recently had an initial public offering of 2.9 million shares, whereas Steelcase Inc., Michigan, had an IPO of 12.2 million class A shares, 9.7 million of which were offered in the United States and Canada.

In order to pay part of its bank debt, Young & Rubicam Inc. decided to sell to the public some 16 million shares, that is, around one fourth of the company, at about $24 a piece.

United Parcel Service of America Inc., the world's largest package delivery service (established in 1907), which is owned by its employees, decided to sell 10 percent of itself to the public for $5 billion. It seems that it found it hard to resist the siren song of Wall Street in a period of instant riches.

DEMOCRATIZATION OF THE ECONOMY

The increase in the number of shareholders leads to the democratization of capitalism worldwide. Gradually and quietly we are transformed into a society of shareholders or a society of democratic capitalism.[11] This transformation has a serious impact on the stock markets and the economies around the world as more and more people invest their money into stocks directly or through mutual funds.

In the United States, in an NBC News/Wall Street Journal poll in October 1997, 51 percent of adults said they own stock shares or mutual funds, whereas 53 percent of registered voters are shareholders. In addition to direct American participants in the U.S. stock markets, there are another 110 or so million indirect participants in the markets. As a result, the demand for stocks and their prices, promoted by the 600 broker-dealer members of the NYSE, increased dramatically. In the last decade and a half, the Dow Jones Industrial 30 accented from 800 to 9,374.72 (on November 23, 1998) and more than 11,000 as of this writing, attracting millions of investors into the market. Likewise the Nasdaq composite index and the Standard & Poor's 500 stock index climbed to very high levels.

Sometimes, cable TV, the Internet, and other mass media are contributing to the popular passion for stocks and also to high nervous tension, similar to that of lottery or casino gambling, sex scandals, and sports, at the expense of the traditional virtues of industry and thrift. In order to cool off transactions and avoid panic, when there are large declines in stock markets, brackets are introduced in the NYSE and other stock exchange markets.

Partial or total privatization of Social Security and putting the money collected from contributions into the stock markets would increase share ownership, domestically and internationally, thereby introducing gradually a global system of shareholder capitalism. The same thing can be said for pension and mutual funds that put their money into domestic and international stock markets.

Nevertheless, the mania for investing in stocks may distort our political and cultural life, create speculative riche, and exacerbates inequality. In such cases, shares may be overvalued, as has happened in the U.S. stock market since 1982, when returns averaged 19 percent per year and 30 percent annually the last three years, compared to around 5 percent on money-market accounts and certificates of deposits or CDs.[12]

People usually prefer money from speculation and inheritance, looking forward to early retirement, over money from earned income and saving. Also, large amounts of money are borrowed through credit cards, margin-requirement (using stocks as collateral), or otherwise to play in the sophisticated casino or the sacred temple of the stock market, not only by the prosperous but the middle class and working people as well.[13]

The idea that work is honorable and economy a virtue becomes less important compared to the practice of short-run speculative riches via the stock market and the sordid behavior for unearned wealth. In pursuing happiness, the citizen investor puts more and more emphasis on the material possessions and not on the elimination of desires, which Plato emphasized some twenty-five centuries ago when he mentioned in his *Republic* that appetites and desires should be subordinated to reason and virtue.

Putting too much emphasis on material possessions may lead to what Thomas Malthus (1798) and later John Maynard Keynes (1936) mentioned, overproduction, as happened during the Great Depression in the 1930s. With the split of wealth through shareholder or democratic capitalism, there will be more flexibility in the market, less defective demand, and a better approach to what is known as Say's law that "supply creates its own demand." In such a case, there will not be much need for public policy and a supportive government role in the economy.

The doctrines of private ownership and free market, advocated mainly by Aristotle (fifth century B.C.), Adam Smith (1776), Jean-Baptiste Say (1803), David Ricardo (1817), and other classical economists, may be better implemented through a system of shareholder or popular capitalism, as modern Saysians may also advocate. This is so, because shareholder capitalists are expected to feel more secure on spending for consumption and investment, thereby avoiding overproduction or inflationary pressures and moving closer to an acceptable balance of supply and demand.

On the political front, shareholder democracy is different from political democracy. In the first case, shareholders have voting rights proportional to their ownership stakes, whereas in political democracy the voting rights are equal for all citizens regardless of property ownership.[14]

Moreover, stock market profits are treated more leniently, as taxes were reduced from 28 percent to 20 percent (1977 budget bill) for capital gains from stocks held more than a year and the U.S. Congress voted to reduce the rate to 15 percent, compared to the top rate of 39.6 percent on income earned. This is an incentive for people to buy shares in order to set up a tax shelter, with the result of weakening the productive work ethic as a dollar gained beats a dollar earned.

With about half of the country in the stock market, inflated stock prices or the "irrational exuberance" of the stock market incorporates the risk of a sudden collapse, which may possibly lead to a recession or depression, as happened in the 1930s. It is unreasonable for an economy to grow at 5 percent a year and a stock market 20 percent or more a year for many years.

Historically, the percentage of American household assets in stocks changed from 16 percent in 1945 to 26 percent in 1968, back to 12 percent in 1990, and as high as 28 percent in 1997, the highest ever and even more later. Stocks accounted for 43 percent of financial assets, including mutual funds, bank accounts and securities, whereas gains on stocks have averaged 8 percent per year, historically, and 30 percent annually for the five years 1995–1999. According to the Federal Reserve, recently employee-controlled plans were half of the more than $3 trillion in corporate pension plans at the end of 1996, compared to one fourth at the beginning of the 1980s. Saving fell to 3.8 percent of disposable income in 1997, and even negative (–0.2) at the end of 1998 and later, the lowest since the Great Depression of the 1930s, compared to 9.5 in 1974. It seems that the new symbols of the American life are "Mom, apple pie, and stocks."

Developing countries with cheap labor tend to use domestic and foreign financial means to invest in labor-intensive projects, whereas developed countries with plenty of capital tend to finance capital-intensive projects. This process would continue until equalization of factor remuneration worldwide, although this requires a long period of time to be realized.[15]

CURRENT ACCOUNTS, MARKET CAPITALIZATION, AND EXTERNAL DEBT

Current accounts, which is the most important part of the balance of payments of any country, includes transactions in goods and services as well as income from investment abroad. As long as there are deficits in current accounts, external debt is expected to increase.

Table 5.1 demonstrates the current account balances and international reserves for a number of developed and developing countries. The United States has the largest deficit in current accounts, followed by Brazil, Australia, Thailand, and Germany. Japan has the highest amount of international reserves, followed by China, the United States, and Germany. Usually, countries with persistent deficits in current accounts end up with large debts, which in turn require sizable international reserves for the payment of debt service.

Table 5.2 shows the population, GNP per capita, GDP deflator, and stock market capitalization for selected developed countries. (For inflation and market capitalization in emerging nations, see Chapter 6.)

Table 5.3 shows countries with heavy external debt in billions of dollars and as percentage of exports. Brazil, Mexico, India, China, and Russia have the highest amount of debt, followed by Argentina, Thailand, Indonesia, and Turkey.

Recently Deutsche Bank, which heads a group of Western banks with $15 billion short-term defaulted Russian debt, as well as the London Club of creditors of $30 billion unpaid Soviet-era debt, and Chase

Table 5.1 Current Account Balance (1996) and Gross International Reserves in Selected Countries (1997)

	Developed Countries			Developing Countries	
	Current account balance ($bn)	Gross international reserves ($bn)		Current account balance ($bn)	Gross international reserves ($bn)
Australia	-15.9	17.5	Algeria	1.1	9.7
Austria	-4.0	22.0	Argentina	-4.1	22.4
Belgium	14.4	20.6	Bolivia	-0.3	1.4
Canada	2.8	18.7	Brazil	-18.3	51.7
Denmark	2.9	19.6	Chile	-2.9	17.8
Finland	4.8	8.9	China	-7.2	146.7
France	20.6	54.7	Colombia	-4.8	9.6
Germany	-13.1	105.2	Egypt	0.5	19.4
Greece	-4.6	13.7	Hungary	-1.7	8.5
Ireland	1.4	6.6	India	-4.6	28.4
Israel	-7.1	20.0	Indonesia	-7.0	17.5
Italy	41.0	75.0	Malaysia	5.8	21.1
Japan	65.9	227.0	Mexico	-1.9	28.9
Netherlands	25.3	32.8	Nigeria	3.1	4.3
New Zealand	-3.9	4.4	Pakistan	-4.2	1.8
Norway	11.2	23.7	Peru	-3.6	11.3
Portugal	-1.5	20.4	Philippines	-2.0	8.7
Spain	1.8	72.9	Poland	-3.3	20.7
Sweden	5.9	12.2	Russia	11.4	17.7
Switzerland	20.5	63.2	Thailand	-14.7	26.9
United Kingdom	-2.9	37.6	Turkey	-1.4	19.8
United States	-148.7	134.9	Venezuela	8.8	17.7

Source: World Bank, *Word Development Report*, 1998/99.

Manhattan agreed to accept 5 cents on the dollar of the face value of the debt in new Russian bonds and rubles.

Brazil, with about half of the South American population and half of the GDP, owes some $230 billion in foreign debt. Nevertheless, as a result of the devaluation of the real and the lifting of the exchange controls, the financial conditions are expected to improve. However, severe fiscal policy measures are needed to reduce the swollen budget deficit of around $65 billion or 8 percent of the GDP and 8 percent unemployment and to lower interest rates, which run at rates over 40 percent. This would increase further foreign direct investment, which increased from $2 billion in 1994 to $35 billion now, and improve foreign reserves, which declined from $75 billion in the summer of 1998 to around $30 billion now.

Table 5.4 shows international debt securities of some major industrial and developing countries, as well as breakdowns of these securities in different currencies.

Table 5.5 shows domestic and international debt securities for seven developed countries. Bonds are the largest part of international debt securities, followed by medium-term notes, Euro-commercial papers, and other short-term notes. The private sector, mainly in the United States, Japan, Germany, and France, holds the largest amount of international debt securities. In the public sector, Canada, Italy, the United

Table 5.2 Population, GNP per Capita, GDP Deflator, and Market Capitalization of Developed Countries, 1997

Economy	Population (millions)	GNP per Capita (U.S.$)	GDP Deflator Average 1990–97 (%)	Market Capitalization (billion $)
United States	268	28,740	2.4	8,484
Japan	126	37,850	0.6	3,089
Britain	59	20,710	3.1	1,740
Germany	82	28,260	2.5	671
France	59	26,050	1.9	591
Switzerland	7	44,320	2.3	402
Canada	30	19,290	1.4	486
Netherlands	16	25,820	2.0	379
South Africa	38	3,400	10.1	232
Australia	19	20,540	1.2	312
Italy	57	20,120	4.5	258
Spain	39	14,510	4.6	243
Sweden	9	26,220	2.6	247
Belgium	10	26,420	2.8	120
Denmark	5	32,500	2.4	72
Finland	5	24,080	1.7	63
Austria	8	24,080	2.9	34
Ireland	4	18,280	1.8	12

Source: World Bank, World Development Report, various issues.

Table 5.3   **External Debt of Selected Nations ($ billion)**

Country	1980	1990	1997	1997 % of GNP	1997 % of Exports
Algeria	19.4	27.9	30.9	67	329
Argentina	27.2	62.2	123.2	38	489
Bangladesh	4.2	12.8	15.1	20	397
Bolivia	2.7	4.3	5.3	51	482
Brazil	71.5	119.9	193.7	23	380
Bulgaria	0.07	10.9	9.9	96	230
Chile	12.1	19.2	31.4	43	211
China	4.5	55.3	146.7	15	80
Colombia	6.9	17.2	31.8	27	292
Ecuador	6.0	12.1	14.9	72	363
Egypt	19.1	32.9	29.8	28	764
Honduras	1.5	3.7	4.7	86	294
Hungary	9.8	21.3	24.4	52	107
India	20.6	83.7	94.4	18	284
Indonesia	20.9	69.9	136.2	62	279
Malaysia	6.6	15.3	47.2	48	64
Mexico	57.4	104.4	149.7	37	127
Nicaragua	2.2	10.7	5.7	244	950
Nigeria	8.9	33.4	28.5	72	274
Pakistan	9.9	20.7	29.7	38	354
Peru	17.4	20.1	30.5	45	555
Philippines	9.4	30.6	45.4	51	155
Poland	8.9	49.4	39.9	27	152
Russia	4.5	59.9	125.6	27	170
Tanzania	2.5	6.4	7.2	77	1028
Thailand	8.3	28.2	93.4	61	174
Turkey	19.1	49.4	91.2	43	347
Venezuela	29.3	33.2	35.5	41	206
Zambia	3.3	7.3	6.8	136	756

Source: World Bank, *World Development Report*; and the International Monetary Fund, *International Financial Statistics*, both various issues

States, and Japan have the largest amounts of debt securities. In domestic debt securities, bonds incorporate the largest amounts of debt for the years considered, followed by treasury bills and other short-term notes. The United States, Japan, Germany, and France have the largest amounts of domestic debt securities in both the public and the private sectors.[16]

THE USE OF TECHNOLOGY

New technology is primarily embodied in new investment. The use of new investment may result in proportionately more capital per unit of output (capital-deepening or labor-shallowing technology) or more

Table 5.4 Outstanding Amounts of International Debt Securities (in billions of U.S. dollars)

	1993	1996
All countries	2,037.8	3,225.9
Industrial countries	1,650.3	2,594.3
Of which:		
United States	176.9	402.6
Japan	340.1	356.7
Germany	120.1	342.4
France	153.1	215.9
Italy	70.2	95.8
United Kingdom	186.7	274.2
Canada	146.9	182.6
Developing countries	121.8	276.3
Offshore centers[1]	11.3	36.3
By Currency of Issue	Amounts Outstanding	
U.S. dollar	836.4	1,245.9
Japanese yen	272.3	517.6
Deutsche mark	192.8	347.1
French franc	92.7	168.1
Italian lira	37.7	99.7
Pound sterling	154.8	237.3
Canadian dollar	81.7	77.0
Spanish peseta	10.6	17.9
Netherlands guilder	44.9	95.3
Swedish krona	3.5	5.2
Swiss franc	149.1	165.7
Belgian franc	2.2	13.4
Other	159.1	235.7
Total	2,037.8	3,225.9

Source: Bank for International Settlements and IMF, *International Capital Market*, 1997, 111.
[1]The Bahamas, Bahrain, Bermuda, the Cayman Islands, Hong Kong, China, the Netherlands Antilles, Singapore, and other offshore centers.

labor per unit of output (labor-deepening technology) or in equiproportional change in capital and labor per unit of output (capital-widening technology). It is a worldwide phenomenon that in periods of high unemployment, politicians and economists may argue in favor of labor-using technology. In such cases, depending on factor endowment and skills available, governments can encourage labor-

Table 5.5 Domestic and International Debt Securities: Amounts Outstanding (in billions of U.S. dollars)

	Amounts Outstanding	
	1994	1996
International debt securities		
Total Issues	2,441.2	3,225.9
Bonds	2,035.2	2,391.8
Medium-term notes	292.0	662.5
Euro-commercial paper	81.5	102.9
Other short-term notes	32.6	68.7
Private sector	1,559.1	2,150.7
Of which:		
United States	204.7	366.2
Japan	341.3	332.9
Germany	179.1	334.6
France	178.9	201.2
Italy	40.2	40.9
United Kingdom	195.4	257.3
Canada	37.4	47.2
Public sector	598.7	756.0
Of which:		
United States	5.0	36.4
Japan	20.0	23.8
Germany	9.4	7.7
France	6.6	14.7
Italy	45.0	54.9
United Kingdom	17.1	16.9
Canada	128.0	135.5
Domestic debt securities		
Total issues[1]	22,823.9	25,829.6
Bonds	18,336.2	20,541.9
Medium-term notes	530.9	664.1
Commercial paper	815.9	1,031.6
Treasury bills	1,876.9	1,964.3
Other short-term notes	1,264.0	1,627.7
Private sector[1]	8,335.0	9,624.9
Of which:		
United States	3,654.0	4,513.0
Japan	1,497.3	1,469.1
Germany	863.9	1,024.6
France	572.7	549.5
Italy	325.4	410.0
United Kingdom	170.0	258.6
Canada	47.2	65.9
Public sector[1]	14,488.9	16,204.7
Of which:		
United States	6,362.3	7,102.0
Japan	3,252.7	3,299.0
Germany	805.0	853.6
France	549.4	689.8
Italy	1,074.0	1,277.8
United Kingdom	354.8	467.3
Canada	410.5	443.3
Memorandum items:		
International debt securities		
Financial institutions	835.9	1,344.4
Government and state agencies	603.1	755.8
Corporate issuers	718.5	806.4

Source: Bank for International Settlements; and IMF, International Capital Market, 1997, 10.
[1]Organization for Economic Cooperation and Development countries plus major emerging markets.

deepening technology, which is using more labor (L) and less capital (K) per unit of output (O). This can be done through subsidies and taxes or other fiscal measures. Also, projects with capital-widening technology can be selected. In that case, the capital/labor ratio remains the same along the expansion line (0, O1, O2, O3) as output moves up the hill to higher levels of production (isoquant curves), as Figure 5.1 shows.

Depending on the availability of factors of production and the relative prices of the services of labor (w) and capital (r), substitution of one factor for the other may take place in the production function. The elasticity of substitution of capital (K) for (L), EKL, in different terms can be expressed as follows:

$$EKL = -d(K/L)K/L : d(r/w)r/w$$

Thus, if the percentage change in capital/labor ratio, d(K/L)/(K/L), is 20 percent and the percentage change in the rental/wage ratio, d(r/w)/(r/w), is 10 percent, then the elasticity of substitution, EKL, is –2; that is,

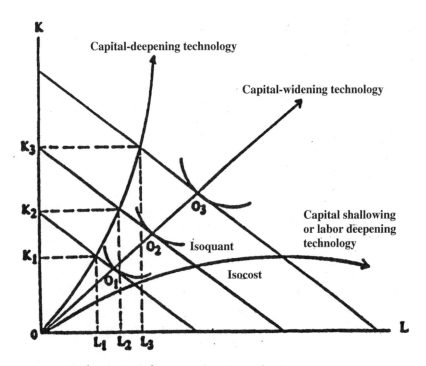

Figure 5.1. Technological change and project selection

$$EKL = -0.20 : 0.10 = -2$$

Or, for each change in rental / wage ratio there is a double change in the capital/labor ratio. Developing countries with cheaper labor tend to use domestic and foreign financial means to invest in labor-intensive projects, whereas developed countries with plenty of capital tend to finance capital-intensive projects. This process would continue until equalization of factor remuneration worldwide, although this requires a long period of time to be realized.

EFFECTS OF NATIONAL POLICIES

National economic policies and fiscal policies in particular not only affect changes in domestic deficits and debts but also have repercussions on the debts of other countries. Measures on multinational corporations and mergers, rules and regulations to minimize government distortions of capital and technology transfers, and controls on foreign exchange rates and financial transactions influence and are influenced by fiscal and monetary policies in other nations. Technical and financial assistance, government guarantees for bank loans, the absence of tax discrimination, and international agreements for business protection and economic cooperation affect world trade and play a significant role in changes in economic, financial, and social conditions in other countries.

The need for international fiscal cooperation and coordination of demand policies requires that the tax equity and tax neutrality principles of public finance be extended from an interindividual to an international level. Government aid and capital transfers among nations should consider the principles of efficient allocation and income distribution as a way of raising economic growth, in the long run, without debt accumulations. Along these lines, investment in sectors and regions with low capital/output ratios is expected to receive priority in capital formation, subsidies, and other incentive policies. In low-income regions and nations, where the private sector hesitates or is unable to undertake the construction of needed infrastructure facilities, the public sector has an important role to play in allocation resources and training people, especially in the early stages of development. However, state enterprises and the public sector in general are responsible for large budget and trade deficits, which bring about big foreign debts.

Laxity in fiscal and monetary discipline, structural rigidities, and biased growth strategies in rich and poor countries, as well as the rise in protection sentiment, are some of the factors responsible for huge external debts and the financial dependency of mainly Third World countries.

To avoid a worldwide financial crisis and to soften economic shocks, which could lead to fiscal and social disruptions, an expanded role of the IMF has been introduced. Such a role includes the introduction of fiscal performance clauses, ceilings on budget deficits, restrictions on bank credit to the public sector, and controls on public enterprise pricing policies. In more practical terms, debt rescheduling and refinancing include provisions that debtor countries introduce austerity measures to balance their public budgets, deflate their economies, and reduce or eliminate balance-of-trade deficits.

Empirical evidence suggests that a one percentage point increase in the ratio of fiscal deficit to GNP would cause a deterioration of the current account by about half a percentage point. Therefore, from the point of view of domestic policy, fiscal restraints, together with currency adjustments, can be applied in order to keep the current account balance from worsening. The urgent priority, therefore, is to reduce budget deficits, which affect current account balances, foreign debt, and currency adjustments.

To prevent an international economic crunch from foreign loan defaults, especially from Latin American countries, budget deficits should be adjusted. This pressure for a possible foreign credit crunch is expected to be severe in the foreseeable future because a number of countries look perilous, for both economic and political reasons.

Continuation of high interest rates because of large budget deficits in many countries aggravates the world debt crisis and threatens widespread protectionism. Countries with large debts, such as Brazil, Mexico, Argentina, Poland, Yugoslavia, Romania, Chile, Peru, Turkey, and the Philippines, ask for long-run debt rescheduling with lower interest rates and other loan fees. The alternative may be widespread defaults and large-scale bankruptcies of creditor banks. More than 800 banks are owed money by Brazil alone. They include large banks such as Chase Manhattan, Morgan Guaranty Trust Company, and Citibank. It would seem, then, that poor people abroad and banks and taxpayers in rich nations share a common interest to stimulate international trade and avoid a world financial crisis. Thus domestic fiscal and monetary policies become more and more intertwined with international economic policies.

Whether we commend or condemn the U.S. fiscal policy, the net capital inflow is not all a simple direct result of the previous budget deficits and the increase in national debt. In addition to the demand for U.S. government securities, the inflow of foreign funds reflects also a significant increase in private-sector deposits and investments in stocks and other financial instruments. On the other hand, U.S. banks have started reducing lending to financially unstable developing nations. This has reduced the supply of dollars abroad and contributed in making the United States a net international borrower. U.S. fiscal and monetary discipline, then, would help world economic growth and lead nations towards a socioeconomic convergence.

According to Vassily Leontief, the Nobel Prize winner for economics in 1973, the cost to U.S. taxpayers of propping up friendly "authoritarian" countries and combating hostile "totalitarian" regimes in developing countries with large debts is expected to increase. On the other hand, record deficits up to recent years have propelled U.S. debts to high levels and are used to pay for themselves. Under such a heavy burden, the government might be unable to rescue defaulting debtor nations and U.S. banks.

REASONS AND PROBLEMS OF FOREIGN DEBT

Emerging countries with small and less advanced financial markets face great risks from relaxing capital controls, because investors easily lose confidence in their economic policies and take capital out of these countries. At times, they get swamped with foreign investment capital, but they are characterized by loose regulations, insider dealing, weak accountability, and crony capitalism. Under such conditions, their financial markets are unstable, and in cases of small disturbances the banking system is in trouble and investors take capital out of these regions.

A number of emerging nations use short-term money from abroad to support public sector expenditures and investment in real estate and other nonexported ventures. With weak exports, foreign debts are growing, local currencies are weakened, and servicing the debts becomes problematic. The usual policies of budget cuts and sharply higher interest rates to avoid currency devaluation may work in the very short term, but they may lead to an economic downturn and panic difficult to reverse.

The financial crisis of October 1997 and later in Asian countries (mainly Indonesia, Malaysia, the Philippines, and Thailand), which spread to South Korea and Japan as well as Russia and other emerging and even advanced financial markets, is related to such unwise policies. As a result of the crisis, the worst in thirty years, Indonesia has 130 million people under poverty in a total population of 206 million and a debt of around $100 billion.

The deficits of the bloated public sector, stemming mainly from money-losing state enterprises and organizations, result in high rates of inflation and large debts, mainly foreign debts. Some emerging nations may achieve a lower rate of inflation at the cost of higher debt. In order to avoid "imported" inflation—inflation due to the rising prices of imports—they may keep their currency overvalued, ignoring the detrimental effects of this policy on the balance of trade and the current accounts deficit. As a result, exports become more expensive, whereas imports become cheaper for the nations, leading to high foreign-trade deficits and more borrowing from abroad.

For decades, politicians have gathered votes by having many unneeded workers placed on the payrolls of state enterprises. As a result, emerging nations end up with many employees, as a ratio to population, compared to other developed countries.

At the same time, they have a small number of university students, related to their population, compared to other advanced countries. For example, there is 1 student in 90 persons in Greece (115,000 students for 10.4 million population), compared to 1 in 18 in the United States (14.3 million students for 264 million population). India and Iran are also among the first countries exporting students.

With large numbers of students studying abroad at any given time, a number of emerging nations are exporters of students to foreign universities, resulting in both a huge immediate drain for the economy and a dramatic brain-drain for society. The establishment of independent nonprofit universities, where the students pay tuition, similar to those in the United States (Harvard, Yale, M.I.T., Columbia, Fordham, N.Y.U., etc.) and other countries, capable of absorbing thousands of good candidates who prefer such universities, is an absolute necessity for such nations with large public sector deficits.[17]

To retain the confidence of investors and to increase productivity, drastic measures are needed by emerging nations to reduce public sector expenditures, through denationalization of public enterprises and the education of their youth for a better future.

To reduce their national debt, governments of emerging nations announce, from time to time, the issue of bonds that may be converted to shares of state-owned enterprises that can be introduced in stock markets. Such bonds can be in local currencies or in hard currencies, like dollars or euros, with interest rates less than that of similar traditional bonds; also, the price of shares, into which the bond will be converted, may be higher than the prevailing price at the time of conversion.

The debt of the public sector in many countries is high mainly because of the large number of employees employed in governmental enterprises and organizations. For example, in Greece there is 1 public employee per 19 persons of the population, compared to 92 in Britain. As a result, the country is among the countries with the highest government sector and the highest per capita public debt. Some 40 trillion drachmas was the debt of the public sector in 1997, or about $130 billion, about $50 billion of which is foreign debt. However, recent measures of privatization and reduction in inflation would enable the economy to enter the euro.[18]

In order to reduce the national debt, the Greek government announced the issue of a new bond that may be converted to shares of state-owned enterprises already introduced in the ASE, or not yet introduced in the ASE but controlled by the government. This bond, with maturity of five to seven years, can be in drachmas or in euros with an interest rate 1.5–2 percent less than that of similar traditional bonds and a price of shares, into which the bond will be converted, 15–20 percent higher than the prevailing price at the time of conversion. The name of the bond was Balantir-bond, from the name of the French Minister of Finance, Edwart Balantir, who introduced such bonds in France in 1993.

The high interest some governments pay to sell their bonds domestically and the overvaluation of their currencies lead to high financial speculation and deterioration of the economy. For example, one could borrow dollars, euros, or other hard currencies with a lower interest rate and invest this money in higher interest bonds domestically, gaining the difference by repurchasing such hard currencies with the relatively constant prices in local currencies.

Some governments find refuge in the erroneous policy of avoiding the depreciation or devaluation of their currency at all cost. This is the result of a pervasive fear to deal decisively with entrenched interests and powerful public sector labor unions. Nevertheless, serious measures are taken to privatize state-owned enterprises and to reduce inflation and debt.[19]

Nigeria, with more than $30 billion foreign debt and a population of 200 million, faces serious problems, mainly fluctuation of oil prices. Some 20 percent of its population is living on less than $1 a day, as are 1.5 billion poor people in the world, in a growing inequality.

Turkey's foreign debt increased significantly, from $19.1 billion in 1980 to $79.8 billion in 1996 and as high as $154 billion currently ($2,444 per capita) or 73 percent of GDP. For the immediate need to service the debt, the Turkish government requested $10–15 billion from the IMF. The heavy debt is mainly the result of heavy budget deficits that reached 15 percent of GDP per annum.[20]

It is estimated that the current foreign currency reserves for Argentina amount to $25 billion, whereas about $34 billion are needed to forestall a currency devaluation. Brazil has only about $47 billion currency reserves, but about $200 billion is needed; Mexico has $30 billion and needs $100 billion, respectively.

To avoid a virulent financial crisis that may send the whole world into a recession or depression, developed countries, in cooperation with the IMF, should support developing countries to avoid a currency devaluation that may affect many other countries including the United States, which exports more than 20 percent of its exports to Latin America, where there are many American factories.[21]

In order to satisfy the International Monetary Fund and prove a stronger government commitment, Venezuela will attempt to modernize its public finances and to increase the rate of economic growth by more than 5 percent annually. The annual non-oil deficit of the government is about 10 percent of Gross Domestic Product, and the IMF would like to see this reduced to about half of that amount in a few years, mainly through a reduction of public sector workers.

6

Emerging Markets

INTRODUCTION

Emerging markets—that is, markets of developing and transitional economies—deal primarily with stocks and bonds. Out of thirty-one emerging markets in the world, ten are in Asia, seven in Europe, seven in Latin America, and seven in the Middle East / Africa. Asia had the largest number of stocks (758 out of a total of 1,424 for all emerging markets) traded in the last week of January 1998, followed by Latin America (270), Middle East / Africa (236), and Europe (160).[1]

From the Asian emerging markets, South Korea has the largest number of stocks, followed by Malaysia, Taiwan, India, Thailand, Indonesia, Philippines, China, Pakistan, and Sri Lanka.

In the European emerging markets, Greece has the largest number of stocks, followed by Russia, Poland, Portugal, Hungary, the Czech Republic, Slovakia, and the Balkan countries.

Although the emerging markets of Latin America are growing, they are still limited in number and sizes. There are some 1,200 public companies in the major markets of Latin America with a combined market capitalization of about $300 billion, with Brazil having the largest number of stocks traded, followed by Mexico, Chile, Argentina, Peru, Colombia, and Venezuela.

In the Middle East / African markets, South Africa has the largest number of stocks traded, followed by Turkey, Israel, Egypt, Morocco, Zimbabwe, and Jordan.

The spread of information technology, together with growing global stability, led to the rapid development of stock markets, including those in Latin America, Eastern Europe, and China, which are expanding rapidly lately. In the 1980s, the entry of Greece, Portugal, and Spain into the European Union, as well as the high economic growth of Hong Kong, South Korea, Singapore, and Taiwan (the four Asian "tigers") stimulated the growth of their stock markets. However, the recent financial crisis in Asia reduced the performance of the stock markets, mainly in Asia, Russia, and Latin America, but growth started again after the financial crisis was over.

As a result of the drop in commodity prices of the Latin American and other developing countries, it became difficult for them to service the loans they took, mainly in the 1980s, from international banks. Although there were some debt-to-equity swaps, where loans were exchanged for equity investment in developing countries, the banks were mostly not satisfied and hesitated to give new loans. In order to avoid an international crisis in financial markets, negotiations were enacted between the creditor banks, which formed the Paris Club, and the emerging nations to reschedule nonperforming debt with a steep discount.

As a result, the Brady bonds, from the name of the United States Secretary of the Treasury, were introduced in the 1990s, which replaced existing government debt with a market value less than the par value of the initial debt. After the emerging nations initiated reforms, approved and funded mainly by the International Monetary Fund and the World Bank, sovereign debt was transformed into tradable Brady bonds, with guarantees (principal or interest collateral) by the United States Treasury, but at a reduced value. About twenty countries have issued such bonds, including Argentina, Brazil, Venezuela, and other Latin American countries. Bulgaria, Nigeria, the Philippines, and Poland also replaced government debt with bonds with a market value less than the par value of the initial debt. The total capitalization of the Brady bonds is about $100 billion, in addition to the Eurobonds and the domestic bonds of far more value emerging nations are periodically issuing.[2]

The total capitalization of the bond markets in the world is more than $16 trillion, about half of which are denominated by U.S. bonds, more than one fourth by European currency bonds, and some 20 percent by Japanese yen bonds.

Eurobonds are bonds placed outside of the country of the issuer and of the currency or denomination, thereby avoiding national regulations. Moreover, the eurocurrency market is the offshore banking market with deposit and loan operations in foreign currencies, as, for example, borrowing and lending American dollars outside the United States.

Table 6.1 shows bond issues, equity issues, and syndicated loan commitments for the emerging markets of the world. Asian emerging

Table 6.1 Emerging Market Bond Issues, Equity Issues, and Syndicated Loan Commitments (in millions of U.S. dollars)

	1990	1996
Bond issues		
Emerging markets	7,789	101,926
Africa	0	1,648
Asia	2,604	43,144
Europe	2,335	7,408
Middle East	0	2,570
Western Hemisphere	2,850	47,157
Equity issues		
Emerging markets	1,166	16,414
Africa	0	781
Asia	900	9,789
Europe	97	1,289
Middle East	70	894
Western Hemisphere	98	3,661
Syndicated loan commitments		
Emerging markets	28,377	79,737
Africa	2,127	2,658
Asia	12,541	49,488
Europe	9,139	11,457
Middle East	1,089	5,836
Western Hemisphere	3,480	10,297
Short-term commitments[1]		
Emerging markets	4,423	30,458
Africa	83	3,701
Asia	3,116	20,374
Europe	775	3,136
Middle East	350	0
Western Hemisphere	100	3,248
Total		
Emerging markets	41,755	228,535
Africa	2,210	8,788
Asia	19,161	122,795
Europe	12,346	23,290
Middle East	1,509	9,300
Western Hemisphere	6,528	64,363

Source: IMF, International Capital Market, 1997, 77.

[1]Commercial paper, certificates of deposit, revolving credits, and trade finance

markets have the largest amounts of equity issues and syndicated loan commitments, Western Hemisphere and European emerging markets have the largest amounts of bond issues, whereas Middle East and African emerging markets have small amounts of such financial instruments.

INFLATION AND MARKET CAPITALIZATION

According to the World Bank classification, emerging or developing nations are the ones with a low or middle level of per capita income, compared to developed nations with high per capita income. Emerging stock markets include the financial markets of developing countries and those growing in size, turnover, and sophistication. The capitalization of all emerging stock markets, which is growing rapidly, accounts for about 12 percent of the total world market capitalization in which developed or advanced markets are included. There is not much concentration in the emerging markets, as a large number of firms are traded in each national market. However, privatization of large state enterprises leads to more concentration and inequality. Although such markets are volatile and risky, the high growth potential, the diversification, and the relatively high return they offer make them attractive.

Table 6.2 shows population, per capita income, inflation, and market capitalization for major emerging markets in Asia, Europe, Middle East / Africa, and Latin America. Before the turmoil in the Asian financial markets, particularly in Indonesia, Malaysia, South Korea, and Thailand, these markets were booming. In Europe, Greece and Portugal try to adjust their markets to those of the European Union, as the Eastern European countries and Russia do, although at a lower pace.

From all emerging markets, Brazil has the largest stock market capitalization (more than $250 billion), followed by South Africa, China, Mexico, India, and Russia. (For inflation and market capitalization in developed countries, see Chapter 5.)

AFRICAN AND ASIAN EMERGING MARKETS

An important group of Middle East / Africa emerging markets includes the countries of South Africa, Turkey, Israel, Egypt, Morocco, Jordan, and Zimbabwe.

South Africa's monetary policy was such that part of the increase in money supply was counterbalanced by the decline in the velocity of money, as Figure 6.1 indicates. As a result of stabilization measures, the stock market is going up and more foreign investment is flowing into the country.

Table 6.2 Major International Emerging Markets: Population; GDP per Capita (US$); Inflation (GDP Deflator, Average Annual % Growth, 1990–1997); Market Capitalization (Billions of US$), 1997

Economy	Population (millions)	GDP per Capita	Inflation Rate	Market Capitalization
ASIA				
China	1,227	860	13.6	206.4
India	961	390	9.4	128.5
Indonesia	200	1,110	8.5	29.1
Korea, Rep.	46	10,550	5.3	41.9
Malaysia	21	4,680	4.4	93.6
Pakistan	137	490	11.4	11.0
Philippines	73	1,220	8.7	31.4
Sri Lanka	18	800	9.9	2.1
EUROPE				
Czech Rep.	10	5,200	17.7	12.8
Greece	11	12,010	11.3	34.2
Hungary	10	4,430	22.5	15.0
Poland	39	3,590	29.5	12.1
Portugal	10	10,450	6.3	39.0
Russian Fed.	147	2,740	394.0	128.2
Slovakia	5	3,700	12.7	1.8
MIDDLE EAST/AFRICA				
Egypt	60	1,180	10.5	20.8
Israel	6	15,810	12.2	45.3
Jordan	4	1,570	3.9	5.4
Morocco	28	1,250	3.7	12.2
South Africa	38	3,400	10.1	232.1
Turkey	64	3,130	78.2	61.1
Zimbabwe	11	750	22.6	2.0

Table 6.2 Continued

Economy	Population (millions)	GDP per Capita	Inflation Rate	Market Capitalization
LATIN AMERICA				
Argentina	36	8,570	13.0	59.3
Brazil	164	4,720	475.2	255.5
Chile	15	5,020	13.6	72.0
Colombia	38	2,280	26.1	19.5
Mexico	95	3,680	18.5	156.6
Peru	25	2,460	288.8	17.6
Venezuela	23	3,450	46.7	14.6

Source: World Bank, *World Development Report*; IMF, *International Financial Statistics*, both various issues; *The Economist: Pocket World in Figures*, 1998, 34; and Bruno Solnik, *International Investment*, 3rd Edition (New York: Addison-Wesley, 1996), 255.

Note: In some cases, earlier years' data were available.

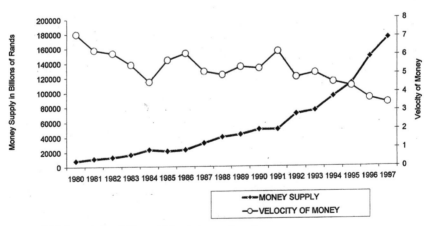

Source: IMF, *International Financial Statistics*, various issues.

Figure 6.1. Money supply (M) and velocity of money (V=GDP/M) for South Africa.

In the Middle East, Israel has a relatively high growth of money supply, but a declining velocity of money, as Figure 6.2 shows, so that stable prices can be achieved.

From the other Middle East countries, Turkey has the highest stock market value, followed by Israel, Egypt, and Morocco. Turkey's market capitalization is around 30 percent of GDP, compared to 40 percent for Morocco, 30 percent for Egypt, and as high as 120 percent for the United States. Some 45 percent of the Turkish stock market value is under foreign ownership, 16 percent for Egypt, and only 3 percent for Morocco, whereas the average daily volume is around $200 million, $31 million, and $6 million, respectively.

The government of Turkey, following a policy of privatization, recently sold 132.4 million shares or 12.3 percent stake in Turkiye Is Bankasi A.S. for $12.2 billion. Salomon Smith Barney managed the sale of the firm, 55 percent of which was sold to foreign investors and 45 percent to Turkish investors. Moreover, Turkcell, a Turkish phone company 41 percent of which is owned by Sonera company of Finland and 50.3 percent by Cukurova, a Turkish financial and industrial big firm, decided to proceed with a big initial public offering (IPO). The IPO stock would be sold domestically and overseas with a partial listing in the New York Stock Exchange or in the London Stock Exchange. The total equity value of Turkcell is estimated at $16 billion.

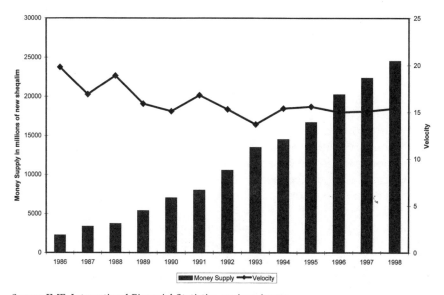

Source: IMF, *International Financial Statistics,* various issues.

Figure 6.2. Money supply (M) and velocity of money (V=GDP/M) for Israel.

Although Turkey adopted the EU's common tariff on most industrial products, reducing the average tariff from 27 percent to 13 percent, further reforms are needed, especially in agriculture, which employs about half the work force, and financial and other services. According to the WTO, more privatization is needed, mainly in telecommunications, banking, and airlines, as well as fiscal discipline and closer budget controls to stabilize the economy and improve the stock market. More or less, similar reforms are needed by other Asian and African emerging nations.

Israel, with a population of 6 million and a per capita income more than $15,000, has a stock market capitalization of more than $45 billion.

The reforms of the Egyptian markets, which are gradually linked to global markets, are improving slowly. However, privatization of banks stimulated the Egyptian Stock Exchange, which has a market capitalization of more than $20 billion. Nevertheless, Egypt, with a population of 60 million, a foreign debt close to $30 billion and direct investment about $1 billion a year, needs further fiscal and monetary reforms.

The Asian financial crisis in 1997 and later has swept the region and hung over the world economies as a dark cloud. The Asian Miracle seems to have faded away, and the emerging markets in the area, primarily South Korea, Malaysia, India, Indonesia, Thailand, China, and even the advanced market of Japan, came under financial turmoil. However, it is expected that after a period of adjustment, these markets would reach stability and eventually high growth again. A similar problem occurred in Mexico, which devalued its peso in late 1994, affecting other countries, including Brazil and Argentina; but with an aid package by the International Monetary Fund (IMF) and the United States, it managed to avoid a further currency crisis.

The Japanese economy also came under a severe financial crisis recently, which was due mainly to huge bad loans by the Japanese banks. Another reason was what John Maynard Keynes called liquidity trap, resulting from a falling demand for goods and services short of the country's production, regardless of how low interest rates are, a phenomenon similar to that of the Great Depression. Presently, though, consumer spending in Japan, as well as in almost all other countries, is high, and the global economy is not expected to face the problem of defective demand or overproduction in the near future.

The IMF and other institutions agreed to a huge bailout for East Asian nations, providing $55 billion for South Korea, which is higher than that of $48 billion for Mexico in 1994. Some $20 billion of that amount came from the IMF, $15 billion from the World Bank, and the rest from the United States and Japan. Also, Thailand received $17 billion, and Indonesia was promised $43 billion.

In order to defend its currency against a large devaluation, South Korea used a large part of its $30 billion reserves, and the government agreed to cut spending by 10 percent, whereas the expected economic growth was reduced from 6 to 3 percent a year. This policy was the result of South Korea's teetering economy and the sharp decline in the leading index of its stock market to more than 50 percent.

The recent worldwide stock market tremors, initiated in Asian countries, proved that global financial markets are interdependent. These tremors affected not only American and European stock markets but more so the markets of Russia, Latin America, and other emerging nations. The chain reactions of such tremors are expected to be rapidly contagious and potentially disastrous in the future, as the global computer networks can transfer huge amounts of money every day.

Gradually, the pain from the financial crisis in the Asian countries was turning to anger as people were suspicious that the West, and particularly the United States, aimed at an economic and intellectual imperialism in the area. They felt that the triumph of Western financial imperialism over Asia was similar to the triumph over socialism after the fall of the Berlin wall and that the crisis was plotted by the West to win trade negotiations, put down China, and increase influence in the region. However, many other people felt gratitude for the American and IMF help and blamed the nonopenness of their economies to international trade and finance for the turmoil. As a result, economic reforms were introduced by the Asian countries, including Japan and China, to attract foreign investment and adjust their economies to the new conditions of globalization.[3]

China's and India's Emerging Markets

China, with a population of 1.3 billion, which switched from the Maoist revolution of 1949 and the communist doctrines to denationalization and other reforms, achieved high rates of economic growth in the last fifteen years. Nevertheless, as the Chinese economy is gradually opening to international trade, it is more and more exposed to financial turmoil. Although China's $134 billion foreign exchange reserves put its currency out of the prospect of devaluation, the $119 billion foreign debt and the reliance of the country on foreign investment may delay the liberalization of the financial sector and other reforms in the economy.

In order to stop paying huge subsidies to inefficient state enterprises, the Communist Party Congress in September 1997 decided to privatize some 3,000 inefficient state enterprises, out of about 300,000 in China, mainly through public sale of shares or transferring control to the managers and workers in the enterprises. The shares, for which each worker pays up to $500 (about three times the average monthly salary), cannot be sold, except to another employee, and have a value in line with the company's assets.

Although only about 700 companies have permission to trade shares in China's young stock markets, mainly in Shanghai and Shenzhen, expectations are that many more companies will have shares in the rapidly growing Chinese stock markets domestically and eventually internationally. Already Nasdaq of the United States and the Shanghai Stock Exchange are doing cross-training and are forging closer ties toward a dual listing agreement.

Another measure to prepare China's industries for international competition is the recent formation of conglomerates through mergers in order to improve operations and reduce deficits in state-owned businesses. Also, to soften the tone toward foreign lenders, China is going to overhaul Guangdong Enterprises, a debt-ridden state company with $5.6 billion in debt.

To speed the sale of state assets and support the fledgling stock market, the Beijing rulers approved regulations for creating investment mutual funds, hoping to stabilize the speculative and volatile young capital markets. There are about 100 small mutual funds operating in China (a retail casino), but it is expected that the new regulations will allow Sino-foreign joint venture investments from the United States, Japan, Korea, and other countries.

Thus, the Microsoft Corporation announced a partnership with China Telecom and the government to link Chinese ministries to the Internet.

Figure 6.3 shows that the money supply in China increased slowly from 1980 to 1991, but rapidly thereafter, whereas the velocity of money declined from 4 to about 1 respectively, so that high rates of inflation and big exchange rate fluctuations can be avoided.

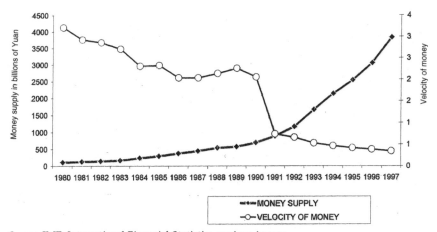

Source: IMF, *International Financial Statistics,* various issues.

Figure 6.3. Money suppy (M) and velocity of money (V=GDP/M) for China.

India's stock market capitalization is about $130 billion. From the standpoint of monetary policy, India, with a population of close to 1 billion, had a gradual increase in money supply but stable velocity of money during the last two decades, as Figure 6.4 shows. This is a policy of avoiding high inflationary rates and currency depreciation. After the gates were opened to overseas investors, more foreign investment is moving into the country, but progress in the financial and other sectors has been modest, mainly because of bureaucratic impediments and the slow implementation of economic reforms.

EUROPE'S EMERGING MARKETS

Russia's Financial Markets

After the fall of the Soviet Union in 1989 and especially after President Boris Yeltsin defeated Communist hard-liners by shelling the Parliament in 1993, Russia's privatization program proceeded rapidly. Shares in thousands of government companies were sold in auctions or given to managers and workers. Many workers, though, quickly sold the offered shares, leaving stocks in relatively few hands. Foreign investors from Wall Street, London, and elsewhere put huge amounts of money in Russian stocks, whereas mutual funds, pension funds, and institutional investors moved rapidly into the wild Russian markets.

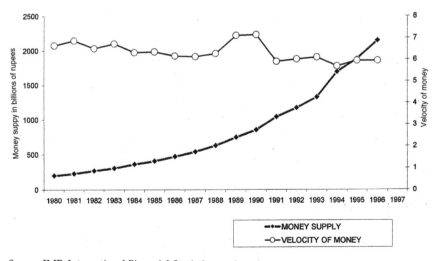

Source: IMF, International Financial Statistics, various issues.

Figure 6.4. Money supply (M) and velocity of money (V=GDP/M) for India.

Because of the mess in the domestic market, equity valuations of Russian companies are in deep discounts. Thus, the market value of Gazprom's reserves was only at $0.20 per barrel of oil equivalent, compared to $11.00 for Exxon's reserves and $8.00 for Amoco's. The reserves of Gazprom, which has sold gas to Western Europe for thirty years, are estimated at 33 trillion cubic meters of gas and 15 billion barrels of oil. About 10 million barrels is the production of oil equivalent per day, which is more than the production of any other company in the world. Gazprom's ADRs were recently priced in Wall Street at $19.90 and its market capitalization is $47 billion.[4]

Moreover, Gazprom decided to place over $3 billion in convertible bonds and Eurobonds in addition to $4 billion in loans. Also there are some twelve additional Russian companies with ADRs, including Lukoil, with market capitalization of $21 billion, and other oil, electricity, telecom, and metal firms, whereas the number of Russian companies entering the American stock markets is growing rapidly.

The stock market of Russia is expected to improve also as Russian companies are acquiring foreign firms. Thus, Lukoil Europe, a subsidiary of the Russian oil giant, bought 51 percent of Petrotel refinery from the State Ownership Fund of Romania for $300 million with the hope to make Romania a key route of oil from the Caspian Sea. Other Russian entrepreneurs also bought Vega, a smaller refinery, whereas Lukoil plans to expand into Yugoslavia.

Russia, the biggest market in Eastern Europe, remains an attractive place for equity investors. With a stock market capitalization of around $130 billion, roughly on a par with India, Russia's dollar-adjusted equity indices went up 130 percent in 1996 and 175 percent in 1997. Although Russia is facing a possible downgrading of its credit rating by Moody Investors Service (mainly in its $6 billion international bonds), political stability and reforms, as well as massive natural resources, would make Russian equities attractive in the near future. As a result of the good expectations of the Russian economy, the IMF relaxed the $10.1 billion loan terms, although required tax revenue targets were not achieved and the value of the ruble and the stock market of Moscow declined.[5]

After breaking from Moscow in 1991, Belarus achieved a good rate of economic growth. However, its policy to defy free market's logic led to financial turmoil. By printing money to support inefficient state enterprises that generate more than 80 percent of GDP brought about high inflation and drastic currency depreciation, from 35,000 to 69,000 rubles per dollar during the first five months of 1998 alone, mainly because of double money supply growth, compared to the previous year. That is why the IMF and the World Bank refused lending to Belarus until reforms are enacted to liberalize the economy.

Emerging Markets of Eastern Europe and the Balkans

All the stock markets of Eastern European and the Balkan countries present good opportunities for foreign investment. Hungary, with an index growth in equity market of 350 percent in 1996 and 130 percent in 1997, as well as a volume 50 percent higher in 1997 compared to 1996, is in the forefront, followed by Romania, with more than quadrupled and Estonia with more than doubled growth in equity markets in 1997.

Poland, with a low price–earning ratio, and the Czech Republic are expected to recover and show a strong position in their stock markets, as are the other Eastern European countries.

The Warsaw Stock Exchange of Poland, with a market value of about $12 billion, is rapidly growing in size mainly because of privatization of state-owned enterprises. Recently, Schroders, the London-based investment bank, in competition with Goldman Sachs and Credit Suisse First Boston, arranged the flotation of Telecomunikacja Polska (TPSA), which has a market capitalization of around $10 billion. Schroders, which also coordinated the flotation of Bank Hadlowy of Poland, first arranged the sale of 15 percent of TPSA's equity and the promotion of a new share issue.[6]

Since the end of communism in 1989, Poland attracted more than $20 billion foreign direct investment. Among other investors, Motorola Inc. agreed to establish a software center in Krakow to make cellular phones and computers worth about $110 billion. The Jagiellonian University in Krakow would provide some 500 well-educated staff in high-tech research and development.

Recently, negotiations started for Poland's membership in the EU, but there are questions regarding the sovereignty sacrifice and economic and financial reforms people are willing to accept. Although the large majority of the population favors the entrance of the country to the EU, some people are willing to accept an association of sovereign states and a strong federation.

Albania, the poorest country in Europe, with a population of 3.3 million, has weak financial institutions. The privatization program, during the transition from the centrally planned to the market economy, necessitated the establishment of the Tirana Stock Exchange (TSE) on May 2, 1996, the first in the history of Albania. As yet, treasury bills and bonds, as well as privatization vouchers, are the only transactions in the TSE. The Commission of Securities is supervising the capital market. The Bank of Albania adopted a floating exchange system in which the Albanian currency, the lek, is determined by supply and demand. In July 1997, 145 leks were exchanged to the dollar, compared to 102 leks in 1993. Because of some 750,000 Kosovar refugees, who return back gradually, the World Bank and other institutions approved $200 million loans and more aid comes from the EU and other countries. As a result of the recent ethnic and religious conflicts in the Balkans, there are more than 30,000 NATO, mainly American, troops in Kosovo, in addition to 32,000 in Bosnia and 26,000 in the former Yugoslavian Republic of Macedonia (FYROM), which are expected to reduce tension and bring stability in the Balkan markets.

Bulgaria, with a population of around 8.5 million people, initiated the first joint stock companies in 1989, which resulted from the privatization of state-owned enterprises. The Sofia Stock Exchange (SSE) started its first trading sessions in April 1992. The Securities and Stock Exchange Commission controls and regulates the Bulgarian stock market. The mass privatization of 1996–1997 and later contributed to the revitalization of the SSE. Some forty-six investment intermediaries have been licensed to facilitate securities transactions. In 1991, the IMF supported the liberalization program of Bulgaria, after price and foreign trade liberalization programs were enacted. The official exchange rate was fixed at the level of 1,000 levs per German mark, or about 0.5 euros.

In the former Yugoslavian Republic of Macedonia (FYROM), with a population of around 2 million, a commodity market with agricultural products, established in 1992, has limited activities, if at all. The first stock market of FYROM was created in 1992. Some 240 stock companies, transformed in the process of privatization, participate in the Stock Exchange of FYROM Inc., in Skopje, which provides regular information for the trading and the quoted companies. However, this highly regulated market is at a low level of development.

Romania, with a population of about 23 million, followed the French model and created the first stock exchanges in Bucharest, Braila, and Galatzi in 1881. However, because of wars and other changes, the normal function of the stock market started after the reforms of 1989. In order to facilitate transactions, ninety-six brokerage companies have already been licensed. In 1997, there were eleven companies with a large number of high-priced shares quoted in the Bucharest Stock Exchange in the first category, and fifty-two smaller companies in the second category. From May 1992, the foreign exchange regime is based on a floating rate of the national currency.

In Yugoslavia, the Belgrade Stock Exchange operated successfully from 1894 to 1941 with its securities listed in the big European financial centers. It resumed its operations in 1990, but the economic sanctions imposed by NATO, because of the conflict over Bosnia, mainly in 1992–1993, and currently over Kosovo, weakened this Balkan financial market.[7]

Greece's Emerging Market

As mentioned earlier, Greece has the largest number of stocks traded in the emerging markets of Europe, followed by Russia, Poland, Portugal, Hungary, the Czech Republic, and Slovakia. The drastic increase of mutual funds is expected to improve the performance of the Stock Exchange of Athens. After a timid beginning in the 1980s, the Greek mutual funds developed rapidly during the decade of the 1990s, accounting for more than 7.3 trillion drachmas deposited ($1 is roughly equal to 300 drachmas) or about 40 percent of all the deposits. The average annual growth of their assets in the last ten years is estimated at 85 percent.[8]

In the Athens Stock Exchange (ASE), which was founded in 1880 and renovated in 1986, traded securities include shares of the listed companies and government and corporate bonds. Derivative products started trading recently, whereas gold pounds and gold bars are rarely traded. In addition to the "main" market, where large companies with a five-year profitable record are involved, there exists the "parallel" market where small companies with a three-year profitable record are involved. The public companies in this rapidly growing emerging market increased from 116 in 1980 to 270 public companies, with their total capitalization of $34.2 billion in 1997. The price–earnings ratio (P /E), that is, the ratio of stock prices divided by the gross returns, ranges from 11.7 to 14, which is among the most attractive compared to the stock markets of other countries. The ASE is supervised by the Capital Market Commission, which has nine members and belongs to the Ministry of National Economy. Brokerage firms with 200 million drachmas assets can be approved by this Ministry.

In order to join the European Exchange Rate Mechanism and eventually join the common European currency—the euro—in 2001, Greece, in agreement with the other members of the EU, devalued the drachma by 14 percent on March 13, 1998. This was the result of the unwise policy of keeping the drachma overvalued for years, although Greek inflation was higher than the average of the EU and other hard currency countries.

Recently, though, Greece introduced for the first time shares of the Organization of Telecommunications of Hellas (OTE) in the New York Stock Exchange (NYSE) with a price of $11 per ADR (two ADRs per share of OTE), which was attractive, as prices moved upward. Also, the National Bank of Greece (NBG), the biggest bank of the country, offered some 4.6 million shares worth $348 million, 25 percent of which went to global investors, mainly through the NYSE. Merrill Lynch and Warburg Dillon Reed were the global coordinators. There are 5 ADRs for each share of NBG, worth around $14 each. As the privatization of state companies continues, more Greek firms are expected to enter the NYSE, including Olympic Airlines.

In order to meet the EU economic and monetary targets, the Greek government announced the privatization and partial flotation of twelve state-owned enterprises. They include OTE telecom and Olympic Catering, Piraeus Port Authority (OLP), Thessaloniki Port Authority, Thessaloniki Trade Fair, Corinth Canal, and the Horse Racing Organization.

LATIN AMERICAN EMERGING MARKETS

The recent crisis in Asia and Russia affected the financial markets of Latin America, particularly those of Brazil, with a population of 160 million and the ninth-largest economy in the world, as well as Venezuela, an oil-producing country. The devaluation of the Mexican peso in late 1994 had a similar result in other neighboring emerging nations. In such cases, the outcome is capital flight from such emerging markets and the pressure of currency devaluation.

The achievements of Brazil and other Latin American countries, which had recovered from the severe debt crisis and high inflation in previous years, came under jeopardy as a result of the Asian turmoil in financial markets, which acted like a wrecking ball, knocking one country after another. Argentina and Brazil, with effective economic reforms, Chile, with successful innovations, and other South American nations, with painful economic and political changes, try to adjust their economies to the new conditions of the global capitalist system.

The Bovespa stock market of Brazil and the Bolsa stock market of Mexico have the highest capitalization in Latin America, followed by the stock market of Chile and that of Argentina (Merval). All these markets and those of the other Latin American countries are expected to soar, as domestic and foreign investors are encouraged by the current high rates of economic growth.

The land reforms of Brazil and other Latin American countries offer hope to landless peasants for higher agricultural productivity, economic and financial stability, and a better distribution of income and wealth. Moreover, recent privatization of state-owned firms, such as that of Telebras, the huge telecom of Brazil from the sale of stakes of which the government raised $19 billion, attracts foreign investment because of high returns due mainly to high risks. Such policies strengthen the stock markets of the countries involved and support the arguments of shareholder capitalism. Already, the Brazilian Stock Market (Bovespa) index rebounded recently in both local and dollar terms, as did the Mexican and other emerging markets.

Winds of economic change are sweeping across almost every corner of Latin America. Argentina and Brazil have privatized their giant oil and telephone companies in recent years in an effort to lower costs and increase their competitiveness in global markets. Mexico has sold off more than 800 state-owned companies in the last decade, and a consensus has arisen among most politicians and voters across the region to press ahead with change.

The waves of privatization affect almost all emerging or developing nations, including the Latin American countries. A number of U.S. and other firms search for profitable investment and move into these nations, acquiring total or partial stakes of related companies. Also, at times, Latin American firms move into other neighboring countries for profitable opportunities.

The Latin American economies have become impressive to investors since they began their turnaround in the 1990s, whereas the governments have a serious commitment to maintain their economic course. Trends in both inflation and growth have been favorable, and the economies are booming. Average growth is expected to be more than 5 percent in Venezuela, Peru, Mexico, Ecuador, Colombia, Chile, Brazil, and Argentina according to Merrill Lynch & Co.

Many Latin American countries are shying away from their anti-Americanism, and their currencies have become closely tied with the dollar. Also, they have taken on the advice from the International Monetary Fund, whereas American and other investors are looking for profits and shift funds around frequently, not only in Argentina and Brazil but in other South American countries as well. Moreover, to boost faith in their banks, they implement reforms and allow acquisitions such as that of the Invertal Bank of Mexico by Canada's Scotiabank and many other financial and industrial firms.

The privatization trend in Argentina, Brazil, Mexico, and other Latin American countries leads to equity offerings by many enterprises, primarily in the form of initial public offerings (IPOs). Private equity funds and foreign investors are buying stakes in banks and other state and private companies at deflated prices, particularly after the Asian financial turmoil in 1997 and later when stock and bond markets in Latin American countries plunged, losing more than a third of their value.

Latin American and other emerging markets became attractive to large institutions and pension funds, such as the Teachers Insurance and Annuity Association (TIAA) and College Retirement Equity Fund (CREF), which expand their overseas investments for greater diversification and better returns. Although under New York State law 10 percent of TIAA's assets can be invested outside of the United States and Canada, billions of dollars of TIAA and more so of CREF, out of more than $250 billion of their total assets, are invested in promising Latin American and other emerging markets.

McDonald's Corporation has planned to invest more than $1 billion in the next three years to double its restaurants in Latin America. Latin America is contributing around $1.5 billion dollars to the company's total sales of about $34 billion a year. Sales in the region are expected to increase significantly in the coming years. Outside the United States, they account for about 50 percent or more than $17 billion of McDonald's total sales and are growing faster than U.S. sales.

United Parcel Service of America Inc. (UPS) agreed to acquire Challenge Air Cargo for an undisclosed price to expand into Latin America. Some 13 percent of UPS total revenue of about $25 billion a year comes from outside the United States.

The boom in Latin America is also evident with the capitalizing of the Latin American appliance market. In an effort to revive its sagging European and Asian operations, Whirlpool said it will cut part of its global work force over the next two years, boost its presence in Latin America, and pull out of two troubled joint ventures in China. Also, the appliance maker plans to sell its financing business to Transamerica Corporation for $1.35 billion.

In order to enlarge and expand to other countries in the Americas, Sleeman Breweries Ltd. of Canada acquired another Eastern Canadian brewery. The Ontario-based Sleeman, which produces a variety of lagers and ales that are sold throughout Canada, received tenders for its earlier offer for 86.5 percent of the shares outstanding in Upper Canada Brewing Co. of Toronto, whereas similar plans are formulated for expansion in Latin American emerging nations.

The French building materials company, Lafarge S.A., agreed to buy a stake in Cementos Molins S.A. of Spain for expansion in Latin American and other countries, for about 800 million francs, or $134 million. Lafarge's Spanish subsidiary, Asland S.A., will acquire the stake from a rival French building materials company, Climents Français S.A. Cementos, based in Catalonia, Spain, has operations in Spain and Latin America. Lafarge is based in Paris and has annual sales of more than 35 billion francs or $6 billion.

Enterprise Oil P.L.C. of Britain was part of a group that bought a North Sea oilfield from Conoco Inc. for $92 million. The consortium consists of the Mobil Corporation with a 50 percent interest, Enterprise Oil with 22.8 percent, the Amerada Hess Corporation with 22.2 percent, and OMV A.G. with 5 percent. Conoco, a unit of DuPont, is based in Houston and plans to expand in Latin America.

Regarding monetary policy in Latin American countries, there is mostly a high degree of instability in money supply and velocity of money, as Figures 6.5–6.8 show, particularly in Argentina, Brazil, and

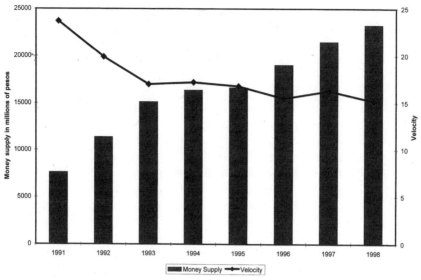

Source: IMF, *International Financial Statistics*, various issues.

Figure 6.5. Money supply (M) and velocity of money (V=GDP/M) for Argentina.

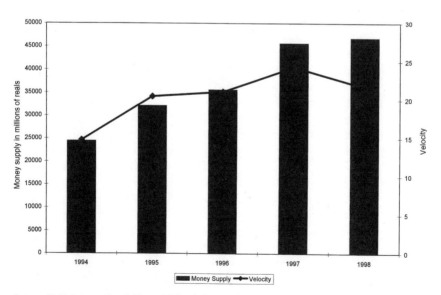

Source: IMF, *International Financial Statistics*, various issues.

Figure 6.6. Money supply (M) and velocity of money (V=GDP/M) for Brazil.

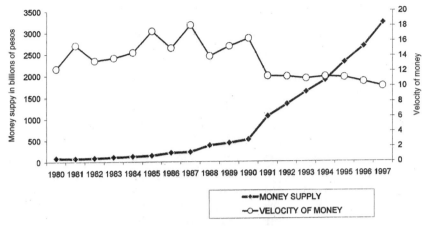

Source: IMF, *International Financial Statistics,* various issues.

Figure 6.7. Money supply (M) and velocity of money (V=GDP/M) for Chile.

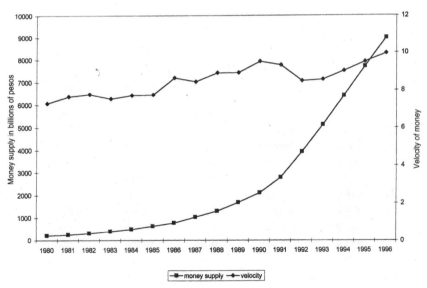

Source: IMF, *International Finance Statistics,* various issues.

Figure 6.8. Money supply (M) and velocity of money (V=GDP/M) for Colombia.

Peru, leading to high rates of inflation. However, financial measures are taken now by almost all Latin American countries for currency stabilization, foreign investment, and economic growth.

Argentina's Markets

The Buenos Aires bourse, with $60 billion market capitalization, is sensitive to changes in the stock market of its giant neighbor, Brazil, to which Argentina exports about 30 percent of its total exports. With a high rate of economic growth (around 7 percent per year), Argentina relies heavily on foreign capital inflows and international liquidity for the growth of its stock market. Although the turbulence in Southeast Asian markets affected Argentina's stock market, the Merval Index increased from 650 in 1996 to more than 850 recently.

In Argentina, domestic demand for stocks is favorable, particularly from private pension funds (known as AFJPs), but more foreign investors are also expected to enter Argentina's stock market (the Bolsa). The hope is that the dollar peg would work, as it did for Mexico during the financial crisis of 1995, and improve foreign trade, thereby uplifting the Merval share index, which dropped from about 900 to around 500 in 1997, mainly as a result of the Asian turmoil, but improved later.

It seems that the recent privatization of the airports and other firms, including parts of the YPF, an energy concern with a market capitalization of $10 billion, which already has been mostly privatized, and the Aerolineas Argentinas, would attract foreign investment. Already, YPF S.A., the Argentine oil firm, agreed to be acquired by Repsol S.A. of Spain for $13.4 billion. Also, foreign demand for Argentine bonds would increase, as happened with 10-year bonds in German marks (DM) bonds, worth DM 1.5 billion, which proved to be very attractive.

Argentina lifted exchange controls in December 1989 and permitted private individuals to keep accounts in foreign currency with local banks or sell property against payment in foreign currency in January 1992. As a result, confidence in the stock and bond markets was restored, and transactions were stimulated. The flow of foreign portfolio and other investments increased, and the government was able to sell billions of dollars in 30-year and other global bonds to replace the less risky Brady bonds, which are backed by the U.S. Treasury.

Brazilian Market and Economic Reforms

The emergence of Brazil as a hemispheric powerhouse initiated a rush of U.S. and European Union companies to capitalize on its promising emerging markets. After the turmoil in Asian markets, when the stock exchange in São Paulo, the region's largest with market capitalization of $256 billion, plunged by more than 30 percent, the Brazilian markets became again attractive and profitable. The fast-moving privatization of state-owned enterprises, including Telebras, the largest phone company in the Southern Hemisphere, increased investor confidence.

The crisis in Asia, started from Thailand in July 1997 and Russia in August 1998, affected to a significant degree Brazil, which devalued its currency, the real (R), by 9 percent on January 13, 1999. However, this did not stop the hemorrhage of dollars and other hard currencies from its foreign reserves and Brazil's stock market from heavy losses. Two days later the Brazilian government lifted exchange rate controls, deviating from the policy of pegging its currency to the dollar, which was used to limit high inflation. As a result, the Bovespa stock market of Brazil rose 34 percent in a day, affecting also upward the Dow Jones and other world stock markets. Nevertheless, in order to avoid further deterioration, Brazil should reduce budget deficits through reduction in spending and increase in taxes.

The privatization of Latin America's electricity industries has taken a step forward with the recent announcement of a combined minimum price of 1.68 billion reals or $1.53 billion for the sale of two electricity distributors in the southern Brazilian state of Rio Grande do Sul. The sales are part of plans to liquidate federal and state electricity assets, expected to raise 45 billion reals. With the addition of telecommunications and infrastructure, Brazil plans to sell assets worth R80bn by the end of the century.[9]

The AES Corporation and a group led by Public Service Enterprises Group Inc. won the bidding for two Brazilian energy companies in the latest round of utility sales. Also, AES, based in Arlington, Virginia, paid $1.37 billion for Centro-Oeste de Distribuicao de Energia Electra, which operates in the central-western region of Rio Grande do Sul. AES plans to own 90 percent in the distributor.

A group consisting of Pension funds, Public Service, which is a utility based in Newark, and VBC Energia S.A., a joint venture of Banco Votorantim, Banco Bradesco S.A., and Camargo Correa Industrial S.A., bid $1.49 billion for a 90.8 percent stake in Norte-Nordeste de Distribuicao de Energia Electra. The company distributes energy in the northeastern region of Rio Grande do Sul.

A group led by Brazil's Light Servicos de Electricidade S.A. made the sole bid for the company that provides power to residents of São Paulo, the world's third-largest city. The sale is part of Brazil's push to attract investors to an industry that suffers from energy losses and blackouts.

El Paso Energy Corporation, a natural gas company in Houston, acquired 50 percent stake in Epic Energy Amazon C., a Brazilian energy company, for $42.1 million.

A consortium of Brazilian industrial and financial companies agreed to pay $3.02 billion, or 70 percent more than the government's minimum price, for Companhia Paulista de Forca e Luz, known as CPFL, which distributes electricity in the state of São Paulo.

Brazil's Communications Minister raised the amount of $4.71 billion by selling private companies the rights to offer Brazilian consumers mobile phone service, known as cellular B-band. Furthermore, the government plans to bring up $40 billion more through the privatization of state-owned Telecomunicacoes Brazileiras S.A., known as Telebras, which holds monopolies in local, national, and international telephone services. This is the largest privatization ever in Latin America.

In São Paulo, Brazil, there is no expectation to limit foreign investment in the three fixed-line holding companies that will result from the massive privatization of the twelve holding companies through the breakup of the state telecommunications company, Telebras S.A.

Because of privatization, the ADR of Telebras hit a high price of $167 in July 1997. Then turbulence from the financial crisis in Asia spread to Latin America, and a sell-off in the Brazilian stock market later. drove the stock down as low as $83. Currently, fears have subsided that Brazil will further devalue its currency, the market has stabilized, and the telephone stock has rebounded. Salomon Smith Barney is guiding the sale of all or virtually all of its remaining stake in the company, which is worth about $25 billion. Also, AT&T, MCI, GTE, Bell Atlantic, Bell Canada, Telecom Italia, and France Telecom are preparing bids for control of the various pieces.

The privatization will help government pay down debt, but it may create a private monopoly and limit competition, which could stunt Brazilian productivity growth and threaten the very same economic plan that it is meant to enhance.

A group led by the DDI Corporation of Japan and Suzano de Papel e Celulose S.A. of Brazil bought a license to offer mobile phone service in Brazil's southern states for at least $802 million.

Another upward move for Brazil is the joint venture of Stora, the Swedish forestry group, with Odebrecht, the Brazilian industrial conglomerate, underlining the trend toward transcontinental consolidation in the paper and pulp industry.

Brazil is aiming to be a leading world car manufacturer in a few years, through the doubling of investments by the big car makers, which are planning to start new assembly lines in the country. Ford expects to invest $2 billion, General Motors $2 billion (along with the construction of a $150-million auto parts plant), and Volkswagen $3 billion in expansion. Fiat has planned to invest $1 billion in Brazil and $600 million in Argentina. Fiat's operation in Brazil is the Italian company's largest and most profitable. Toyota plans to produce 200,000 cars a year in Brazil for the domestic market in the next decade. Although sales were plunging more than 30 percent during the Asian financial crises, most of Brazil's auto industry only temporarily shut down or reduced output.

Texton Inc. agreed to buy Brazaco Mapri Industrias S.A. of Brazil, a maker of fasteners for the automobile industry, for $70 million. Brazaco, which is based in São Paulo, has about $100 million in annual sales. Its operations will be combined with Camcar Textron, a division of Textron's fastening-systems unit based in Rockford, Illinois, that has annual sales of $1.5 billion. At full capacity, Brazaco can generate $150 million in sales.

Brazil's market is ripe, and Wal-Mart Stores revised its merchandising in Brazil and Argentina and made other innovative changes even though it is still operating in the red.

The consumer goods conglomerate Unilever N.V. paid $930 million to acquire Brazil's largest ice cream business, Kibon, from the Philip Morris Companies. Kibon, based in São Paulo, controls 60 percent of the Brazilian ice cream market with annual sales of about $330 million. Unilever has operated since 1929 in Brazil, where its Gessy Lever consumer goods business is the country's tenth-largest company.

Carrefour is a French retailer that has recently moved into Brazil and is now that nation's biggest retail chain. However, what was seen as a success story is now being viewed as a potential liability. Analysts say Carrefour's problem is not its food sales, because food consumption will hold up well, crisis or no crisis. Where the retailer could run into trouble is on the nonfood side of its business, particularly its hypermarkets.

One of Brazil's largest insurance companies is preparing to sell shares to international investors, the first global offering by a Latin insurer. Also, Porto Seguro Cia de Seruros Gerais, a São Paulo-based firm specializing in automobile insurance, will offer a minority stake of about $200 million in shares, depending on market conditions.

Scores of global insurers, including American International Group Inc., Liberty Mutual Group, and Cigna Corporation, have entered the Brazilian market by buying stakes in local companies or setting up joint ventures.

Sul America Seguros, Brazil's largest insurer, began a joint venture with Aetna Inc. Bradesco Seguros, the second largest company, announced a joint venture with Prudential Insurance Company of America.

Telefonica International of Spain agreed to acquire Telerj Celular and Telest Celular, as well as Telebahia Celular and Telergipe Celular, of Brazil.

Reforms in Other Latin American Countries

Changes and adjustments are usual also in other South American countries. Regarding fish business, for example, Chile's salmon farmers could soon be punished for doing exactly what the United States is promoting in South America. The U.S. government is always talking about free and fair trade, but more time is needed for adjustment. Objections are raised by the executives of such firms as the Eicosal S.A., a fish-farming company that is based in Chile and has annual sales of $22 million.

In Chile, strikes by organized labor are unusual because the country has the Western Hemisphere's lowest levels of unionization and collective bargaining. Chilean law crimps labor's leverage by effectively limiting collective bargaining to unions representing workers at individual companies rather than across entire industries. The law also provides scant protection against blatantly antiunion practices and a divide-and-conquer strategy.

In its efforts to avoid a further economic decline, the government of Colombia decided, on June 28, 1999, to devalue its currency, the peso, by 10 percent. Its value now is around $0.85. The main reason for the devaluation was the selling pressure on the peso and the reduction of the $8.5 billion in foreign reserves for the defense of the peso. This devaluation has a serious impact on neighboring countries, mainly Ecuador and Venezuela, whose currencies are under devaluation pressures.

Central American nations are now moving quickly to make up for lost time by allowing new trade treaties like the North American Free Trade Agreement to be negotiated quickly with other Latin nations. Mexico and the northern triangle countries of Central America—Guatemala, Honduras, and El Salvador—decided to sign a wide-ranging trade accord.

Guatemala has made less expansive trade agreements with Mexico in the past. In previous years, there were more Mexican imports from Guatemala, compared to present imports, although Guatemala's total exports of goods of more than $2 billion were more than double the level of ten years ago, according to the Inter-American Development Bank.

In Kingston, Jamaica, the governing People's National Party of Prime Minister P. J. Patterson won a majority in Jamaica's recent elections, getting forty-eight seats in the sixty-member parliament compared with only nine for the opposition Jamaica Labor Party. This means that the people of Jamaica approve of the economic reforms policy of the party in power. However, in Georgetown, Guyana, riot police officers fired shotguns and tear gas to disperse hundreds of demonstrators who said election fraud helped an American expatriate to take a strong lead in the presidential vote.

Peru, in order to have access to a $4.5 billion IMF fund and improve its markets, is implementing privatization and other fiscal measures, as Chile, Mexico, and other South American countries do.

Canada's Cambior Inc. had promised to develop the giant La Granja copper mine in Peru, but it would not proceed until the price of the metals begins to rebound. Canada's goal is to have the equivalent of 80 percent of Peru's entire output, which is the world's fifth-largest producer of copper.

In Uruguay, the government still monopolizes electricity, oil refining, and all but cellular telephone services, because most people voted to keep it that way. The cradle-to-grave welfare state dates from 1903 and still offers all citizens catastrophic health insurance. Governmental agencies run the railroads, operate gas stations, supply water and mail service, even produce rum and whiskey and manage casinos. One in every five workers is employed by the state, and government spending, including a sweeping pension system, represents a quarter of the gross national product, more than that of any other Latin American or Caribbean country except Cuba. Recently, though, the president pushed a law that will open the way for private companies to generate and transmit electricity.

Figure 6.9 shows the trend of money supply and velocity of money for Venezuela. After 1993, the money supply of the country increased significantly. However, velocity of money declined, thereby mitigating the rates of inflation.[10]

Eventual political stability in the area would help improve financial markets in all Latin American nations, which are expected to join NAFTA, MERCOSUR, or other common markets toward their economic growth and sociocultural development.

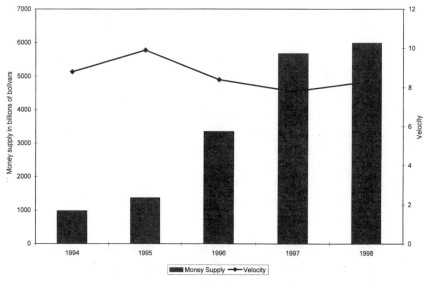

Source: IMF, International Financial Statistics, various issues.

Figure 6.9. Money supply (M) and velocity of money (V=GDP/M) for Venezuela.

Foreign Investment and Cross-Border Mergers and Acquisitions

INTERNATIONAL CAPITAL FLOWS

The capital flows around the world bring economic benefits to all countries involved because more efficient allocation of savings and investment is normally achieved. Reductions in capital controls increase the opportunity for higher investment returns and diversify risk through the spread of investors' portfolios. With a mere computer keystroke, large amounts of money move across borders in order to enjoy higher returns. As a result, the divergence in interest rates among countries, without capital controls, is fallen and movements of currencies against each other, as well as arbitrage opportunities, are reduced.

Nevertheless, expected inflation differentials may lead to changes in interest rates and subsequently to changes in exchange rates, particularly when there is high government spending or monetary expansion. Moreover, if the confidence of investors is undermined and they start pulling out of a country, selling its currency, then interest rates are raised to stop the trend of capital flight.

After the 1980s, capital flows changed direction from the United States to the emerging nations, primarily to Asia and Latin America. Privatization of state-owned enterprises, elimination of capital controls and other financial regulations, higher productivity, expansion of mutual funds and banks, and the electronic linkages of different financial markets are some of the main reasons for such a change. Moreover, the development of repurchase agreements (repos), bonds, and options, on a global scale, provide a better portfolio diversification and greater investment opportunities. This is so especially with futures because "the future belongs to the futures," as young urban professionals (yuppies) claim.

Private investment in developing countries increased significantly in the 1990s, according to the World Bank, from around $40 billion in 1990 to $200 billion in 1995 and $280 billion in 1997. Although there was a decline thereafter because of the financial crisis, mainly in Asia, Russia, and Brazil, the upward trend is expected to start again in the near future. Not only did long-term foreign direct investment in developing countries increase from some $20 billion in 1990 to $150 billion in 1997, but short-term investments in stocks and bonds in these countries increased from around $10 billion to close to $100 billion, respectively, as did commercial loans from some $20 billion to $50 billion.

For comparative reasons, the present value of the costs and benefits of a project in domestic or foreign markets can be determined by employing the discounting principle. In the cost-benefit analysis used in investment decisions, projects in different countries can be ranked according to the difference of the present value of the stream of benefits (B) minus the present value of the stream of costs (C), that is, $(B - C)$. Thus, the present value of a benefit stream B1, B2, . . . , Bn for n years, discounted at the rate of discount, r, is:

$$B = B1/(1 + r) + B2/(1 + r)^2 + B3/(1 + r)^3 + \ldots + Bn/(1 + r)^n$$

The same holds true for the stream of costs.

The present value (PV) of a project is equal to the stream of benefits minus the stream of costs, discounted. That is,

$$PV = \sum_{t=1}^{n} (Bt - Ct)/(1 + r)^t$$

A project that gives a positive present value can be expected to be approved. If it gives a negative value, it should be rejected.

Moreover, the ranking of projects can be determined according to the ratios of their discounted benefits over their discounted costs, as follows:

$$B/C = \sum_{t=1}^{N} Bt/(1 + r)^t / \sum_{t=1}^{n} Ct/(1 + r)^t$$

Where Bt and Ct are benefits and costs in year t, respectively, n is the life of the project, and r is the rate of discount. Projects with benefit-cost ratios greater than 1 are profitable and deserve approval, whereas projects with a ratio of less than 1 should be abandoned, regardless of the country involved.

Ceteris paribus, the rate of return on investment (r), which affects the interest rate, is determined by the difference of revenue (R) minus the cost (C) over investment (I), that is,

$$r = (R - C)/I$$

Comparatively speaking, countries with a higher rate of return on investment, assuming other things the same, would attract more capital investment than other countries with a lower rate of return. This trend would continue until equalization of the rate of return in all countries considered.

The marginal rate of transformation (MRT) of factors of production is equal to the ratio of the value of their marginal product (MP) or their prices (P), that is, wages for labor (L) and interest for capital (K), as follows:

$$MRT_{LK} = MP_L/MP_K = P_L/P_K = w/r$$

where w stands for the factor price of labor (wages) and r for the factor price of capital (interest).

Depending on the availability of factors of production and the relative prices of labor (w) and capital (r), substitution of one factor for the other may take place in the production function. The elasticity of capital (K) for labor (L), E_{KL}, in differential terms can be expressed as follows:

$$E_{KL} = -(dK/K)/(dL/L) = -d(K/L)/(K/L) = d(r/w)/(r/w)$$

Thus, if the percentage change in capital/labor ratio, $d(K/L)/(K/L)$, is 10 percent and the percentage change in the rental/wage ratio, $d(r/w)/(r/w)$, is 5 percent, then the elasticity of substitution, E_{kl}, is –2, or,

$$E_{kl} = -0.10/0.05 = -2$$

That is, for each change in the rental/wage ratio there is a double change in the capital/labor ratio.

Figure 7.1 shows the production effects of capital transfer between two countries. Capital supply in nation 1 is 0A, with a rate of return 0C and total output 0FGA, determined by the marginal product of capital (MPK_1) line. Likewise, in nation 2, capital supply is A0' with a rate of return 0'H and total output 0'JMA. The transfer of capital AB from nation 1 to nation 2 equalizes the rate of return to capital at BE. This

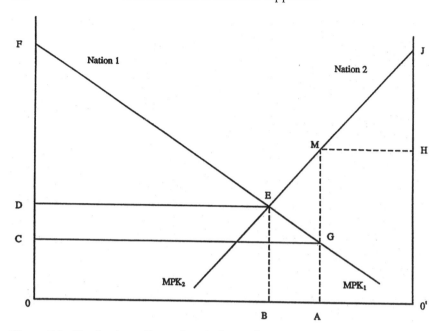

Figure 7.1. Production effects of capital transfer

decreases total output in nation 1 to 0FEB and increases it in nation 2 to 0'JEB, for a net increase in world output of EGM.

FOREIGN INVESTMENT AND MULTINATIONAL CORPORATIONS

The flow of foreign investments from industrial countries, mainly the United States, provides overhead capital, jobs, and technology for the receiving developing countries and raw materials as well as returns on the outflowing capital for the investing countries.

One of the most important issues of economic development in recent years has been the emergence and growth of big corporate enterprises of an international character. The growth of such giant corporations requires expansion in many nations. They not only sell but, typically, also make or buy large numbers of different products and are involved in a number of other commercial, financial, and even political activities in a number of different countries.

There are mainly two schools of thought concerning the growth and expansion of big corporations. The first school supports such an expansion on the grounds that it helps the spread of technological know-how and stimulates economic development in poor as well as in rich countries. The second school criticizes the spread of big corporations, especially in developing countries, because it leads to economic and eventual political domination. This section deals with recent questions raised as a result of foreign investment and expansion of multinational corporations.

Criteria and Trends of Foreign Investment

Poor overpopulated countries cannot save enough to finance new investment projects because their limited income is primarily used for consumption. They have to rely, therefore, on foreign sources for their needed capital. On the other hand, large corporations and individual investors in rich countries may benefit themselves and the poor countries by investing abroad. Opportunities abroad may be more profitable than at home. This was the process that investors from western Europe followed in the nineteenth and early twentieth centuries by investing heavily in the United States, Russia, Latin America, and other areas. (England, for example, used to invest abroad as much as half of her saving, which amounted to around 7.5 percent of the national income.) It must be pointed out, however, that conditions for investing abroad during that time were better than today. Immigration was free, and people moved together with their investments to the colonies. Confiscation, tariffs, and other restrictions were limited or nonexistent. Concessions from widespread bribery, the prevailing international gold standard, and the unexplored mining and other resources were additional reasons for the favorable climate in foreign investment.

Foreign investments and trading have been provided by large firms, such as Singer Machines, General Motors, Ford, and Unilever, even before World War II. But an impressive jump of investment abroad can be observed primarily after the war. The continuation of this trend of foreign investment requires that favorable socioeconomic conditions prevail. Such conditions include

1. Socioeconomic stability and protection of life and property. To some extent, the latter requirement can be met through insurance by a governmental agency or by a private firm, initially subsidized by the government of the creditor or the debtor country.[1]
2. Opportunities for profitable investment. Such opportunities depend, among other conditions, on the size and structure of the market, the existence of public utilities and economies of scale, and the availability of relatively low-cost production methods.
3. Guarantees for the remittances of profits and interest, allowances for depreciation, and capital reimbursement in the event of nationalization, as well as free immigration of foreign personnel.

4. Absence of discrimination in taxes, competitive practices, administrative controls, and treatment of foreigners.

The main reasons for investment abroad are the following:

1. Labor costs in the home country, in some areas of production, are higher than in other countries.
2. Resource availability in certain countries provides for cheap raw materials.
3. Antitrust enforcement is, at times, far tighter in some home countries than in others. However, certain nations, such as France and Japan, support the formation of cartels and export companies for competition with enterprises based in other countries.
4. Trade unions are weaker in other countries than in the home country, and strikes are much shorter and less damaging. In some cases, for example, 75 percent of the union members must support the strike.
5. The cost that investing corporations must pay, incurred as a result of antipollution and consumerism drive, is comparatively less in other countries.
6. Because of imitation in technology, anticipated market expansion, and unexploited opportunities abroad, as well as maturity of business at home, factor productivity in general and investment return in particular may be expected to be higher in other countries.[2]
7. Credit facilities offered by other nations are a consideration. Recently, large companies have been successful in raising foreign capital to supplement their needs. They have also been offering equity participation in their subsidiaries to foreign investors, so that they can enjoy greater financial independence. In fact, big foreign firms are criticized for draining the available financial resources, leaving inadequate room for borrowing by domestic firms.[3]
8. Another reason for extensive direct investment in foreign countries is the production of substitutes for imports in these countries. Foreign firms want to keep their share in the markets of other countries. If they do not invest there, they will lose part or all of the market of the same or similar goods to the import-substituting industries.

Some countries, however, may have limited capacity to absorb foreign investment either because of lack of well-planned projects, or because complementary factors and facilities are not available, or because of the lack of markets where the products could be sold. Furthermore, developing countries change policies, from time to time, toward encouraging or discouraging foreign investment on their soil, using higher taxes or tax exemptions, allowing a higher or lower percentage of invested capital and profits to be taken out, and encouraging faster growth of exporting industries compared to import-substituting industries or vice versa. In Latin America, for example, before the great depression of the 1930s, development was stimulated from abroad by the gradual increase of exports. During the postwar years, however, industrial investment supported by internal sources was emphasized, and tariffs and other protective measures were raised.[4] Recently though, both the export-propelled growth and the import-substitution phases of development declined.

Depending on the need for foreign exchange, developing countries can be selective with regard to foreign investment. Thus, provisions to gradually train local personnel for skilled technical and administrative positions, to invest primarily in export-increasing or import-decreasing manufacturing industries where domestic investment and technology are inadequate, and to admit domestic capital at all stages of the venture may be made in agreements between individual governments and foreign investment firms. Because of such restrictive investment provisions, the risk of confiscation and the expected instability in developing countries, foreign firms, primarily from the United States, prefer to invest in developed countries, such as those of western Europe and Canada, where ownership is secured even though technology is well-known and investment returns lower compared to developing countries.

Regional and Sectoral Allocation of Foreign Investment

Before World War II, foreign investments were flowing mainly from western European countries to colonial areas producing minerals and other raw materials. After the war, large amounts of foreign investments were flowing mainly from the United States to the rest of the world.[5] Percentage-wise, western Europe, especially the European Union countries, absorbed the greatest amount of American investment, followed by Canada, Latin America, and to a limited extent Asia and Africa.

The sectoral allocations of foreign investments depend mainly on the resource endowment of each country and its stage of development. Canada and Latin American countries for example, with rich mineral resources, have large amounts of foreign investment in mining and smelting, compared to Europe where manufacturing has absorbed great amounts of U.S. direct investment. In the earliest stages of development, exploitation of mineral resources by foreign capital is more profitable than manufacturing. At higher stages of development, however, investment in manufacturing is more attractive, since by then the required skills and public utilities have already been established.

In the past, foreign investment in developing countries has been directed mainly to locations with mineral deposits and areas suitable for plantations. Economic and social contact with the local economy and the indigenous population was limited. Under such conditions, stimulation of economic development through backward and forward linkages was either limited or nonexistent because there was either no enlargement of demand for inputs from industries providing other raw materials or no cheaper cost for forward industries. A small portion of local labor could have been hired, if any. The gap in wages between the foreign and the domestic sectors was enlarged, and local entrepreneurs were gradually pushed aside.

Foreign enterprises are usually encouraged by poor countries to invest in industries producing heavy machinery, paper, chemical products, synthetic oil, pharmaceuticals, steel, and aircraft. It is argued that investment in manufacturing provides external economies, absorbs labor migrating from the villages into the cities, and provides advanced skills needed for rapid economic and social development. Commerce, however, is equally or even more important in training entrepreneurs and personnel how to keep accounting books, organize stores, and manage offices, hotels, and warehouses. All these and a host of other commercial activities may be necessary even before the process of industrialization can start.

Notwithstanding the large amount of total U.S. investment, private foreign investment in less developed countries followed a declining path throughout the years. Thus, outstanding direct investment in these countries was 50 percent of the total U.S. foreign investment during the period 1914–1950; by 1960, however, it declined to 40 percent and in recent years to less than 30 percent. This trend of channeling an ever greater proportion of foreign investment to advanced countries, rather than to low-income countries that desperately need capital formation, has tended to widen the gap between rich and poor nations, bringing on many undesirable worldwide social and economic repercussions.

Potential new sources of domestic capital can be generated and greater flow of foreign capital may be attracted by an organized capital market mechanism. However, the immediate questions to be asked are: What are the proper devices to facilitate capital investment in poor nations by foreign countries? What policy measures must be introduced to attract such investments? Do developing countries have the capacity to absorb foreign capital investment in development projects? How can they provide security, essential for such investment, against inflation and other risks?

A number of suggestions have been made in connection with the recycling of surplus funds. The most important suggestions are the following:

1. The surplus nations should lend some of their funds to the International Monetary Fund (IMF) or the World Bank, which would re-lend them to countries in need. Given the proper interest rate and the right exchange rate guarantees, the IMF can recycle the extra reserves efficiently into productive projects. The United States would prefer that the IMF's regular currency resources be used, supplemented by additional funds established by the industrial nations.

2. A special agency could be established to purchase collectively products in short supply and sell them to the consuming nations. The mechanism of Special Drawing Rights might play a vital role in such a scheme. A surcharge might be collected from such a procedure, the revenue from which could be lent or given to developing countries.

3. Capital markets could be created in developing countries, ready to attract surplus capital from countries with excess reserves. This would help the rapid economic development of poor countries, increase the export of capital goods from industrial countries, and stabilize the international monetary mechanism. To avoid the undesirable effects of inflation, some form of indexing for investment in securities could be provided.

An efficient stock market in developing countries can be a good vehicle for capital investment into their territories. It may be the most efficient way of achieving an orderly economic development. The establishment or improvement of intermediate financial institutions can provide credit for underwriters, market makers, and local entrepreneurs for investment.

The creation of effective capital markets can solve the problem of borrowing of many developing and even some developed countries. This is particularly important at the present time because of the new financial problems in the emerging nations. Excess capital reserves are searching for secure and profitable investment. Such reserves could be invested directly in developing countries, which, in turn, could finance the cost of needed machinery imported for developed countries.

As yet, surplus countries do not seem to prefer investing their excess capital in developing countries per se. On the contrary, they prefer primarily developed countries. However, reliable wholesale commercial banks can attract such excess capital by providing high-yielding and fully liquid securities, ready to be traded in any capital market, relending the funds to many smaller banks in developing countries. Such wholesale banks and stock exchanges could even be established in poor countries with the support of world associated institutions such as the World Bank, the International Monetary Fund, and the Asian and African Development Banks. Intermediate institutions such as these could not only stimulate economic development but promote regional, economic, and political integration.

Foreign Investment and Taxation

In recent years, many countries have enacted legislation concerning tax exemption or tax reduction to attract foreign investment. Also, international tax treaties have been concluded between the major capital-importing and capital-exporting countries to promote such investment. Different tax systems inevitably distort allocation. They create opportunities for foreign investors to maximize net profits after taxes by departing from the optimal allocation of resources on a before-tax basis. Therefore, international treaties and laws that eliminate tax differences and promote uniformity and equality are of great importance for the efficient allocation of international investment.

Domestic taxation gets instant attention by the taxpayers and the fiscal policymakers, but taxation on foreign earnings appears to be of remote importance, even though it may have serious long-term repercussions upon the economy. Corporations with overseas earnings are customarily taxed by two countries: the foreign country where earnings take place and the country of residence in which the citizens or corporations receive the earning. To implement the two main principles of taxation that (1) all the citizens and corporations with the same income should pay the same amount of tax (tax equity), and (2) taxes should be paid on all income earned (tax universality), many countries have enacted laws with credit provisions.

The tax credit permits companies and citizens to subtract from their tax on income earned abroad the amount of tax they paid to a foreign country on the same income. By juggling their books, so to speak, and arranging their worldwide income distribution, big corporations may manage to pay little or no domestic income tax. For example, royalties paid by a company to a host country may be converted to income taxes and be subtracted from taxes paid to the home country. This means a transfer of tax revenue from the home to the host country without affecting the company. Such tax credit provisions are criticized on the grounds that they are loopholes in favor of companies investing abroad, reducing income and employment at home.

However, restricting foreign operations through heavier taxation upon firms investing abroad would probably lead to an elimination of present and future markets and loss of efficiency for greater comparative advantages as well as loss from more dynamic management and future technological advances. The use of foreign sources for the financing of these firms and the increase in total earnings for operations abroad are additional reasons in support of foreign ventures. Some countries, such as Canada, Germany, and the Netherlands, do not even tax foreign earnings of their multinational companies; France and Japan have very small tax rates in dividends from abroad. Nevertheless EU member nations are to implement common taxation on foreign investment.

In addition to tax reductions and, in some cases, tax exemptions, other measures, such as tariff reductions on imported capital goods and high rates of depreciation allowances, have been taken by capital-importing countries to attract foreign investment. Personal income tax exemptions for foreign personnel, especially managers and technicians, have been introduced by poor countries, such as India and Pakistan, to promote capital investment and foreign ventures. Furthermore, developed countries, such as Germany and the United Kingdom, in addition to the United States, have introduced measures for deferring tax liabilities on profits abroad until repatriation, thus encouraging reinvestment. Long-term credit insurance for sales of capital equipment and against losses from currency depreciation, exchange controls, nationalization, and similar risks have been introduced by capital-exporting countries to protect and facilitate the regular flow of capital to developing countries. Another incentive for investment might be the granting of permission to average profits, for tax purposes, over long periods of time.

Tax deferral, which prevails in some developed countries including the United States, means that taxation is levied on dividends remitted to the country rather than on income earned. This is a form of an interest-free loan for the government to the corporations, who will thus reinvest profits in low-tax countries to defer tax payments until their liquidation. In that event, they would be paying less taxes on the accumulated profits, which are considered long-term capital gains.

Transfer-price manipulation or price adjustment is another device used between parent companies and their affiliates to save taxes or to repatriate more profits than the amount permitted. A number of firms are accused of charging their affiliates exorbitant prices in order to reduce taxes and primarily to shift profits that have been frozen in other countries back to the home countries. To achieve a fair income tax policy, negotiations between governments and companies involved have been enacted periodically.

Given that government policies are different in various countries, foreign investors may have to face the policies of two or more governments. Such policies may be in harmony with each other or may be in conflict. The policy of the host country may favor capital inflow and reinvestment of profits, while the home country may favor investment abroad but with profit and capital repatriation and not extensive capital outflow. Comparatively speaking, the policies of the United States, for example, are favorable to multinational expansions. To harmonize diverging national policies toward foreign investment, an international code of national behavior and business ethics may be needed. Common antitrust policy, common custom duties, transportation rates, benefits, and taxation may be included in such a harmonized code. Technological progress in our supersonic era makes the world smaller and the corporations bigger, and very soon we may emphasize not independent national economic policies but unified international policies.

Multinational Expansion

The basis for the creation of the modern national and international corporation lies in the old Roman system of laws that recognized the existence of juristic or artificial persons with rights and obligations similar to those of natural persons. Such legal entities have privileges, as well as responsibilities, that emanate from contractual agreements, property acquisitions or disposals, and activities that physical persons can undertake. As a result, the first joint stock companies of an international nature were established toward the end of the Middle Ages. Such companies were the East India Company (chartered in England in 1600) and similar ones in Spain, Denmark, Sweden, and Austria, the Eastland Company, the Merchant Adventurers, the Muscovy Company, the Hudson Bay Company, and the House of Rothschild (German bank). Their main function was to expand trade and investment between the mother countries and their colonies then existent. Toward the end of the nineteenth century and afterward, the growth of the corporate form of enterprise was extensive, particularly in North America.

An enterprise may consist of one or a number of individual units and carry out business operations in one or more countries. In the latter case, each component unit of the enterprise becomes a resident of the territory of a sovereign state with separate legal identity. When an enterprise is composed of units that reside in many sovereign states or nations, it is referred to as a multinational enterprise. The individual units of such an enterprise are linked by ties of ownership and / or other economic and contractual links. In any case, the word multinational implies many nations (the minimum is two) and, in recent literature, is associated with large, integrated enterprises.

The term "multinational" or "multikorp," which made its appearance in the dictionaries in the early 1970s, means, therefore, a firm with divisions in more than two countries, with a global strategy for investment and market share, and awesome in size and power. It is different from the term "international," which is too broad, including even small firms such as import-export and foreign retail selling companies.

Once a company has decided to enter a country for business, the first problem to be considered is in which of the following possible alternatives it shall choose to conduct its operations:

1. To market its product through foreign middlemen or to establish sales branches in the host country, in which case little risk, investment, and effort are required by the exporting producer. However, the exporter must pay tariffs and may be subject to trade restrictions.
2. To authorize a foreign manufacturer to produce the merchandise, that is, by licensing. In this case the company avoids the problem of tariff, quota, and other restrictions but creates a potential competitor who will acquire the know-how and then proceed to operate independently after the licensing agreement expires.
3. To build or otherwise acquire its own production facilities in the host country either in the form of a joint venture or a wholly owned subsidiary. In the case of a joint venture or consortium, the company is a partner with a person or company or public institution in another country. Depending on the extent of ownership, the company does not have real control and decision-making authority if its ownership is less than 50 percent and vice versa if it owns more than 50 percent.
4. To integrate foreign and domestic operations into one worldwide company with a number of plants spread throughout different countries. Each plant may be concentrated in the production of a product, or parts of it, or a number of products.

Alternatives 3 and 4 are related to foreign investment, which is the main function of multinationals, whereas alternatives 1 and 2 involve primarily international marketing. Investment, in turn, takes the form of buying shares in an existing operation or physically constructing a new plant and starting from scratch.

Multinational companies are gradually transforming the planet into a global supermarket. Thus one can meet gas stations with such trade marks as "Mobil Oil" or "Shell" and other oil companies in scores of countries. Banks with titles such as "Citigroup," "Chase Manhattan," "Manufacturers Hanover Trust," and "Continental Bank International" can be seen in many capitals and large cities all over the world. The same thing can be said for TWA, IT&T, General Electric, Toyota, Volkswagen, Singer, Nestle, and scores of other giant companies.[6]

Most of the multinational firms, such as General Motors, RCA, IBM, Westinghouse, Goodyear, Dow Chemical, Motorola, Honeywell, and other blue chips, are based in the United States.[7] Recently, however, many firms in countries other than the United States, such as Japan and Europe, have engaged in worldwide operations and compete with American firms. Still other foreign and American companies have formed joint ventures and invest and produce all over the world.[8]

In an effort to move industry to the fuel rather than the fuel to the industry, many corporations intend to build factories in the countries where fuel is plentiful. Firms such as Marcor, Hercules, General Motors, Kaiser Industries, and other petrochemical concerns seek the opportunity of investing in joint ventures of oil, steel, aluminum, and fertilizers, primarily in oil-producing countries. At the same time, oil and other raw-material-producing countries are interested in foreign technology and the markets of the industrial countries. Such gradual flow of capital and technology to countries producing minerals may reduce the risks for unilateral actions, stimulate development, and give a global economic concept to the production and trade of oil and other important raw materials.

The spread of multinationals creates an opportunity for some oil countries to invest the billions of dollars that they are amassing. These countries cannot possibly invest such huge amounts of money within their own borders. However, they can invest their surplus petrodollars in many other countries through multinationals. Kuwait, for example, invested in joint ventures in such countries as Egypt, Sudan, Mauritania, Guinea, and Brazil. Joint ventures were also enacted between Arab nations and such ex-communist countries as Hungary, Romania, Yugoslavia, and other countries in Eastern Europe, which helped build low-cost housing and provided equipment and experts for industrial projects in these and other developing countries where oil nations are investing. Also, France agreed with Iran to establish steel mills, Renault car-plants, chemical plants, housing projects, color television networks, and even subway networks.

Multinational economic expansion, in many cases, originates or is supported by governmental agreements. Such agreements are enacted not only between market economies, but between market and ex-planned economies as well, mainly Eastern European countries. A number of Western corporations, such as Occidental Petroleum and Fiat, have operations in Russia and other republics of the former Soviet Union, and even in communist China.

Even though the U.S.-based companies hold a commanding lead in the multinational world, companies based in other countries are also spreading rapidly. Thus, more than 700 major manufacturing firms in the United States are owned by foreign companies. There are more than sixty foreign banks operating in the United States. Furthermore, large foreign investments in the United States create new problems from the viewpoint of ownership and control of business enterprises. From a national point of view, this trend may have serious implications for the United States and some other countries because they expect owner countries to increase control over their companies.

CROSS-BORDER MERGERS AND ACQUISITIONS

In their efforts to position themselves in the world markets, many companies merge with or acquire foreign existing companies. Instead of starting from scratch with direct investment, they can achieve better results through mergers and acquisitions (M&A's), thereby acquiring local expertise, clients, and business contracts for many years. Such M&A's may involve two or more firms in the same line of business (horizontal) or upstream toward the production of raw materials or downstream toward the production of consumer goods (vertical) or finally may combine firms of different lines of business (conglomerates). Usually, M&A's take place when there is a gain, that is, when the value of the new, single firm is higher than the sum of the values of the two firms operating individually. In these values, equity plus debt are calculated. Moreover, large firms can achieve economies of scale, as costs increase less than proportionately with output, because fixed costs are spread over a larger volume of output, through sharing central services in management, research, and the like. However, such activities may lead to less competition and more unemployment. The next section discusses some important international M&A's. There are more M&A's in the United States listed in Chapter 9. For M&A's in the banking sector, see Chapter 2.

From the United States to Europe

In order to tap into a multibillion-dollar telecommunications market, Motorola Inc., based in Illinois, and Siemens A.G., based in Munich, agreed to manufacture and distribute cable-telephone systems around the world. Already they produce together computer memory chips in Virginia, but they plan to move aggressively in other countries, mainly in the European Union, which forced member countries to open their telephone markets to competition from the beginning of 1998.

Wal-Mart Stores Inc., the biggest retailer in the world, based in Arkansas (USA), agreed to buy seventy-four supermarkets from Spar

Handels A.G. of Germany, in addition to 21 stores bought from Wertkauf previously. Terms of the deal were not disclosed.

Among the 14 shareholders the Italian Treasury Ministry has chosen to participate in the stable shareholding core of 9 percent stake (worth $3.25 billion) of the Telecom Italia SpA are the AT&T corporation and Unisource NV. They will each buy 12 percent of Telecom Italia and agreed to hold their shares for three years.

Because worldwide demand is around 50 million vehicles but capacity to produce is about 70 million, further big mergers are expected in the auto industry. The main potential acquirers include Ford Motor of the United States and Volkswagen A.G., of Germany, which acquired Rolls-Royce recently, whereas potential targets for acquisition include Nissan Motor of Japan, Bayerische Motoren Werke of Germany, and Volvo A.G. of Sweden.

DP Mann Holdings Ltd. of Britain was purchased by General Re Corporation, a big reinsurance firm of Connecticut, which in turn was acquired recently by Berkshire Hathaway for $22 billion. The price of the deal was not disclosed. Ford Motor Company plans to buy BMW of Germany for $17 billion.

Price Waterhouse, a Swiss auditing firm, and Coopers & Lybrand of New York completed their $13 billion merger deal after the approval of the European Union authorities. In order to be effective in auditing among banks and multinationals, the new company, named Newco, is expected to have a combined staff of some 400,000.

Seagram completed its $10.4 billion bid for Polygram, a Dutch music and film company, after the U.S. Securities and Exchange Commission approved the deal. This is the value of 75 percent of Polygram, which Seagram bought from Philips, the Dutch electronics firm.

PacifiCorp, a U.S. utility firm, agreed to buy The Energy Group, a UK company, for $8.5 billion. Citibank, J.P. Morgan, and Goldman Sachs provided the loan package, which was greater than the stock market capitalization of PacifiCorp.

Ford Motor Company of the United States agreed to buy the passenger car operations of A.B. Volvo of Sweden for $6.5 billion. This is another acquisition of an independent firm by a giant multinational for a better global distribution.

The Cendant Corporation, which provides travel, auto, shopping, and other services and owns Howard Johnson, Avis, and other brand names, agreed to buy the National Parking Corporation, which operates parking garages and emergency car services in Britain, for $1.34 billion. Also, it agreed to buy the American Bankers Insurance Group Inc., which is based in Miami and sells credit insurance, for $3.1 billion.

Renault of France and Fiat of Italy agreed to merge, creating a world leader in automotive components. Although financial details were not announced, annual sales of the combined foundry activities are about $2 billion.

The DSC Communications Corporation of the United States was acquired by Alcatel Alsthom of France, a large telecommunication equipment maker, for $4.4 billion in stock. DSC is in competition with Ciena Corporation, a young growing company, which recently agreed to be acquired by Tellabs Inc. for $7.1 billion in stock. For each share of DSC stock, shareholders of DSC will receive 0.815 of an Alcatel ADR.

Houston Industry of the United States announced its merger with PowerGen of Britain worth $3.4 billion, thereby creating one of the biggest electricity groups in the world.

Akzo Nobel, a Dutch company, agreed to sell two smaller coating businesses to PPG, a U.S. paint maker, for $2.98 billion, after the decision by Sanbanci of Turkey not to buy 50 percent stake in the industrial fibers subdivision of the Dutch company.

Du Pont, a U.S. chemical company, acquired Herberts, the paints arm of Hoechst of Germany.

ITT Industries of the United States sold its electrical systems business to Valeo, an automotive components group of France for $1.7 billion, expecting to use the proceeds to buy stock and support its business in fluid oil technology.

The Koch Industries, an oil and gas refiner based in Wichita, Kansas, with some $30 billion revenue and 16,000 employees worldwide, plans to acquire most of the assets of Trevira, the international polyester business of Hoechst A. G. of Germany. Koch, which is involved in financial investment as well, is a 50-50 partner with Groupo Xtra, a textile, agriculture, and real estate firm, in Mexico City.

Owens-Illinois of the United States, which is partially owned by Kohlberg Kravis Roberts, a U.S. financial buy-out group, bought BTR, a British glass and plastic bottling firm, for $3.67 billion. BTR, facing pressure from the Asian turmoil, agreed to this acquisition, after the approval of the European Union regulators, also giving Owens-Illinois presence in the Australian glass-bottling market.

The Microsoft Corporation, which is under investigation by the U.S. Justice Department and the European Commission for anticompetitive practices in Windows operating systems, agreed with ICL P.L.C., a British information systems developer, to market Microsoft products throughout Europe. ICL, which has operations in some seventy countries, is 90 percent owned by Fujitsu Ltd. of Japan. It is expected that more than 1,000 new jobs will be created as a result of this alliance, mostly in Britain. WordPerfect and Lotus, which is owned by IBM, had the largest share in the market about three years ago. Microsoft has about 90 percent of software business now.

Volvo A.B., the Swedish automaker, sold half of its holding, or 9.9 million shares, in Pharmacia & Upjohn Inc., an American-Swedish drug-producer, in order to concentrate on auto interests.

Prologis Trust, a large real estate investment firm based in Denver (USA), which bought Meridian Industrial Trust in Atlanta for $1.32 billion and $650 million recent investment in Europe, agreed to buy Garonor S.A., a French developer, with operations primarily in Paris and Marseilles, for $317 million.

From Europe to the United States

Merger mania continues on a global scale. Even law firms are affected. Thus, Clifton Chance, the London-based firm with more than 2,000 lawyers, agreed to merge with Rogers & Wells, a New York-based firm with 366 lawyers and big clients such as Merrill Lynch, Citigroup, and Prudential securities. The new cross-border law firm is in negotiations to unite with Mallesons Stephen Jacques, a big Australian firm. Their main advice is on global mergers, banking finance, and other corporate services.

In competition with the Bell Atlantic Corporation, which plans to merge with GTE Corporation for a $53 billion stock swap, Vodafone Group P.L.C. of Britain agreed to acquire Airtouch Communications Inc. of the United States for more than $60 billion. This is the largest cross-border acquisition ever, which will make more mobile phone operations not only in the EU countries but all over the world.

SmithKline Beecham and Glaxo Wellcome plan their $165 billion merger into a new company named Glaxo SmithKline, the world's biggest drugs firm. The shareholders of Glaxo would have 59.5 percent of the new company, in which about 10 percent job losses are expected, mainly in Britain.

Royal Dutch/Shell Group plans to takeover Chevron Corporation for $65 billion in stock, or $100 a share. Moreover, in addition to the huge merger of Exxon and Mobil, Texaco, Phillips Petroleum, and Arco are searching for mergers in order to reduce cost of production.

British Petroleum (BP) acquired Amoco for $60.2 billion, with headquarters in London and Chicago, respectively, forming a new company known as BP Amoco in a merger worth $110 billion (combined market capitalization). The new company, with some 100,000 employees, launched the largest issue of American Depository Receipts (ADRs), used for non-U.S. companies, listing its shares with the New York Stock Exchange. The ADRs of the new firm are worth about $60 billion, overtaking Royal Dutch/Shell and Unilever, with $26 billion and $13 billion, respectively. BP Amoco, in turn, agreed to acquire Atlantic Richfield Company (ARCO) for some $25 billion.

In order to win approval of its $37 billion acquisition by Worldcom Inc., MCI Communications Corporation offered to sell parts of its Internet business, in addition to the $625 million deal with Cable and Wireless P.L.C. For the approval of the acquisition by the European Commission and the U.S. Department of Justice, MCI , the second-largest long-distance telephone company, sold part of its business. The European antitrust regulators approved the takeover in June 1998. The merger would create a company with some $70 billion in sales a year.

Daimler-Benz A.G., the German giant car firm, acquired Chrysler Corporation, the American big auto firm, in May 1998 for $36 billion. This is the largest industrial merger ever, leaving the car industry in an oligopolistic condition with a few big firms controlling the largest part of the global car market. One of the hurdles of the deal was cleared after Daimler's shareholders exchanged 97 percent of the shares for stock in the new firm. Although German laws require that Daimler's workers sit as members of its corporate board, such problems are expected to be overcome by the new DaimlerChrysler A.G. company. Moreover, Daimler is discussing links with Nissan Motor Company of Japan, which would include cooperation in development, production, and sales of vehicles and components worldwide.

Astra, the Swedish pharmaceuticals group, plans to take control of Merck, the U.S. drug manufacturer, for $10 billion, with an initial payment of $1.5 billion, followed by further payments to Merck over a ten-year period. In the joint venture, named Astra Merck, Astra lifted its share from 50 percent to more than 90 percent. The main product that the company markets in the United States is Losec, the antiulcer drug.

Aegon N.V., a life insurance and pensions company of the Netherlands, agreed to buy the Transamerica Corporation, the sixth-largest U.S. life insurer, for $9.7 in stock and cash.[9]

Other large foreign acquisitions of U.S. companies include Bay Networks by Northern Telecom for $9 billion, and Federated Stores by Campeau for $7.8 billion.

Scottish Power P.L.C. of Britain agreed to buy PacifiCorp, a provider of power in the northwest United States, for $7.5 billion. The stockholders of PacifiCorp will have some 36 percent shares of the new company. Scottish Power will run PacifiCorp as a subsidiary and plans to buy the Florida Progress Corporation and the Cinergy Corporation of Cincinnati.

Reed Elsevier, an Anglo-Dutch publisher, agreed to buy from Times Mirror, which publishes the *Los Angeles Times* and *Newsday*, the Matthew Bender legal publishing unit and 50 percent interest of Shepard's Company for $1.65 billion. Such consolidations are the result of recent international mergers in the publishing industry in order to survive stiff competition in the field. Reed, which is jointly owned by Reed International of Britain and Elsevier of the Netherlands, had also purchased in

1994 Lexis-Nexis, a large U.S. company providing on-line information services in the legal, government, and business areas.[10]

Olivetti S.p.A. merged its information technology systems with Wang Laboratories of the United States, transforming the Italian company into a large telecommunications firm. Olivetti also controls Omnitel, a cellular telephone operator that has partnership with Mannesmann of Germany and Airtouch and Bell Atlantic of the United States, and agreed to buy Cellular Communications International Inc., based in New York, for $1.4 billion.

Pearson P.L.C., the British media conglomerate, agreed to buy the education division of publishing imprints of Simon & Schuster of the United States for $3.6 billion. Growing student enrollment meant an increase in spending on textbooks and instructional material, mainly by the 9,000 American library systems, worth more than $20 billion a year.

Bertelsmann, the German media group, agreed to buy Random House, the New York-based publishing firm, for an estimated $1.4 billion, thereby creating the largest publishing company in the English-speaking world. Bertelsmann bought Doubleday Dell in 1986 and may buy other publishing firms such as HarperCollins and Simon & Schuster, which are also up for grabs, to increase profitability through economies of scale and strengthen its position in the United States. As a result of the acquisition of Random House, about one third of the group's turnover of $13.7 billion will be in the United States. With the imprints of the companies bought, Bertelsmann will be one of the seven oligopolies that dominate the U.S. publishing markets, most of them foreign, much the way steel, automobile, and other industries dominate their fields.

Also, the German Holtzbrinck owns St. Martin's, Henry Holt, and Farrar, Straus & Giroux. Some 28 percent shares of the total publishing market in the United States are already in foreign hands. However, there are complaints by the Authors Guild that such publishing colossi reduce the number of choices at bookstores of literary books that are chosen for book reviews and prestigious prizes. Although there are antitrust questions, Bertelsmann is determined to proceed with new acquisitions if necessary.

Because of the withdrawals of governments from financing retirement plans, insurance and investment firms are expanding rapidly. Thus, AXA Investment Managers, a unit of the AXA S.A. of France with more than $600 billion under management, agreed to buy 60 percent of Barr Rosenberg Investment, which is based in California and manages about $7 billion in assets, for $125 million.

Ispat International NV of the Netherlands agreed to buy Inland Steel Co., a subsidiary of Inland Steel Industries of the United States for about

$900 million. Inland Steel Co. is a member of the LNM Group with operations in Canada, Germany, Ireland, Mexico, and Trinidad.

L'Oreal, the beauty giant based in Paris and operating in more than 150 countries, agreed to buy Soft Sheen Products Inc., based in Chicago.

Mergers and Acquisitions in Europe

Record merger activities can be observed in Europe as well.

The Airbus companies of Europe decided to merge and expand from civilian to military aircraft as well. Daimler-Benz Aerospace of Germany, Aerospatiale of France, British Aerospace, and Casa of Spain agreed to reorganize and form a single European aerospace and military company able to compete effectively on a global scale.

The EU approved the takeover of Mannesman A.G. of Germany by the Vodafone Air-Touch P.L.C. of Britain for $180 billion.

Zeneca Group P.L.C. of Britain agreed to buy Astra A.B. of Sweden for $35 billion, creating the fourth-largest pharmaceutical firm in the world.

Ciba Specialty Chemicals AG and Clariant AG agreed to merge and create the largest specialty chemical company in the world. The market capitalization of the new firm, known as Clariant AG, is $14.6 billion (SFr.20 billion). Hoechst A.G. of Germany holds a 45 percent stake in Clariant. For the financial arrangement of the deal, Warburg Dillon Read acted for Clariant and Credit Suisse First Boston acted for Ciba.[11] However, because monopoly commissions overseas might force them to divest assets, this merger presents problems.

DaimlerChrysler is in talks to buy Volvo A.B. of Sweden for $11 billion.

Moreover, Hoechst A.G. of Germany agreed with Rhone-Poulenc S.A. of France to combine their agricultural and pharmaceutical units into a new company named Aventis, which will be the top seller of agricultural products and the second pharmaceutical maker in the world.

Total S.A., the second oil company, after Alf Aquitaine, of France, agreed to buy Petrofina S.A., a petrochemical firm of Belgium, in a stock swap worth $13 billion. Total follows the consolidation of the global oil industry, mainly because of the decline in crude oil prices. The new company, called Tota Fina, has some $52 billion revenue, around the same as ENI S.p.A. of Italy, which is the third-largest oil firm in Europe.

LVMN Moet Hennessy Louis, a French company, plans to take control of Gucci, the fashion house, which issued shares to an employee fund and diluted the LVMN holding to 25 percent.

Stora A.B., a large Swedish forest-product company, and Enso Oyl, a similar firm in Finland, agreed to a $8.5 billion stock swap. The new company, called Stora Enso, will be the world's largest paper and board maker, more powerful than the International Paper Company.

Polygram N.V., 75 percent of which is owned by Royal Philips Electronics N.V., was acquired by Seagram Company for $9 billion. The shares of Seagram, which owns MCA and Universal Studios, trade on the New York Stock Exchange.

I.C.I., a specialty chemical company, bought a similar business of Unilever for $8 billion.

Akzo Nobel NV, a Dutch chemical group, plans to acquire Courtaulds of Britain for $3 billion.

GE Capital Corporation, a unit of General Electric Company, plans to buy 24.9 percent of the GPA P.L.C., an Irish aircraft-leasing firm. GE had rescued GPA from bankruptcy in 1993.[12]

Telecom Italia formed an alliance with BSkyB television group, owned by Rupert Murdoch, in partnership with TF1, which is controlled by Bouygues, a media firm of France. Meoliaser S.p.A.of Italy and Kirch Group of Germany agreed to create a pan-European television network worth $1.1 billion.

The British Sky Broadcasting Group plans the takeover of the Manchester United team, a wealthy soccer club in Britain, for $1.05 billion. However, the British Labor Government asked the Monopolies and Mergers Commission to study the effects of the deal on the field's competition.

Rolls-Royce, a prestigious British company, which was established in 1906 and was separated into jet engine and automobile divisions in 1971, announced in 1997 that it is for sale. In competition with BMW, Volkswagen, the German car company, decided recently to buy Rolls-Royce of Britain from its parent company, Vickers P.L.C., for $704 million, ending the long takeover odyssey. BMW, which provides 30 percent of each Rolls-Royce car's components, threatened to sever supply lines for the engines and other parts. It is expected that a big surge in exports in the United States will take place, mainly because a stronger dollar, relative to the mark, makes German cars cheaper in the American markets.[13]

Greece, as a member of the EU, is expected to play a vital role in joint ventures and investment into the other Balkan countries. Thus, the Organization of Telecommunications of Hellas (OTE) and the Deutsche Telekom plan to buy the Bulgarian Telecom, the financing of which comes primarily from bank loans and cash. Also, the Latsis shipping and banking company plans to move into joint ventures with other companies in neighboring countries, such as the Post company of Bulgaria. The new measures to reduce the debt of public enterprises (some 2.8 trillion drachmas) and the subsidization of the protesting farmers, as well as the implementation of the privatization program, would improve the economic conditions of the country and make Greece a business and financial center, attracting EU and American investment for the whole Balkan region.

The Balkan countries are relatively small, and their economies are weak. This suggests that they should join the large group of the EU for their protection and rapid development. As Thucydides said some twenty-five centuries ago, "In the judgment of human beings, justice counts when there is equal power for implementation, but if it does not occur, the powerful do whatever their power allows and the weak retreat and accept" (translated from Hellenic).

Closer relations with and eventual membership in the EU would stabilize the economies of the Balkan nations and increase trade and investment in the area. This, in turn, would eliminate ethnic and religious conflicts, particularly in Bosnia, Kosovo, and other republics of former Yugoslavia, and make people look forward to an effective union with the rest of Europe, instead of quarreling about regional borders.

MERGERS AND ACQUISITIONS IN LATIN AMERICA

Argentina, which pegs the peso at par to the dollar, faces problems of weakening exports, mainly Peugeot cars and other products to Brazil and other countries, and balance-of-payments deficits. Although domestic demand for stocks is favorable, particularly from private pension funds (known as AFJPs), foreign investors hesitate to enter Argentina's stock market (the Bolsa). The hope is that the dollar peg would work, as it did for Mexico during the financial crisis of 1995, and improve foreign trade, thereby uplifting the Marvel share index, which dropped from about 900 in 1997 to around 600 later, mainly as a result of the Asian turmoil.

It seems that the recent privatization of the airports and other firms, including parts of the YPF, an energy concern with a market capitalization of $10 billion, which already has been mostly privatized, and the Aerolineas Argentinas, would attract foreign investment. Also, foreign demand for Argentine bonds would increase, as happened with the 10-year D-Mark bonds worth DM 1.5 billion, which proved to be very attractive.[14]

In order to cover budget and foreign trade deficits and avoid stock market declines, some Latin American countries sell state enterprises to the private sector and foreign investors. Thus, revenues from privatization in Brazil (which is a member of the MERCOSUR trade block, along with Argentina, Paraguay, and Uruguay) reaches $80 billion by the end of the decade. Also the social security system was reformed, setting a minimum retirement age of 60 for men and 55 for women and a minimum contribution period of thirty-five years for men and thirty years for women. More or less the same trend can be observed in Argentina, Chile, Peru, Venezuela, and other Latin American countries, which, together with the other Western Hemisphere nations, except Cuba, committed themselves to a Free Trade Area of the Americas (FTAA) by 2005 at the summit in Miami in 1994 and in Santiago in April 1998.

To attract foreign investment and stimulate economic growth, these countries take measures to transform local operations into globally competitive business. As a result, foreign companies, primarily from the United States and Europe, are buying up Latin American firms and enterprise shores at record levels. The value of all completed mergers and acquisitions in Latin America increased from around $10 billion in 1991 to more than $40 billion in 1997, about half by foreign companies.

Credit Suisse First Boston, the Swiss-American investment bank, and Robert Fleming of Britain, among others, were given permission to acquire Brazilian banks. Robert Fleming was authorized to buy up to 100 percent of Banco Graphus, a Brazilian investment bank, whereas Caterpillar Financial Services, the financial arm of the U.S. heavy equipment firm, is setting up its own leasing finance company in Brazil.

In the recent steps of Brazil's wide-ranging privatization program, Cemat, an electricity distribution firm in the state of Mato Grosso, was sold to a consortium led by Grupo Rede, a utility company of Brazil, for US$352.8 million (R$391.5 million). Cemat was the third electricity firm to be privatized, after CPFL in São Paulo and Enersul in Mato Grosso do Sul.

Mobil Corporation's ties to South America go back to 1918, but presently Mobil holds major positions in Brazil, Colombia, Chile, and Peru. It plans to team with Brazil's Petrobras to explore deep-water and on-shore fields for oil and gas, as well as to explore the shores of Argentina and Venezuela for petrochemical products. Nevertheless, Brazil makes serious attempts to revitalize a controversial program to replace gasoline with ethanol distilled from sugar cane. Such a replacement saved Brazil more than $20 billion during the last twenty years and helped improve its currency and its stock market.

The Sprint Corporation and Bell Canada bought telephone connections from Brazil for $80.4 million (115 million reals). The two groups plan to invest more than 3 billion reals to compete with Embratel, a company carved out of Telebras and privatized in 1998. Moreover, the Bonair Holding Corporation, including France Telecom and National Grid of Britain, bought a phone connection for 55 million reals.

Chile, with a more open economy than other Latin American markets, cannot escape the waves of mergers and acquisitions. Thus, Arthur

Andersen, a leasing global firm, plans to merge with Coopers & Lybrand (C&L), Langton Clarke, Deloitte Touche Tomatsu, Price Waterhouse, and KPMG and Ernest & Young. This merger is under consideration by regulators in Brussels and in Washington for possible antitrust violations regarding inward investment from Spain and other stock market operations.

Other Global Mergers and Acquisitions

Global Crossing, a communications carrier of Bermuda, agreed to merge with U.S. West Inc. in a stock swap at $37 billion and to buy Frontier corporation, a U.S. telephone company, for $11 billion in stock.

Japan Tobacco agreed to buy the international tobacco business of RJR Nabisco for $80 billion. Also, Renault S.A. of France agreed to buy 35 percent of Nissan Motor Company of Japan for $5 billion. Nissan is in trouble, with more than $30 billion in debt.

Japan Telecom Company agreed to sell 20 percent stake to the British Telecom and 10 percent to AT&T for about $1.3 billion. British Telecom already has a joint venture with Marubeni Corporation and AT&T with twenty-five Japanese firms, including Hitachi Ltd., Fujitsu Ltd., and the KDD Corporation, offering Internet and other services in competition with MCI Worldcom.

Goodyear Tire and Rubber Co. of the United States acquired 10 percent of Sumitomo Rubber Industries Ltd., a Japanese tire maker, and effective control of its U.S. and European operations. Sumitomo will receive $1 billion and a small stake in Goodyear. GE Capital, a subsidiary of General Electric of the United States, taking advantage of the Global Crossing, a communications corner of Bermuda, agreed to buy Frontier Corporation, a U.S. telephone company, for $10.8 billion in stock.

Nomura International P.L.C., a unit of Nomura Securities Company of Japan, in competition with PacifiCorp and Texas Utility Company of the United States, plans the acquisition of Energy Group P.L.C. of Britain for some $10 billion.

Tyco International Ltd., one of the largest manufacturers of fire protection systems based in Bermuda, agreed to acquire a majority stake in CIPE France S. A. and expects to make an offer for the remaining shares of this French security alarm company. Also, it agreed to acquire Williams P.L.C. of London for $5.8 billion, as well as the U.S. Surgical Corporation for $3.3 billion and the American Home Products Corporation for $1.77 billion.

In order to increase sales in Europe, Brazil, and the United States, General Motors Corporation, the world's largest auto producer, agreed with Isuzu Motors Ltd. of Japan to produce a pickup truck, as well as sport utility vehicles. Already, General Motors owns 37.5 percent of Isuzu, which will provide the chassis, including the engine and the frame, according to the agreement.

The Ford Motor Company, the American automaker, and its affiliate, the Mazda Motor Corporation of Japan, plan to bid for 51 percent of the Kia Motor Corporation, the bankrupt South Korean auto producer, in which Ford and Mazda together own 16.9 percent stake.

Texas Utilities Co. agreed to acquire the retail operations of Kinetic Energy and the distribution business of Westar of Australia for $1.02 billion, in a privatization auction.

Electricite de France agreed to build two gas-fueled stations in Egypt for $760 million.

Citroen, the French carmaker, in partnership with Peugeot, Mitsubishi, BMW, and others agreed to invest in assembly plants in Egypt.

Volvo, the Swedish vehicles and industrial firm, acquired Samsung Heavy Industries of South Korea for $500 million in order to expand in southeast Asia.

Placer Dome Inc., the second-biggest producer of gold bullion in Canada, would buy a 50 percent stake in assets owned by Western Areas Ltd. of South Africa, worth US$235 million, thereby doubling its ore reserves to 60 million ounces.

Loblaw Companies, based in Toronto, agreed to buy Provigo Inc. of Montreal, the third supermarket chain of Canada, for $1.8 billion.

Endesa of Spain plans to buy a further 32 percent of Enersis of Chile for $1.45 billion, as it wants to expand throughout Latin America.

Fairfax Financial Holdings Ltd. a Canadian insurer, agreed to acquire TIG Holdings Inc. of New York for $840 million.

Manulife Financial, a big life insurance firm of Canada, plans to form an alliance with Daihyaku of Japan with a capitalization of $832 million (Y100 billion).

Celanese Canada agreed to be acquired by Hoechst A.G. of Germany for $306 million.

Litton Industries agreed to buy Denro Inc., the air traffic control communications firm, from Firan Corporation of Canada, for $60 million.

Perez Compac S.A. of Argentina bought a 10 percent stake in Distrilec Inversora S.A. from Energy Corporation, which is based in New Orleans (USA), for $101 million.

Northern Telecom Ltd. of Canada and United Utilities PLC of Britain agreed to transmit Internet service to several electric utilities in Asia and Europe, including German giant RWE and other utilities in Scandinavia. They expect to transmit Internet and data services over electricity cables many times faster than the current speed. Also, Northern Telecom agreed to acquire Bay Networks Inc. for $9 billion.

Telus Corporation, Toronto, plans to buy a two-thirds stake in AT&T Canada Long Distance Services Company, from three banks, for US$706 million. The other one third of AT&T Canada is owned by AT&T Corporation of New York, which is the maximum percentage permitted by Canadian regulations.

The Homestake Mining Company, a U.S. mining firm, offered to acquire the remaining 49.4 percent stake in Prime Resources Group, a precious metals firm in Canada, for $300 million. However, the British Columbia Supreme Court and Prime's shareholders must approve this acquisition.

Abitibi-Consolidated Inc. of Canada agreed to a joint venture, worth $1.35 billion, with Norske Skog of Norway and Hansol Paper Company of South Korea and created the biggest newsprint company in Asia, with each firm controlling one third of the venture.

Olivetti S.p.A. of Italy and its partner Mannesmann A.G. agreed to buy Cellular Communications International Inc., based in New York, for $1.4 billion. Moreover, Olivetti plans to take over Telecom Italia, a former state-owned firm for $60 billion, using stocks and cash.

Royal Philips Electronics N.V., a music company of the Netherlands, is expected to sell its 75 percent ownership of Polygram N.V. to the Seagram Corporation for about $10 billion. However, another group, consisting of the Forstmann Little & Company and the Thomas Lee Company, may offer a higher amount.

Germany's Allianz Assurance Generales de France go to the altar. The marriage of the two big insurance companies was cleared by the European Commission and will overlap business in several markets, primarily France, Spain, and Belgium. Heidelberg Druckmaschien A.G. of Germany agreed to buy the copier manufacturing operations of Eastman Kodak Company of the United States.

PRIVATIZATION, INVESTMENT, AND TRADE FOR THE BALKAN COUNTRIES

After the drastic changes in East European countries and the former Soviet Union since 1989, the winds of freedom and democracy are blowing through the Balkan region as well. Although ethnic rivalries, which were suppressed under communism, surfaced again, gradual and painful efforts are being made toward a market economy, through privatization of public enterprises.

Greece made many efforts to bring the Balkan countries together for closer cooperation, especially in the 1930s and 1970s and more so recently. Now, as a full member of the EU, Greece can play a decisive role for economic and geopolitical developments in the region.

There are many economic opportunities for trade and investment in the area, and scores of Hellenic and other EU and American companies are moving into the profitable Balkan markets, primarily in joint ventures with local enterprises. The growth of big corporate enterprises requires expansion in many countries, and the Balkans cannot be excluded from this economic intercourse. For these reasons, the government of Greece provides tax and other incentives to Hellenic enterprises that invest in the northern Balkan countries. Such a policy strengthens the economic conditions of the countries involved and creates economic bridges between the EU and the Balkan nations. In this effort, a number of Hellenic banks, as well as the European Investment Bank, participate in investment expansion, with needed loans and venture capital.

Moreover, the Cross-Balkan and Euxene Center in Salonika provides information and other services to companies that want to invest in the Balkan and the Euxene countries. The Union of Euxene Countries, a similar formation of which was called "The Common Market of Euxene" by Aristotle (fifth century B.C.), includes the neighboring countries of the Black Sea, primarily Armenia, Bulgaria, Georgia, Greece, Romania, and Turkey.

Albania, a tiny and poor country, producing mainly agricultural products, such as chrome (the world's third-largest producer) and oil (about 20 million barrels a year), started privatizing state enterprises and forming joint ventures with EU and other companies. Such joint ventures include the Albkrom state enterprise, producing chrome, with six British companies (including GEC-Alsthom and Compair Holman) and the American Mecalloy Corporation.

Also, Chevron, a big U.S. petroleum company, agreed with DPNG, an Albanian petroleum enterprise, to search out and produce coal and petroleum products in an area close to Tirana, the capital of Albania, whereas the Coca-Cola Company began operations in the country, opening a $10 million bottling plant.

Recently, the former Yugoslav Republic of Macedonia (FYROM) introduced legislation for privatization of state enterprises. Firms with fewer than fifty employees were to be sold to the highest bidder, with preference given to the basic buyer who should obtain 29 percent of the capital at the first stage. For big companies, 10 percent of the capital value is sufficient, provided that this first buyer will eventually obtain at least 51 percent of the total.

The Bulgarian Organization of Privatization plans to privatize more than 300 state enterprises, in addition to more than 100 sold previously. However, Bulgaria, with the largest part of its economy still in the hands of inefficient state firms, is slow in the process of privatization. Among the state firms that have been sold or are under privatization are the Elcabel Company, which produces wires and similar products; the Eltos Company, which produces machines and tools; the Plastchin Company, which produces plastic products; and the Panoyot Volvo Company, which produces plastics. The Euromerchant Balkan Funds takes minority stakes in some Bulgarian and other Balkan companies, mainly focusing on food processing and retailing. Also, the Global Finance of Hellas, in association with Baring of Britain, is engaged in investment ventures in Bulgaria, with some capital contributed by the International Finance Corporation and the European Bank for Reconstruction and Development (BERD). Moreover, Bulgaria and Greece signed an agreement for the construction of a pipeline carrying Russian oil to Greece, by tankers from the Black Sea to the Bulgarian port of Burgas and, by pipeline, to the Hellenic port of Alexandroupolis. Through the EU PHARE and TACIS programs, EU firms increased their investment activities in Bulgaria, mainly from Greece and Germany.

Although the pace of privatization in Romania is slow, there are more than half a million small state enterprises sold. Foreign investment is not encouraged, but a number of foreign firms enter Romania and form joint ventures. The previously unproductive centrally planned economy of Romania, with its guarantee of permanent employment but many surplus workers in state firms and a low standard of living for all, is exposed to efficient but often brutal capitalism. As the joke used to go, "They pretend to pay us, and we pretend to work."

Foreign investment in Romania includes the Triton and Ellconsult Hellenic firms with investments concerning expansion of the Black Sea ports; the BNP French bank, in alliance with the Dresdner Bank of Germany, which created a subsidiary in Bucharest; and the PSA Peugeot Citroen of France, in joint venture with Automobile Dacia (a state-owned carmaker of Romania), to assemble small family cars. Moreover, New Holland, a subsidiary of Fiat of Italy, acquired 60 percent of Semanatoarea, a Romanian state-owned group, to make tractors for Eastern Europe.

From an economic point of view, the creation of a Balkan common market and the infant Union of Euxene Countries are not expected to have impressive results, mainly because these countries produce primarily competitive products. Nevertheless, from a sociopolitical standpoint, such unions may prove to be beneficial for further cooperation, as pioneering movements toward an eventual pan-European union, under the auspices of the EU. Already Greece is a full member and Turkey an associate member of the EU, whereas the other neighboring nations are also expected to become associate members in the near future. Again, a closer cooperation with the EU may be more beneficial, although painful, for a transitional period of economic and political adjustment. In the meetings in Athens and other places, the Balkan and the Euxene countries pledged further cooperation among themselves and the EU.

Economic and Financial Integration

EFFECTS OF REGIONAL AND INTERNATIONAL COOPERATION

Economic cooperation and formation of common markets and financial unions for economic development are not a recent phenomenon. Some important economico-political organizations established throughout history were, for example, the Achaean League established in Peloponnesus by twelve city-states in ancient Greece (Hellas), which, according to Nietzsche, provided the nucleus of European civilization, during the sixth century B.C. until its defeat by the Romans (229 B.C.). This league resembled modern federal systems and economic unions similar to the present European Union (EU) and the North American Free Trade Agreement (NAFTA). Also, the Greek Commonwealth in the eastern Mediteranean area (the Delean League, similar to the present NATO), mainly under Athens, was formed around the fifth century B.C. Moreover, the medieval guilds between the feudal states appeared during the Middle Ages, the German unions (Zollverein) in the 1830s, and more recently the British Commonwealth of Nations.

Since the end of World War II, the number of such organizations increased considerably. Some of them, such as the United Nations Relief and Rehabilitation Administration (UNRA), United Nations Educational, Scientific, and Cultural Organization (UNESCO), World Health Organization (WHO), United Nations Children's Fund (UNICEF), and Food and Agricultural Organization (FAO), were or are under the auspices of the United Nations. A few other regional organizations or commissions, established by the United Nations, include the economic commissions for Europe (ECE), Asia and Far East (ECAFE), Latin America (ECLA), and Africa (ECA).

In order to manipulate the oil supply and increase their revenue, five leading oil-exporting nations (Iran, Iraq, Kuwait, Saudi Arabia, Venezuela) established, in 1960, the Organization of Petroleum Exporting Countries (OPEC). Other oil-producing countries (Abu Dhabi, Algeria, Ecuador, Gabon, Indonesia, Libya, Qatar, and United Arab Emirates) joined OPEC later, and by 1973 there were thirteen members. The main result of this organization was a drastic increase in oil prices (from $2 to more than $30 per barrel, declining to around $10 per barrel later and growing again to about $26 per barrel at the end of 1999), affecting the economic and financial conditions of almost all other countries.

Grants, interest-free loans, and other forms of aid, as well as special funds and banks to serve oil-importing developing countries, were since advanced by OPEC nations (which amassed over $100 billion per year), but with limited results. As a result of the oil price increases, the current account deficits of the petroleum-importing countries increased dramatically thereafter.[1] That is why efforts were and still are made to recover oil shale, coal, sunrays, winds, tides, and mainly hydroelectric and nuclear power.

The most important international institutions now are the International Monetary Fund (IMF), the World Bank, and the World Trade Organization (WTO), mentioned earlier, and the less effective International Labor Organization.

It seems that the future belongs to economic and political federations. This verifies what Pierre-Joseph Proudhon predicted in 1863, that in the twentieth century the era of federations will begin. This can be seen not only in Europe but in the Americas and other parts of the world. One can predict that in the twenty-first century the era of integration and globalization will begin.

TRADE CREATION AND TRADE DIVERSION

The creation and enlargement of trade groups normally lead to trade creation, as part of the domestic production by some member nations would be replaced by lower-cost imports from other member nations. This is so because of more specialization, as a result of the principle of comparative advantage and the enlargement of the markets among the members of trade groups.

Moreover, as long as lower-cost imports from outside the trade group are not replaced by higher-cost imports from member nations, trade diversion, which reduces welfare, will not occur. Thus trade associations and integrations lead to trade creation rather than to trade diversion, as long as domestic tariffs among members fall and tariffs on imports from the rest of the world do not rise. Therefore, the greater the number of member-countries and the larger their size, the lower the cost of production and the higher the welfare of the countries involved.[2]

Figure 8.1 shows the effects of trade creation in a customs union when a part of domestic production of a member country of the union is replaced by lower-cost imports from another member country. Point E indicates the equilibrium of supply (S) and demand (D) of a product. With tariffs, total consumption of the country before the formation of the customs union is shown by the line BB', domestic production is BF, and imports are represented by FB'. The tariff revenue collected is the rectangle FGHB'. After the formation of the union, consumption is AA', domestic production AC, and imports CA', whereas the sum of the two triangles CFG and A'B'H is the net gain of the country.

Trade diversion is the case when lower-cost imports from outside a customs union are replaced by higher-cost imports from union members. Line AA' , in Figure 8.2, shows the position of the country under free world trade, with J'A' representing imports. A nondiscriminatory tariff shifts line AA' to CC', with FC' imports. After reducing or eliminating tariffs among customs union members, the imports of the country in question are JB'. The welfare gain of the country is the summation of the two triangles FGJ and B'C'I, whereas the welfare loss from trade diversion is the rectangle GHIK. Therefore, the difference between the rectangle GHIK and the two combined triangles FGJ and B'C'I is the net welfare loss.

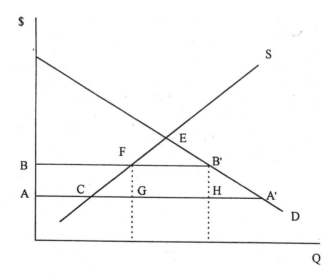

Figure 8.1. Trade creation

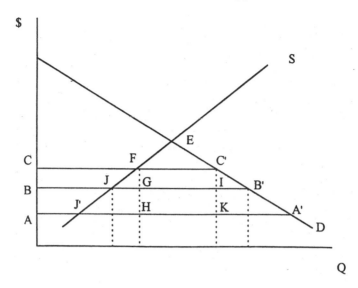

Figure 8.2. Trade diversion

As tariffs or other barriers on trade among members of a customs union are reduced or eliminated and trade policies are harmonized with the rest of the world, trade creation and trade diversion may occur. Trade is normally created and welfare increased among member nations of a customs union. But trade diversion and welfare reduction can be expected to occur in nonmember nations, as a result of the formation of a customs union and the less efficient use of their resources.

Nevertheless, the welfare of nonmember countries may increase through higher exports as a result of the increase in real income of the members of the union. As long as a customs union does not raise tariffs or other trade barriers to outside nations, then the reduction of barriers among members will normally increase trade and welfare, not only for members but for nonmembers as well. However, depending on the relative elasticities, there may be reductions in the union's demand for imports from, and its supply of exports to, the nonmember nations and an improvement in its collective terms of trade.

EURODOLLAR MARKET

The Eurodollar market began officially in 1957, when the Moscow Norodny Bank of the former Soviet Union deposited dollars in its branch in London and in another bank in Paris, whose telex was "Eurobank," mainly because of the fear of possible freeze or confiscation of Soviet funds by Americans during the Cold War. Other Eastern European countries and American and other banks and corporations followed this example, depositing dollars in Europe, which were and still are called Eurodollars.

Other European banks continued the practice of accepting dollar deposits and lending them out to other European banks and corporations, thereby financing world trade in dollars outside the United States.

This was the result of the efforts of the banks to escape national controls. In order to regulate the participation of U.S. banks in this market, the Kennedy administration enacted the Interest Equalization Tax, taxing the differences in interest, without effective results, regarding the outflow of dollars.

Then, United States banks increased their operations in Europe, where they established branches to tap the Eurodollar market. Other regulations and controls, requiring foreign investment to be financed from abroad, were removed in 1974, and transactions in dollars in Europe continued to thrive. Thereafter, dollars were and still are deposited and redeposited in Europe to enjoy high interest rates and other privileges.

Although the Eurodollar multiplier is not expected to be large, there is some influence upon inflation depending on the velocity of Eurodollar transactions. However, if the Fed attempted to absorb dollars by selling bonds domestically, this policy might be undermined by domestic banks through loans from the Eurodollar market, thereby nullifying partially or totally the results of contraction of money and credit. In addition, more and more American corporations and investors become foreign holders of dollars, and this means less business and profits for American banks and other companies.

EUROPEAN INTEGRATION

Europe is in the process of economic and political unification. Six central European nations formed the European Economic Community (EEC), also known as the European Common Market, in Rome in 1957. This "Inner Six" group included Belgium, France, Germany (W), Italy, Luxembourg, and the Netherlands. Initially, it was formed to gradually reduce internal tariffs.

Three years after the formation of the EEC, later named European Union (EU), that is, in 1960, the European Free Trade Association (EFTA) was created in Stockholm. It included Austria, Britain, Denmark, Norway, Portugal, Sweden, and Switzerland. The EFTA (the "Outer Seven") as well as the EU ("Inner Six") were formed to gradually

reduce tariffs and encourage investment. But EFTA permitted the reten-
tion of individual external tariffs, so that imports from the rest of the
world could enter a low-tariff member of EFTA, thereby avoiding the
higher tariffs of the other member nations (trade deflection).

Because EFTA was not as successful as the EU, Britain and Denmark,
as well as Ireland, joined the EU in 1973. On the other hand, Iceland
joined EFTA in 1970, as did Finland and Lichtenstein in 1986 and 1991,
respectively. Greece became the tenth member of the EU in 1981. In
January 1994, the EU and EFTA (except Lichtenstein and Switzerland)
formed the European Economic Area (EEA) for eventual free movement
of commodities, services, capital, and people among the seventeen
member countries. Portugal, together with Spain, joined the EU in 1986,
whereas Austria, Finland, and Sweden became members of the EU in
1995.

Table 8.1 shows the central government expenditures, budget deficits, and debt of the EU member countries. Greece, Netherlands, Italy,
Belgium, Ireland, and Sweden have the highest central government
expenditures as a percentage of GDP, followed by France, Portugal,

**Table 8.1 Government Expenditures, Budget Deficits, and Debts of
the European Union Countries (percentage of GDP)**

Member Countries	Central Gov't Expenditures		Budget Deficits		Debt	
	1980	1997	1980	1997	1996	1997
Austria	33.3	38.6	3.3	4.1	69.3	73.3
Belgium	45.9	45.9	8.0	3.2	132.7	127.2
Britain	36.4	39.8	4.6	5.3	49.3	56.5
Denmark	35.9	40.0	2.6	1.9	81.6	70.4
Finland	25.2	38.5	2.2	6.3	62.5	60.2
France	37.4	44.6	0.1	3.5	55.0	56.6
Germany	...	32.1	...	1.4	60.1	63.2
Greece	25.7	28.5	4.1	8.5	113.3	104.5
Ireland	40.4	34.4	12.5	1.4	80.0	76.0
Italy	37.8	45.4	10.8	3.1	121.4	122.9
Netherlands	48.2	46.0	4.6	1.7	79.5	76.0
Portugal	28.7	36.2	8.4	2.3	72.6	67.6
Spain	23.6	34.9	4.2	6.0	65.5	68.9
Sweden	37.5	43.2	8.1	1.3	79.5	78.5

Source: World Bank, *World Development Report,* various issues; *National Herald,* February
22–23, 1997.

Denmark, and Finland. Regarding budget deficit, almost all countries tend to have less than 3 percent deficit, which is required by the Treaty of Maastricht to enter the European Monetary Union (EMU) and the common currency, the euro. Greece, with high deficits previously, achieved the target of less than 3 percent of GDP budget deficits, required for joining the euro. But, many EU countries have public sector debt above the 60 percent of the GDP required by the EMU, although some flexibility is permitted. Recently, the EU annual budget was reported by a panel of experts as mismanaged. The twenty members of the European Commission, the executive body of the EU, linked to fraud, quit and were replaced by others.

Agricultural Subsidies

One of the most important European Union (EU) programs is that of agricultural subsidies from the Common Agricultural Program (CAP). Germany pays most of the expenses, whereas France and Spain receive billions of euros of the subsidies, which amount to 40 billion euros (about $41 billion) a year. To avoid this divisive political problem, 15 EU farm ministers achieved a compromise to reduce support prices for cereal grains and beef by 20 percent and for milk by 15 percent between the years 2000 and 2003. This problem would be severe when Poland, Hungary, and the Czech Republic would enter the EU because they sell grain, meat, and dairy products at low prices.

Agricultural subsidies are about 30 percent of the agricultural output for the United States (or about $35 billion), 50 percent for the EU (or around $80 billion), 70 percent for Japan (or about $30 billion), and as high as around 80 percent for Switzerland (or $5 billion), compared to about 45 percent (or around $180 billion) for all industrial countries. Such subsidies are the main source of dispute mainly among the United States, the EU, and Japan. Nevertheless, the trend for free international trade and globalization is gradually forcing the reduction of agricultural subsidies in many countries.

Effects of Monetary Policy

In order to be able to keep their currencies, and eventually the euro, stable, the monetary authorities of the EU member states should adjust their policies accordingly, until the European Central Bank takes over all the related monetary policies. Using the classical equation of exchange ($MV = PQ = GDP$), in an incremental sense, the percentage change in money supply (dM/M) plus the percentage change in velocity (dV/V) must be equal to percentage change in the price index (dP/P) plus the percentage change in the quantity of production (dQ/Q) or the percentage change in real GDP, that is, $dM/M + dV/V = dP/P + dQ/Q$. Therefore, if money grows by 4 percent, velocity by 2 percent, and real production by 3 percent, then dP/P or inflation is 3 percent ($0.04 + 0.02 = dP/P + 0.03$ and $dP/P = 0.06 - 0.03 = 0.03$). Ceteris paribus, the depreciation of the currency, in this case, is expected to be equal to the rate of inflation, that is, 3 percent.

Table 8.2 shows the equity markets of the EU countries, compared to those of the United States and Japan. Figures 8.3–8.8 show the relationship of the money supply and the velocity of money in some EU countries. For Austria, France, Italy, Spain, and to some extent Hellas (Greece), velocity of money remained relatively constant but declined in Germany for the last two decades. This means that all these countries financed their nominal GDP through increases in money supply.

Table 8.2 Equity Markets of the European Union Countries, United States, and Japan (1996)

	Listed Companies Domestic Foreign (In units)		Domestic Market Capitalization (In millions (In percent of ECU's) of GDP)		Annual Turnover Domestic Foreign Total (In millions of ECU's)			Domestic (In percent of GDP)
Markets in EU countries								
Amsterdam	217	216	302,452	96.10	149,587	653	150,241	47.53
Athens	217	0	18,988	19.64	5,695	0	5,695	5.89
Brussels	146	145	95,752	45.40	17,849	2,914	20,763	8.46
Copenhagen	237	12	57,281	41.46	29,111	698	29,810	21.07
Dublin	61	10	27,659	52.29	4,711	3	4,714	8.91
Germany	681	1290	531,553	28.34	621,454	18,778	640,231	33.13
Helsinki	71	0	49,444	50.41	17,538	0	17,538	17.88
Lisbon	158	0	19,706	23.40	5,658	0	5,658	6.72
London	557	833	1,368,000	153.61	335,644	580,777	916,421	37.69
Luxembourg	54	224	25,910	164.53	604	17	620	3.83
Madrid	357	4	194,681	42.25	63,869	18	63,888	13.86
Milan	244	4	206,997	21.79	82,532	18	82,551	8.69
Paris	686	187	472,426	38.48	220,608	4,828	225,436	17.97
Stockholm	217	12	194,045	97.42	106,434	5,021	111,455	53.44
Vienna	94	35	25,719	14.16	8,265	281	8,546	4.55
EU total	3,997	2,972	3,590,614	52.83	1,669,560	614,006	2,283,566	24.56
Other markets								
New York	2,617	290	5,395,889	90.23	3,014,383	190,392	3,204,775	50.41
Nasdaq	5,138	418	1,192,290	19.94	2,505,177	98,767	2,603,944	41.89
Tokyo	1,766	67	2,374,733	64.88	738,711	1,214	739,925	20.18

Source: IMF, International Capital Markets, 1997, 198.

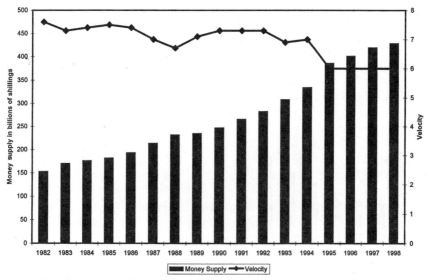

Source: IMF, *International Financial Statistics,* various issues.

Figure 8.3. Money supply (M) and velocity of money (V=GDP/M) for Austria

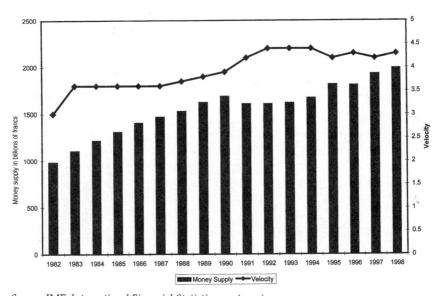

Source: IMF, *International Financial Statistics,* various issues.

Figure 8.4. Money supply (M) and velocity of money (V=GDP/M) for France

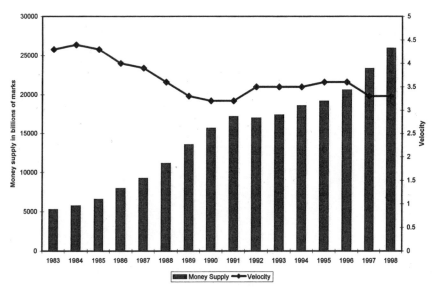

Source: IMF, *International Financial Statistics,* various issues.

Figure 8.5. Money supply (M) and velocity of money (V=GDP/M) for Germany

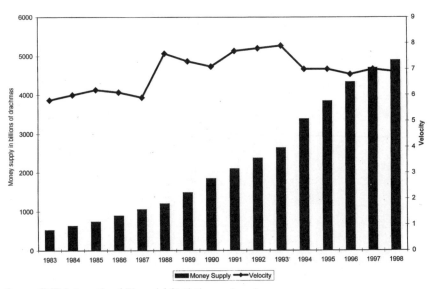

Source: IMF, *International Financial Statistics,* various issues.

Figure 8.6. Money supply (M) and velocity of money (V=GDP/M) for Greece

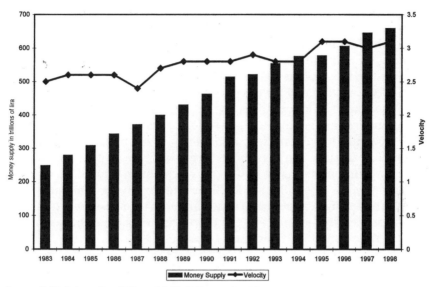

Source: IMF, *International Financial Statistics,* various issues.

Figure 8.7. Money supply (M) and velocity of money (V=GDP/M) for Italy

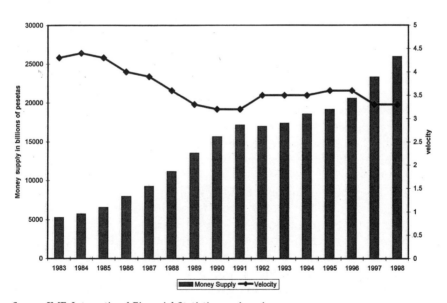

Source: IMF, *International Financial Statistics,* various issues.

Figure 8.8. Money supply (M) and velocity of money (V=GDP/M) for Spain

EUROPEAN MONETARY UNION

In the EU summit meeting in December 1995, member states confirmed that 1999 would be the year of monetary union. However, it became obvious that as long as differences among members persist, it would be questionable for the monetary merger to be smooth in practice. The convergence criteria set by the Treaty of Maastricht, regarding inflation (around 2 percent), budget deficits (3 percent of GDP or less), and particularly government debt (60 percent of GDP or less) are difficult to maintain in practice. To achieve the happy marriage of monetary union, the fiscal house of each member should be in order. However, high unemployment, disparities in living standards, and social unrest might appear as a result of the strict measures required by the Maastricht agreement and the proposed average public-sector deficits of 1 percent of GDP instead of 3 percent.

Potential benefits of the European monetary union include the elimination of troubles of doing business in many currencies and increase in cross-border investment because a single monetary unit eliminates instabilities from devaluation, which price out of the market goods of countries with stable currencies. It is estimated that about $30 billion is wasted annually from shuffling and exchanging different currencies. However, member states with uncompetitive industries would not have the potential of gaining competitiveness through currency depreciation, thereby facing industrial deterioration that would lead to large cross-border movements of capital and labor. This might drive some member countries out of alignment. In any case, it is too late to retreat and, through monetary union, expectations are that Europe would swallow Germany and not the other way around, as some critics argue.

In May 1998 the EU Commission decided which countries qualify to be members of the European monetary union and join the common currency, the euro, on January 1, 1999. They are Austria, Belgium, Finland, France, Germany, Ireland, Italy, Luxembourg, Netherlands, Portugal, and Spain, which met two of the criteria of the Maastricht agreement of 1991, dealing with low inflation and long-term interest rates. Three other countries—Britain, Denmark, and Sweden—did not like to join on January 1, 1999, and Greece did not qualify, but all four member nations are expected to join the euro in the near future. All members now meet the requirement that public deficits not exceed 3 percent of GDP. Some members, though, mainly Belgium, Greece, and Italy, have difficulties reducing public debt at 60 percent of GDP or lower, but as long as there is evidence that this can be achieved within a reasonable period, this requirement will not be an obstacle.

Nevertheless, the European Central Bank opened its business on June 1, 1998. The dispute, mainly between France and Germany, regarding the head of the central bank to run the euro was solved. Wim F. Duiesnberg of the Netherlands agreed to retire four years after the start of an eight-year term, and Jean-Claude Trichet, the president of the central bank of France, would take over by mid-2002.

The participating eleven countries in the euro are giving up part of their sovereignty to the central bank of the EU, and this was the main reason why the other three countries, mainly Britain, postponed participation probably until 2002, when the euro will replace national currencies. However, serious problems may appear in the near future regarding fiscal and monetary policies of the member countries and the differences in unemployment, which may affect related exchange rates and the currency parities to the euro. The floating euro, which replaced the European Currency Unit (ECU) on January 1, 1999, has a value equal to around $1.00 ($1.01 on December 23, 1999 and $0.90 on May 22, 2000).

THE EURO

The idea of a common currency in Europe, which was a vision of diplomats like Jean Monnet of France and many other politicians and economists, became a reality. On January 1, 1999, the euro was officially introduced as a single currency of the eleven European Union (EU) countries (Austria, Belgium, Finland, France, Germany, Ireland, Italy, Luxembourg, Netherlands, Portugal, and Spain), which fulfilled the required criteria. It is the result of the creation of the European Monetary Union (EMU), which is perhaps the most important monetary event in the world in the post–Bretton Woods period.

The main criteria established by the EU, which member countries must meet to participate in the euro, are

1) Inflation should not be higher than 1.5 percent of the average of the three best performing countries, that is, less than 3 percent,
2) budget deficits should not be higher than 3 percent of Gross Domestic Product (GDP), and
3) government debt should be no more than 60 percent of GDP.

With the serious problems of the Japanese economy and the yen, it is expected that the euro will be the second reserve currency in the world in the near future and, depending on the efficiency of the European Central Bank (ECB), it will compete with the dollar for first place.

The board of the ECB, which includes the president of every central bank participating in the euro, is responsible to determine the common monetary targets, such as currency conversion rates, interest rates, reserve requirements, and the like. By January 1, 2002, euro coins and bills will circulate, and by July 1, 2002, national coins and bills will be replaced by them. Nevertheless, there is the risk that one or another elected government may blame the ECB policies, over which it has no control, for its economic problems and threaten to withdraw, thereby creating a crisis, as the EU rules say that no country can withdraw once it enters.

Assuming financial stability in Europe, the euro, as a common currency of Europe from the Arctic Circle to the Mediterranean, will help promote economic and political unification. Although coins and notes are to be introduced in 2002, a euro-bonanza evolution is expected to make the euro-zone an attractive place for international investment. In a global survey, by Merrill Lynch, 60 percent of fund managers favor the euro and believe that it will be a stronger currency than the dollar and the yen. From that standpoint, great benefits are expected for the equity and bond markets. Because of privatization and cross-border mergers, mainly in banking and telecoms, which are stimulated by the euro, global fixed and portfolio investments in the euro zone are expected to increase significantly.[3]

Already, operations among banks and transactions in equities and bonds in the EU countries, particularly in Germany and Italy, are largely denominated in euros. Investment by insurance companies in their own governments' bonds is about $1 trillion, plus some $350 billion by pension funds, whereas American and other banks and investment companies are moving rapidly into the promising euro zone. The total value of the government bond market in the euro zone is about $3 trillion, while the corporate bond market is valued at about $1 trillion, a drastic increase from $230 billion in 1990 and as low as $30 billion in 1980. However, the strict requirements of the Maastricht criteria, particularly on budget deficits and public sector debt—3 percent and 60 percent of GDP, respectively—would reduce the EU government bond issues. The same thing can be expected with U.S. government bonds if surpluses in the governmental budgets continue.

Asset securitization, that is, packaging assets into securities and selling them to investors, is becoming common in continental Europe. This is the process followed in rescuing troubled banks and other firms, as well as in corporate restructuring as a result of mergers and acquisitions, which are growing rapidly all over the world. The combined bond market of Germany and Italy is the largest in Europe. More than half of the Eurobonds are issued by non-European borrowers, mainly U.S. companies, as the Americanization of European capital markets, through securitization of assets and junk bond issuing, continues.

The dissolution of the Warsaw Pact and the gradual weakening of the American commitment to NATO increased the desire to broaden the EU eastward. The monetary union and the establishment of a single currency, the euro, would help the EU expansion, particularly to the new democracies of Eastern Europe, although an uncoordinated monetary policy might dig a deep ditch between the EU and other candidate countries in the near future. Moreover, a successful EU could be the forerunner of a similar union of an expanded NAFTA.

In an analogy to the Spartan and the Athenian monetary systems (fifth century B.C.), the international acceptance of the euro and its stable relation to the dollar requires the fiscal discipline of the economies of the EU members, which would be the "Damocles' sword" of the euro's future. Nevertheless, the American strong dollar would prevail until a United States of Europe (USE), including Eastern Europe, is established.[4]

Other countries willing to enter the EU should adjust their tax systems and business regulations regarding competition and labor policies, as well as their monetary policies, to those of the EU. In the meantime, travel agencies, hotels, restaurants, and other stores are pricing their products in both euros and local currency.

In order to improve economic conditions, reduce debt, and be able to enter the EU, other countries need more domestic and foreign investments, so that the per capita income would be enhanced and closer economic and financial cooperation would be the outcome. The per capita GDP growth per year (gd) depends on the rate of investment (j), the incremental capital/output ratio ($v = dK/dQ$) and the rate of population growth (n). That is, $g = j/v - n$. For example, if the rate of investment is 15 percent ($j = 0.15$), v is constant and equal to 3 (three units of capital are required per unit of output) and population growth is 2 percent ($n = 0.02$), then the per capita growth is 3 percent ($g = 0.15/3 - 0.02 = 0.05 - 0.02 = 0.03$).[5]

Although Vladimir Lenin described foreign investment as economic imperialism and developing economists as neocolonialists, mainly in banana republics, almost all countries of the world invite such investment. In this investment intercourse, Europe, considered "Fortress Europe" some years ago, currently absorbs large amounts of U.S. investments, thereby helping the stabilization and improvement of the euro.

OTHER COMMON MARKETS IN EUROPE

The former Soviet Union and East European nations formed (in 1949) the Council for Mutual Economic Assistance (CMEA or Comecon), a similar but less effective organization than the Common Market of Europe or the European Union. As a result of the disintegration of the former Soviet Union, the former Soviet republics, which were incorporated voluntarily or through annexation in 1922 or later, formed the Commonwealth of Independent States (CIS) for further investment and trade cooperation. On December 8, 1991, the republics of Russia, Ukraine, and Belarus created the CIS, whereas the remaining republics (Armenia, Azerbaijan, Estonia, Kazakhstan, Kyrgyzstan, Latvia, Lithuania, Moldavia, Tajikistan, Turkestan, and Uzbekistan), except Georgia, joined the CIS a little later.

However, the CIS has not proved to be effective as yet, and a number of the republics, particularly Russia and those close to western Europe, expressed their desires to join the EU. Moreover, some Muslim former Soviet republics (Azerbaijan, Kazakhstan, Kyrgyzstan, Tajikistan, and Uzbekistan), together with other Muslim countries (Afghanistan, Iran, Pakistan, and Turkey), formed the Economic Cooperation Organization (ECO) in November 1992, but with not much effectiveness to counter the EU.

Also, the neighboring countries of the Black Sea—mainly Armenia, Bulgaria, Georgia, Greece, Romania, and Turkey—agreed to create "the union of Euxene countries." Aristotle, in his writings about wonderful hearings, named a similar formation at that time (fifth century B.C.) the common market of Euxene.[6] From an economic point of view, this infant union is not expected to have impressive results, mainly because these countries produce primarily competitive products.

A similar intrabloc common market for the Balkan countries (Albania, Bulgaria, Greece, Romania, Turkey, and former Yugoslavia) is also impractical, because the beneficial effects of trade creation may not exceed the detrimental effects of trade diversion. But such a union may prove to be beneficial for further cooperation toward an eventual pan-European union under the auspices of the EU, as was indicated in the meeting of the Euxene countries in Athens in April 1995. Already Greece is a full member and Turkey an associate member of the EU; the other neighboring nations are also expected to join the EU in the near future.

Negotiations for new entrants in an enlarged EU began in November 1998. The first countries eligible to enter the EU, probably by the end of 2002, include Poland, Hungary, the Czech Republic, Slovenia, Estonia, and Cyprus. Comparisons of the candidates' policies with the EU rules are used as criteria for entrance. They include telecommunications and information technologies, science and research, education and training, industrial policy, culture and audiovisual policy, common foreign and security policy, and small- and medium-size undertakings. The second wave of countries eligible to join the EU later include Romania, Bulgaria, Lithuania, and Latvia.[7]

WESTERN HEMISPHERE INTEGRATION

Canada, Mexico, and the United States agreed in August 1992 to create the North American Free Trade Agreement (NAFTA), which took effect at the beginning of 1994, to gradually eliminate tariffs over fifteen years and establish a free trade zone. A few years before (1988), the Canada–United States Free Trade Agreement (CUSTA) had been created between Canada and the United States, which was incorporated into the NAFTA agreement.

Rich Canadian resources, low-cost Mexican labor, and U.S. advanced technology make North American industries and financial institutions more competitive vis-à-vis those of the EU and Japan. NAFTA created the largest common market in total production, with some 380 million consumers. However, some U.S. politicians and labor unions are against NAFTA, mainly because of the big differences in wages. Minimum wages in Mexico are about $4.60 per day, compared to $5.15 per hour in the United States, with expectations to be $6.15 per hour in the near future. Therefore, many companies and factory jobs are expected to move into Mexico and many Mexican workers to eventually emigrate to the United States.

Regarding monetary policy, Canada had a relatively high growth of money supply after 1990, whereas Mexico had a big increase in money supply after 1990, as Figures 8.9 and 8.10 show. Mexico had a high instability in the velocity of money, but Canada had a declining velocity of money, except for the years 1986–1991.

As Figure 8.11 shows, in the United States there was a significant increase in the money supply in 1990–1993, but not much increase

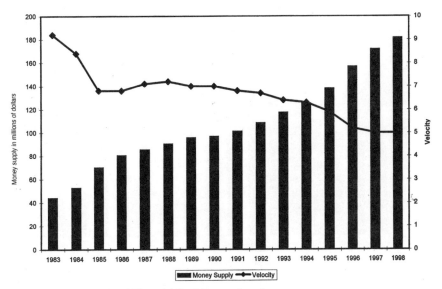

Source: IMF, *International Financial Statistics*, various issues.

Figure 8.9. Money supply (M) and velocity of money (V=GDP/M) for Canada

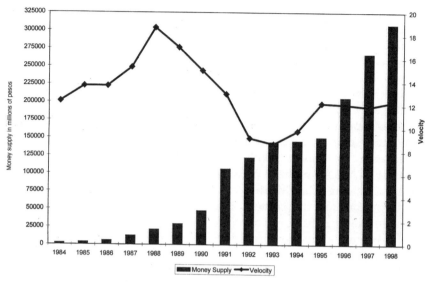

Source: IMF, *International Financial Statistics,* various issues.

Figure 8-10. Money supply (M) and velocity of money (V=GDP/M) for Mexico

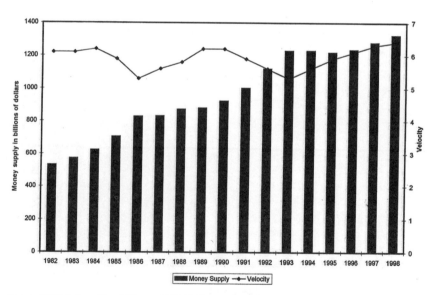

Source: IMF, *International Financial Statistics,* various issues.

Figure 8.11. Money supply (M) and velocity of money (V=GDP/M) for the United States

thereafter. Ceteris paribus, the growth of money is related to the increase in the nominal Gross Domestic Product (GDP), that is, the real GDP plus inflation. Velocity of money, the speed by which the average dollar changes hands in a year, or the ratio of GDP over money supply, M, was relatively constant and around 6 in the period 1980–1990 (except 1986), declining until 1993 and growing thereafter to be 6.4 in 1998 (that is, $GDP/M = 8.51/1.33 = 6.4$). However, there was a gradual increase in velocity during the 1960s and the 1970s. This supports the argument that the velocity of money is not constant over time as the monetarists argue. From that standpoint, inflation, particularly in the 1970s, was largely due to the increase in velocity of money, which is mainly the result of fast spending promoted by advertisement and the advanced monetary system of the United States.[8]

THE DOLLAR AND THE EURO

As the competition between the dollar and the euro is expected to be strong worldwide, there is a trend in South American countries toward dollarization of the economies, primarily in Argentina, Brazil, and Venezuela. Argentina was a pilot country in pegging the value of its currency, the peso, 1 to 1 to the dollar, in 1991. It is also suggested that Brazil is proper to follow the same policy and eventually the entire Western Hemisphere to introduce a common currency, preferably the dollar, like the euro in the European Union. Argentina in particular is considering making the U.S. Federal Reserve Bank (Fed) the central bank of Argentina as well, making the dollar its own currency, as Panama and Liberia have done. However, the Fed is skeptical about allowing foreign banks to borrow from it and about conducting monetary policies for other countries.

The possibility of euroization instead of dollarization of the economies of Latin America, the Caribbean, and other countries is rather remote, because more time is needed for the international acceptance of the euro. The growing use of the euro in the EU countries, though, would greatly affect trade and financial markets for Latin American and other countries in the near future. Nevertheless, it is questionable if and when these countries would substantially diversify their reserve holdings. Otherwise, countries in the Western Hemisphere move toward economic integration, through the NAFTA and the MERCOSUR common markets, and most of them are strongly related with the United States through political links. When the euro becomes a stable currency, then some investors in these and other countries may increase their euro holdings, thereby freeing themselves from "the tyranny of the dollar," as some in emerging nations say. However, since its introduction on

January 1, 1999, the euro depreciated from $1.20 to around $1, although the European Central Bank tries hard to stabilize prices.[9]

Although the euro is used as an accounting unit as yet, the rapidly growing trade and financial activities with Latin America (about $40 billion imports and around $60 billion exports annually) and other countries would make the euro more useful in transactions, reserve holdings, and drawing invoices in a single currency. Also with an integrated EU money market, exchange rate risks would be eliminated and transaction costs would be reduced.

Because of the growing cases of privatization and financial liberalization, portfolio and primarily direct investments to emerging nations are rapidly growing, mainly in Latin America and the Caribbean, where about 40 percent of all foreign direct investment in developing countries, or about $50 billion a year, is flowing in. Moreover, companies in the euro area and other developed nations may feel squeezed competitively and seek new markets through mergers and acquisitions so that mutual financial flows would be stimulated among different regions.

In addition to the use of the euro as a major reserve currency, euro-denominated debt might eventually account for a significant part of the total foreign debt. This might be so in the long run, because only a small part of the foreign debt is presently in the currencies of the euro-area countries, whereas in Latin America only 8 percent of foreign debt is in euros.[10]

MERCOSUR

Many emerging nations of South America, following the example of the EU and NAFTA, formed customs unions and trade agreements for further growth of trade and economic development. One of these groups is the Southern Cone of Common Market (MERCOSUR), which includes Argentina, Brazil, Paraguay, and Uruguay, which was formed in 1991 and became a common market in 1995. Bolivia and Chile are associated members.

Although trade expanded significantly between the MERCOSUR members, from $4 billion to more than $20 billion a year, the fact that they produce mostly primary competitive products suggests that not much progress is expected from the standpoint of industrialization and closer economic integration. Moreover, differences in monetary policies make things worse. For example, the Brazilian real depreciated in 1999 from about one real to more than two reals per dollar. But the Argentine peso remained pegged 1 to 1 with the dollar. This made Brazilian products cheaper for Argentina, which faces severe problems of trade financing with Brazil, as the peso, vis-à-vis the real, became overvalued.

Recently, the leaders of the MERCOSUR countries called upon the United States and the European Union to reduce trade barriers and increase their imports of agricultural products from South America. European Union exports to MERCOSUR nations increased from $6 billion to $23 billion—that is, about 400 percent—during the period 1990–1996, but MERCOSUR exports to Europe increased from $14.4 billion to $18 billion or only about 25 percent during that period. If quotas were eliminated, EU and U.S. imports from MERCOSUR could double. Now the United States absorbs half of Brazil's $20 billion farm exports per year.

President Bill Clinton endorsed MERCOSUR, the Brazilian-led South American customs union, which has faced criticism from U.S. officials. Moreover, Brazil has reaffirmed its commitment to begin negotiations for a thirty-four country Free Trade Area for the Americas after a summit in Santiago and plans to play a leadership role in the process, but it does not want talks on cutting off tariffs to start immediately. Moreover, in June 1999, the EU and the MERCOSUR countries had an important conference for trade and investment cooperation.

With the treaty of Chaguaramas on July 4, 1973, the Caribbean Community (CARICOM) was established. Barbados, Guyana, Jamaica, and Trinidad and Tobago, which had created the Caribbean Free Trade Association (CARIFTA) in 1968, were transformed into CARICOM. The combined population of the fifteen member-countries, including 7 million people of Haiti, which is expected to join CARICOM soon, is 12 million. This group includes Guyana and Suriname, which are located in South America, and Belize, located in Central America. This trading bloc is moving toward a single currency, in a similar way as the EU has done and as the MERCOSUR and the Andean Pact plan to introduce. Anguilla, the British islands, and the Turks & Caicos Islands are associated members, whereas the Dominican Republic is an affiliated trade member. Cuba may be invited to join CARICOM, and the whole group is expected to join NAFTA in the future.

In 1958, the Central American Common Market (CACM) was formed by Costa Rica, El Salvador, Guatemala, Honduras, and Nicaragua, but with not much success thereafter. In 1967, Bolivia, Chile, Colombia, Ecuador, Peru, and Venezuela formed the Andean Pact. This was a subgroup of the Latin American Free Trade Area (LAFTA), which was initially created in 1961 by Argentina, Brazil, Chile, Mexico, Paraguay, Peru, and Uruguay, whereas Bolivia, Colombia, Ecuador, and Venezuela joined later. LAFTA was successful in obtaining agreements on tariff concessions and multilateral-payments clearing during its first years, but after 1965 further movement was very slow. For this reason, the Andean Pact was created by the six Latin American countries.

OTHER CUSTOMS UNIONS

Many African, Asian, and Middle East countries formed custom unions or common markets for regional cooperation and development, but with limited effectiveness, if at all.

In Africa, the Brazzaville Group was formed in 1961 by former French colonies (Cameroon, the Central African Republic, Chad, Dahomey, French Congo, Ivory Coast, Madagascar, Mauritania, Niger, Senegal, and Upper Volta). In 1964, Chad, Gabon, and the Central African Republic formed their own customs union, the Central African Economic and Customs Union (UDEAC). Later, Chad and the Democratic Republic of Congo created the Union of Central African States. Dahomey, Ivory Coast, Mali, Mauritania, Niger, Senegal, and Upper Volta formed (in 1966) the Customs Union of West African States, which had a further cooperation meeting in May 1999. This group joined Ghana, Liberia, Sierra Leone, and Togo to establish the West African Economic Community. Moreover, Kenya, Tanzania, and Uganda created the East African Community in 1967. However, such emerging nations are interested primarily in their own national problems. Furthermore, they produce mainly primary competing products, and cooperation is difficult.

In Asia, Malaya, the Philippines, and Thailand formed the Association of Southeast Asia (ASA), which was succeeded by the Association of Southeast Nations (ASEAN) in 1967 with Indonesia, Malaysia, the Philippines, Singapore, and Thailand as members. In a recent meeting with the EU, the group negotiated further cooperation in trade and investment. Other plans to merge Malaya, Singapore, and British Borneo and to create other trade groups, such as the Pacific Free Trade Area (with Australia, Hong Kong, Japan, New Zealand, and the Asian members), were considered but without practical success. Moreover, the Asian-Pacific Rim is another trading bloc in East Asia under the leadership of Japan and plays an important role in another large trade bloc (the Asia Pacific Economic Cooperation or APEC), which includes Australia, Brunei, Canada, China, Indonesia, Japan, South Korea, Malaysia, New Zealand, the Philippines, Singapore, Taiwan, Thailand, and the United States. It seems that the world economy moves towards a tripolar competitive system—that is, EU, NAFTA, and the Asian-Pacific Rim.

Comparatively speaking, Japan had a more or less constant growth of money supply and a constant velocity of money, up to 1994, as Figure 8.12 shows. Thereafter, and up to 1998, Japan had a higher growth of money supply but a declining velocity of money, so that inflation remained under control.

Similar plans with limited implementations were proposed for Iraq, Jordan, Kuwait, Syria, and Egypt to create the Arab Common Market

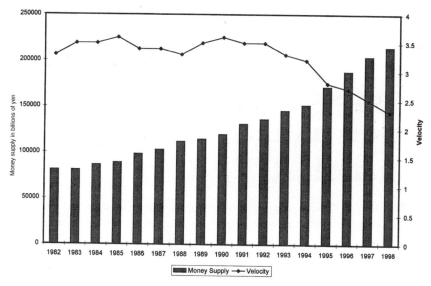

Source: IMF, *International Financial Statistics,* various issues.

Figure 8.12. Money supply (M) and velocity of money (V=GDP/M) for Japan

for coordination and development programs and tariff reduction on certain products.

In the Middle East, the Economic Cooperation Organization (ECO) for regional development was created by the Islamic Republic of Iran, Pakistan, and Turkey in 1985, which were joined by a few other states of the former Soviet Union in 1994, but with not much effectiveness. Also, the United States–Israel Free Trade Agreement was created in 1985. Furthermore, Lebanon and Syria agreed to cut customs duties by 25 percent on industrial goods in January 1999 and gradually to eliminate all tariffs over four years.

Effects of Macroeconomic Policy on International Finance

EFFECTS OF TAXES AND EXPENDITURES

Similarities and Differences in International Taxation

In recent years many countries have enacted legislation concerning tax exemptions or tax reductions to attract foreign investment. Also, international tax treaties have been concluded between the major capital-importing and capital-exporting countries to promote such investment. However, different tax systems still in existence inevitably distort allocation. They create opportunities for foreign investors to maximize net profits after taxes by departing from the optimal allocation of resources on a before-tax basis.

Consequently, international treaties and laws, which eliminate tax differences and promote uniformity and equality, are of great importance for efficient allocation in production and distribution. Furthermore, the existence of tax inequalities leads to self-defeating policies, because foreign corporations will prefer investment in privileged countries. Actually governments compete to attract investments in their countries by offering advantages in the form of tax exemptions, employment benefits for foreign personnel, and easy capital repatriation. Thus, developing and developed countries, one after another, adopt favorable tax measures and favor investment by foreign corporations. In making tax concessions, however, care must be taken not to give foreign firms extensive competitive advantages over existing domestic firms. Presently, some governments are considering the placement of limitations on foreign acquisitions of certain industries, which are increasing rapidly in cases of currency depreciation or devaluation.

Domestic taxation draws instant attention from the taxpayer and the fiscal policymakers. But taxation on foreign earnings appears to be of remote importance, even though it may have serious long-term repercussions upon the economy. Corporations with overseas earnings are customarily taxed by two countries: the foreign country where earnings take place and the country in which the citizens or corporations receiving the earnings belong. Here two main principles of taxation must prevail: tax equity, that is, all the citizens and corporations with the same income should pay the same amount of tax; and tax universality, that is, taxes should be paid on all income earned.

Many countries have enacted laws with credit provisions. Thus the U.S. tax law provides for tax credit for income taxed in another country. The tax credit permits companies and citizens to subtract from their U.S. tax on income earned abroad the amount of tax they paid to a foreign country on the same income. Thus, assuming that the foreign tax on $100 income earned abroad was $30 and given that the highest U.S. tax liability is $34 (34 percent on taxable corporate income), then only $4 should be paid to the U.S. government.

The problem of double taxation, that is, taxation on the same income by the host country and by the home country, is not a new phenomenon. Prior to 1918, foreign income taxes were allowed by Congress to be deducted from gross income earned in other countries. After 1918, taxes paid abroad by U.S. corporations with foreign branches were permitted to be deducted from the U.S. tax liability, thus becoming a tax credit. In 1921, the foreign tax credit was extended to cover corporations that owned a majority of voting stock in a foreign subsidiary. After 1951, the tax credit was further liberalized to cover corporations that own 10 percent or more of the voting stock of a foreign subsidiary from which they receive dividends. The idea was to spread the U.S. system, to increase trade, and to replace aid. As a result of foreign tax credit, it is estimated that the U.S. government collects only about 6 percent of the taxable foreign-derived income, while foreign governments collect 40–50 percent on the same taxable income. Moreover, by juggling their books, so to speak, and arranging their worldwide income distribution, big corporations frequently manage to pay little or no domestic income taxes.

Multinational corporations are affected by taxation abroad in their allocation of management and services costs and the adjustment of transfer price by tax authorities. However, Western industrial (OECD member) countries have agreed that enterprises operating in their territory and controlled by nationals of another member country should be treated as domestic enterprises in like situations. At times, royalties paid by a company to a host country on oil or other products might be converted to income taxes and be subtracted from taxes in the home country. This means a transfer of tax revenue from the home country to the host country without affecting the company.

The foreign tax credit provision is criticized on the ground that it is a loophole in favor of the companies investing abroad. It is claimed that taxes paid to another country on income earned abroad should be deducted from the total income, not from the tax liability.

Arguments to repeal the U.S. foreign tax credit intend to treat taxes paid to another government in the same way as taxes paid to different states within the United States. However, the supporters of the foreign tax credit argue that the U.S. system is such that the federal government does not have the power over the individual states to regulate state taxes, especially in some states, such as Texas, Nevada, Washington, and Wyoming,

The U.S. personal income tax rates for the year 1998 were as follows:

| | For taxable income up to: | |
For single persons	For married persons filing jointly	Rates
$ 25,350	$ 42,350	15.0%
61,400	102,300	28.0
128,100	155,950	31.0
278,450	278,450	36.0
For higher income (for both groups		39.6

The U.S. corporation tax rates for the year 1998 were as follows:

For taxable income up to:	Rates
$ 50,000	15%
75,000	25
100,000	34
335,000	39
10,000,000	34
15,000,000	35
18,333,333	38
For higher income	35

For both personal income taxes and corporation income taxes, the tax rates refer to the brackets from the lower to the higher income.

Recent Trends

Buying or selling different currencies or other financial assets depends also on the tax system of the countries involved. Ceteris paribus, countries with low income tax rates, such as Mexico, Canada, and

Brazil, are expected to be more attractive for such transactions than are France and Germany with high tax rates.

Comparatively speaking, Brazil has low personal income tax rates varying between the lowest, 15 percent, and highest, 25 percent; Canada 17 and 29 percent; Mexico 3 and 35 percent; United States 15 and 39.6 percent; Britain 20 and 40 percent; Japan 10 and 50 percent; Italy 22 and 51 percent; Germany 34.8 and 53 percent; and France 12 and 56.8 percent, respectively.[1]

Revenue in the EU member countries from the value added tax (VAT), as a percentage of gross national product, varies from about 6 for Italy and Spain, to around 7 for Germany and Britain, and 8 to 10 percent for France, Denmark, and Greece.

Top national corporate tax rates vary from 28 percent for Sweden, 33 percent for Britain, 33.33 percent for France, 35 percent for Spain and the Netherlands, 36 percent for Portugal, 37 percent for Italy, 38 percent for Ireland, 39 percent for Belgium, and 45 percent for Germany, compared to mainly 34 percent for the United States.

Switzerland (with 3.6–9.8 percent corporate income taxes), Hong Kong (16.5 percent), Taiwan (25 percent), Canada (28 percent), Brazil (30 percent), and Russia (32 percent) have relatively low corporate income tax rates, whereas Mexico (with 35 percent), Japan (37.5 percent), Australia (39 percent), and Poland (40 percent) have relatively high basic corporate taxes.[2]

A number of EU countries, including Belgium, Denmark, Greece, Netherlands, and Sweden, as well as Australia, Brazil, Canada, South Africa, and Venezuela, have a tax system of "territorial expansion," that is, the home country excludes foreign income from taxation and does not permit income deductions for expenses outside the country. Other countries, including France, Germany, Ireland, Japan, and the United States, have a system of "tax credit," that is, the home country is taxing repatriating investment income, such as dividends, interest, rent, and royalties. However, credit is given for taxes paid to foreign countries.

Differences in tax rates among countries affect decisions of multinational corporations regarding the funding of their activities, particularly the use of internal or external sources and reinvestment from depreciation and other cash-flow transactions. So far, American corporations are allowed to deduct offshore losses from their income taxes. But, as of this writing, the American government is considering ending this loophole, which permits firms to use offshore losses to avoid large amounts of tax liabilities.

Also, domestic tax policies may affect external financial support, as happened with the IMF's loans to Russia. Although the IMF relaxed the tax collection targets for loans, Russia is taking fiscal measures to reduce the budget deficit from around 8 percent to 4 percent of the GDP to stabilize its economy and restore credibility.

In order to stimulate the economy and increase employment, economic policymakers may increase government expenditures more than the increase in revenue (taxation), or may reduce taxation without reducing expenditures. The result is high budget deficits, which are financed by government borrowing or by printing more money. Such policies affect inflation and exchange rates. Assuming full employment or very low unemployment in the economy, an increase in spending more than revenue tends to raise inflation and reduce the value of the country's currency versus other currencies.

Moreover, budget deficits, which may partially be financed by investors from other countries who buy government securities (mainly bonds, notes, and bills), increase the governmental debt. This is what happened in the United States primarily in the 1980s, when the federal government debt increased significantly to $5.6 trillion or about 70 percent of the gross domestic product (GDP). The sizable interest payment of this debt is a serious burden upon the American economy and is expected to remain for years to come, because to pay taxes is always unpopular although to extinguish a debt is almost always favored, as Alexander Hamilton, the first U.S. Secretary of the Treasury, said.[3] The same phenomenon can be observed for many other countries with heavy debts.

Effects of Social Insurance

The social insurance systems mainly for the elders is growing in importance, mainly because the life expectancy at birth is increasing and the ratio of the number of people receiving retirement benefits over those who work and contribute to the system's financing is declining, all over the world. In order to keep the system sound, there are suggestions in the United States and elsewhere to privatize, partially or totally, Social Security and use the revenue to buy shares in the stock market. However, stock market fluctuations may lead to instability in benefits.

To avoid extensive government involvement and high instability, all or part of the shares could be distributed to the beneficiaries under the provision to keep them for some time, collecting dividends. Also more international agreements are needed to pay benefits to individuals working in different countries for less number of years than that required for benefits (ten years or more in the United States).

Another suggestion is to take Social Security out of the governmental budget and establish an independent institution, in a way similar to the Federal Reserve Bank, as many other countries do. Then the governments cannot easily use the surplus of the social security to cover deficits from spending for other programs as the U. S. government has done constantly since 1984. Such accumulated U. S. Social Security surpluses are about $1 trillion now and are expected to be $3.2 trillion by 2012, as they are expected to grow every year from $126 billion in 1999 to $171 billion in 2004 and $217 billion 2009. There would be no budget surplus to spend, as the surplus belongs to Social Security. This would change Cassandra-type of pessimistic announcements by politicians and the press, using the phony crisis of Social Security, to scare the baby boomers and other future retirees. Presently, though, the Federal government budget is balanced without spending Social Security money for the first time since 1960.

An independent Social Security institution will use surpluses to cover future deficits. If deficits persist, then the government can increase the age of full retirement benefits, say to 70 years, as it did previously from 65 to, gradually, 67 years for those born in 1938 and later and retiring in 2027. For those retiring at 62, the benefits would be reduced gradually to 70 percent, instead of 80 percent of full benefits. Thus, for those born in 1938 and retiring in 2000 the benefits are 79.17 percent and so on. Also, it can raise tax rates as well as the income ceiling up to which payments for Social Security are made. Such a policy would save Social Security and stabilize interest rates and capital markets internationally. Nevertheless, differences in Social Security tax rates affect foreign investment, and proper coordination among countries is needed to encourage productive international investment and economic growth.

Differences in Social Security contributions play an important role in international investment. Ceteris paribus, multinational corporations would prefer to invest in countries where payments for social security and other labor costs are comparatively lower. For example, the United States with lower rates (15.3 percent on wages and salaries, half by the employee and half by the employer) would be more attractive for investment than the European Union, for example, with high rates (up to 30 percent).

Since it was created in the 1880s by Germany and later by other countries, social security has been an intergenerational commitment to provide retirement and disability benefits to the most vulnerable of citizens. In the United States, the Social Security Act of 1935 introduced 2 percent tax rates (half by employees and half by employers) on the first $3,000 of earned income. Thereafter, they were increased to the present rate of 15.3 percent on $72,600 of earned income (1999).

Because of the gradual increase of life expectancy at birth all over the world, all nations face long-term financial problems for the survival of the system. Thus, for the United States, life expectancy at birth increased from 40 years for males and 42 for females in the 1850s to 74 and 80, respectively, in 1996. Some 44 million Americans received a total of $380 billion in retirement, survivor, and disability benefits in 1998.

Although the Social Security trust fund has an accumulated surplus of close to $1 trillion now and is expected to rise to about $4 trillion by the year 2020, thereafter it would gradually be reduced. Once the 76 million baby boomers (those born from 1946 to 1963) leave the workplace, Social Security would take in revenue to pay only 75 percent of the obligations starting around 2032. Similar and even worse financial problems would be faced by many other nations, particularly the emerging nations, which may resort to international borrowing as their tax revenue would be insufficient to finance social security programs.

In addition to the proposals of partial or total privatization and putting the money collected from contributions into the stock markets in a fashion similar to the pension funds, other proposals want the U.S. government to devote part of the accumulated surplus of Social Security to buy shares. However, if large amounts of money are put in the markets, the government's ownership of industry would increase (back door socialism) and stock prices would go up, domestically and internationally. Moreover, when the government sells large parts of shares to finance the baby boomers' retirement, stock markets might plunge, leading the U.S. economy, as well as other economies, to severe recessions or depressions. Furthermore, gyrations in the stock market may lead some retired people (particularly the elephants of Florida) to nervousness and even heart attacks, as their benefits may go up and down, accordingly. This may be an indirect and polite way of implementing the strict laws of Lycurgus in ancient Sparta (ninth century B.C.) when very old and incapacitated people were thrown over the cliff (Keada). Nevertheless, such policies of social security privatization might be introduced by other countries as well, thereby supporting the arguments of international shareholder capitalism.

EFFECTS OF MONOPOLISTIC CONCENTRATION

International Repercussions of U.S. Fiscal Policy

Fiscal policy measures are frequently used by the United States and many countries to stimulate industrial productions and to increase exports. In many instances, though, industrial and agricultural expansions create unneeded and duplicative projects with high proportions of idle capacity that threaten to initiate slumps on a worldwide scale. To reduce unemployment and to increase income and public revenue, governments try to implement such policies as investment tax credit, faster write-offs of capital assets, and similar changes, all of which will speed economic growth and grasp foreign markets.

As spending, relative to foreign spending, rises through expansionary government policies, domestic demand is pumped up, relative to foreign demand, and the current accounts are worsened. On the other hand, fiscal deficits, financed by sales of bonds and other government securities, tend to overvalue the exchange rate by raising real interest rates, which attract capital inflows, appreciating the currency and worsening the current account balance. It would seem therefore, that fiscal deficits, domestic demand pressures, and real exchange rates are closely interlinked and tend to rise together with deficits in current accounts.

Capital inflow from abroad affects and is largely affected by public finance policies. A large part of all current net investments, about 40 percent in the United States, is financed by foreign capital. If foreign investors become unwilling to continue such financing and funds from abroad shrink, real investments rates will decline and fiscal measures will have to change. The unprecedented inflow of capital has increased total foreign assets in the United States to about $1.5 trillion and has made the country the largest net debtor nation in the world.

Foreign funds, arriving rapidly (at the speed of a telex) in the United States from Europe, Latin America, Asia, and the Arab countries for security and high earnings, help mitigate the problem of budget deficits and foreign trade deficits. However, from an international point of view, U.S. deficits help the economic recoveries in other countries and stimulate the entire world economy. It looks like a stimulative Keynesian policy on the international scales.

Rising profits, high real interest rates, and stability in the economy attract large amounts of foreign capital and help relieve domestic financial markets and budget deficits, exacerbating, though, the country's obligation for future interest payments to service the growing external debt, along with amortization. However, if the flow of foreign capital stops, as foreigners reach limits on funds available, or reverses itself for different economic and political reasons, the interest rates would go further up and deficits financing would be a serious problem.

Yet high interest rates due to high budget deficits in an important country, such as the United States, force other countries to keep their interest rates high or face capital flight and massive currency depreciation. Therefore, a decline in interest rates, which could come from reductions in budget deficits and coordination of policies with other nations, could be the major remedy of widespread contraction that threatens to cripple the economies of many countries.

From time to time, budget appropriations are needed for contributions to the International Monetary Fund (IMF), the World Bank, and other institutions that provide loans and advice to the countries concerned. Because delinquent debtor countries are cut of from private bank loans, IMF seems to be the last resort for borrowing. But IMF needs higher contributions by its member countries to be able to function in worldwide credit crises. Thus, an increase in the U.S. contribution of $18 billion has been appropriated by Congress recently. Such financial support would help not only debtor countries but also U.S. commercial banks that have extended risky loans in their efforts to increase their profits mainly in developing countries, many of which have large debts. A similar credit trap occurred in the 1840s, when nine U.S. states suspended interest payments on their debts to European banks. The same thing happened also during the Great Depression of the 1930s and may happen in the near future if corrective measures are not taken.

To help avoid a worldwide credit and monetary crisis, industrial nations could support the establishment of a multilateral agency to buy up foreign debt at a discount or to reschedule long-term payments at low interest rates. This would be beneficial to exports of the industrial nations and trade. It would also bail out banks engaged heavily in foreign loans, thereby reducing the pressure on the government budget.

In spite of the arguments that budget deficits are immoral, prevent recoveries, and cause inflation and national bankruptcy, such deficits became common in many countries and continue to pile up debts. Fiscal virtue and the golden rule of budget balancing became remote concepts or empty slogans, particularly in emerging nations. On the contrary, growing debts from annual deficits absorb domestic and foreign savings and crowd out private investments.

From the point of view of capital flows, the introduction of an interest equalization tax, that is, a tax on outflows of capital to offset the interest gap, may be appropriate. Such a tax, though ineffective, was applied in the 1960s by the United States and is contemplated presently in other countries.

Although budget deficits were higher than trade deficits in many countries, foreign trade deficits may rise faster than the structural budget deficits and the drag from trade deficits will outweigh the stimulus of budget deficits. To deal with this imbalance, domestic economic policies should be designed in light of their impact on foreign trade and international relations. Modern nations should acknowledge the close links of domestic economies to the world economy, particularly on matters of investment, fiscal measures, and currency fluctuations.

In addition to the chronic federal budget deficits in the United States, up to the recent years, U.S. trade deficits are more alarming. Since 1893 and until 1970—that is, for seventy-seven consecutive years—the United States enjoyed surplus in its merchandise trade with the rest of the world. However, since 1971 the United States has had deficits in foreign trade, especially with Japan, Canada, Germany, Britain, France, and Italy and ever with China, Brazil, Mexico, Singapore, and Korea. Now they amount to more than $200 billion a year.

The U.S. budget deficits, and the relatively high interest rates they have produced in the past, are blamed for the huge trade deficits. Yet the merchandise deficits are going up although interest rates have come down somewhat. Even with a weak dollar, the United States had foreign trade problems. Although some complaints that unfair trade practices of other nations may be justified, the globalization of the economy and severe international competition may be considered the main reasons for the U.S. trade deficits.

Nevertheless, greater private saving, which will pay future taxes for debt servicing, may offset increased government borrowing and interest rates without affecting investment. This may be so if budget deficits are not large in relation to the rate of economic growth. On the other hand, higher taxes, which are required to pay interest on a large debt, have distorting market effects and impose a deadweight burden on the economy. Moreover, the financing of budget deficits through capital imports, practiced largely by the Reagan administration in the 1980s, led to pressure by special interests and politicians to deploy protection measures in favor of particular U.S. industries. Such measures included tariffs (motorcycles, cheese, textiles), trigger prices (steel), corporate bailouts (Chrysler, Lockheed), quotas (auto, textiles), government allocation of private credit, and other policies to protect certain industries from going off the cliff. Perceptively, the adoption of a prop-up-the-losers policy may lead to the erosion of U.S. competitiveness and to "a strategy for failure and lemon socialism."

A good foreign trade policy requires a sound budget, which can be achieved through taming budget deficits and reducing interest rates, both of which make the economy and the nation vulnerable to foreign competition. Such competition is damaging to certain industries and sectors that require government support as happened, for example, with the agricultural subsidies for 1985–1988. This, in turn, keeps budget deficits high, thus maintaining high trade deficits so that the country enters a vicious circle of domestic and foreign sector deficits. Given this interactive cycle, it may be that deficit reduction and eventual budget balancing will preoccupy economic policy for the years to come.

The huge U.S. budget and foreign trade (twin) deficits as well as the growing dependence on capital inflow make the country turn inward and lose its international economic dominance. Like Britain after 1890, the United States is gradually losing its position as the lender of last resort. This may lead to a financial crisis similar to those of 1873, 1890, and 1929, which produced deep depressions. Jointly with Western Europe and Japan, however, the United States can yet play the role of an important borrower and lender of last resort, so that economic equilibrium can be sustained. In a sense, the financial underpinning of global expansion can be a symbiotic mixture of U.S. hedonism, oriental thrift, and the European balancing force.

The U.S. government spends sizable amounts of money to defend other Western countries (some $120 billion a year for Western Europe alone). This allows other governments, including Japan, to use tax savings to subsidize their exports and compete with the United States. A reduction of such spending for the defense of allied advanced countries and the sharing of their responsibilities would permit reductions in budget and trade deficits and / or transfer of funds toward the developing debtor nations.

In short, budget and trade deficits will predominate economic thinking for years to come. Debtor countries will continue to face serious problems of paying back maturing debts and interests and will repetitively ask for new loans or debt rescheduling. But, as Swiss bankers stress, loans should never be given for interest payment because debts would pile up without the possibility of repayment. A liquidity crisis might thus be concealed under a thick financial ice upon which the world economies are skating. Growing domestic and foreign debts, as well as leveraged buyouts, index futures, junk bonds, and other financial instruments, will continue to create unstable economic conditions.

Although there are budget surpluses in recent years, previous budget deficits have acted like a worldwide mega-Keynesian stimulus as other countries have stepped up their exports to the United States and increased their economic growth. It seems that the United States uses foreign saving to stimulate its economy and, in turn, to end recession for foreign countries as well. It assembles energy from all over the world and feeds energy to the rest of the world. However, in the long run a growing portion of productions should be devoted every year to service the debt that is incorporated in the exported IOUs. It should be pointed out, of course, that about 30 percent of U.S. imports come from U.S. corporations operating abroad.

A gradual correction of budgetary imbalances and a smooth landing of the dollar could restore financial and economic stability in both the U.S. and the international markets. It seems that whereas budget deficits generate employment, trade deficits export jobs, especially in manufacturing.

To harmonize diverging national policies toward foreign investment and taxes, an international code of government behavior and business ethics may be needed. Common customs duties, antitrust policies, transportation rates, benefits, and taxation may be included in such a harmonized code. Technological progress and robotization in our supersonic era make the world smaller and the corporation bigger so that very soon we may emphasize not independent fiscal policies but unified international policies.

The Romance of Budget and Trade Deficits

Excessive government expenditures and fiscal deficits play a significant role in external trade deficits and vice versa. When budget deficits are financed in inflationary ways, as has frequently happened in the past, demand for foreign products increases and trade deficits rise. In many instances, reductions in trade deficits are the results of reduced fiscal deficits. On the other hand, when trade deficits rise, the main reasons are increases in government spending and budget deficits.

The gap between national savings and investment (or that between domestic income and expenditure) is related to the foreign trade position. Therefore, external trade deficits can affect and be affected by policies that change net private sector savings and those that influence government deficits. From that point of view, economic policies to reduce trade deficits must be consistent with domestic targets. They should include fiscal policies that will diminish budgetary deficits through changes in tax rates and government expenditures and alter private saving and investment behavior primarily through changes in interest rates and exchange rates. In addition, exogenous factors may affect internal fiscal deficits and external trade deficits. They include changes in the terms of trade, fluctuations in foreign demand, and sociopolitical disturbances. Nevertheless, there seems to be a high correlation between changes in domestic budget deficits and changes in external trade deficits. This means that improvements in the foreign trade position are related to improvements in the government budget position.

In the United States, foreign trade deficits follow the trend of budget deficits up to recent years. This became obvious after 1969 and especially after 1973, when both variables followed a dramatic upward trend. If trade deficits continue, the U.S. economy will have to pay out large amounts of interest and dividends, instead of collecting them (as it had done for the last sixty-five years up to the early 1970s). Then political power and international influence would be unfavorably affected by such a change in economic power and the dollar could be undermined, forcing fiscal and monetary policies that might have worldwide destabilizing effects.

To promote greater currency stability in the world, major Western nations are trying to conclude a new monetary agreement that could give the IMF a significant role in coordinating related domestic policies. Through a new International Open Market Committee, the IMF could set "target zones" for exchange rates and then encourage countries to adopt fiscal and monetary policies for their implementation. Such coordinated policies would stop certain currencies, notably the dollar and the euro, from changing drastically and ease the debt repayment problems of debtor nations.

Statistical Regression

A regression analysis of trade deficits on budget deficits for the United States shows a close relationship of the two variables for the period 1970–1996. The regression coefficient, 0.45, indicates that for each dollar change in the budget deficit there is a 0.45-dollar change in the foreign trade deficit.

Although correlation does not establish causality, this statistical result shows that when budget deficits increase by a certain percentage, trade deficits increase by almost half of that percentage and vice versa. Therefore, ceteris paribus, reductions in budget deficits are expected to bring about reductions in foreign trade deficits. Also, persistence of deficits in the governmental budget, caused by spending that has been higher than taxation, could perpetuate trade deficits. This means that a growing governmental debt could increase foreign debt as well.

The statistical results of the correlation of budget and trade deficits are satisfactory. The fit of the regression is good. The corrected coefficient of determination is high ($R^2 = 0.752$), indicating that the budget deficit is a good explanatory variable of the trade deficit. On the other hand, the Durbin-Watson (D-W) statistic (1.76) is high enough to exclude serial correlation, and the result should be interpreted with confidence.

For a further review of the relationship between trade deficit and a few of the most important variables affecting it, multiple regression analyses were conducted for the same years. The dependent variable was the trade deficit. The independent variables were the budget deficit, gross national product, inflation, and unemployment.

Comparatively speaking, the regression coefficient of foreign trade deficit on budget deficit (0.38) for 1960–1986 was higher than that on private consumption (0.061), inflation (0.036), and GNP (0.021); whereas the regression coefficient of trade deficit on unemployment was far higher (7.73). This means that for the United States a change of 1 percent in unemployment was associated with a change of 7.73 percent in trade deficit. Also, a unit change in budget deficit was associated with 0.38 unit in trade deficit and so on for the other variables.

The corrected coefficient of determination in this multiple regression was high (0.826), indicating a very good correlation. However, the Durbin-Watson statistic (D-W) at a 5 percent level of significance was not enough to signify the nonexistence of serial correlation, and the results should be interpreted with caution.

MONOPOLISTIC CONCENTRATION AND ANTITRUST LEGISLATION

Gigantic Mergers and Acquisitions

Multibillion-dollar mergers and acquisitions (M&A's) occur in many countries for financial and strategic reasons, as well as for geographic expansion. The prevailing idea is that bigger is better from the standpoint of technological innovations, cost reduction, and international competition.[4]

Some accomplished or planned acquisition megadeals in the field of communications include: two acquisitions of SBC Communications with Ameritech (worth $72.4 billion) and with Pacific Telesis (worth $16.7 billion); Bell Atlantic (which bought earlier NYNEX Corporation of New York for $23 billion) merged with GTE worth $71.3 billion; Worldcom with MCI worth $37 billion and MFS Communications worth $14 billion; three sizable AT&T deals with Tele-Communications (worth $69.9 billion), McCaw Cellular (worth $12.6 billion), and British Telecom (worth $10 billion). Also, AT&T, in partnership with Microsoft Corporation, won the battle against Comcast Corporation and acquired MediaOne Group Inc., a big cable television company, for $60 billion.[5] For cross-border mergers and acquisitions, see Chapter 7.

Global Crossing agreed to merge with U.S. West to create another telecom giant worth $68 billion, known as Global Crossing, to be based in New York. Also, Global Crossing agreed to merge with Frontier for $11 billion; Qwest Communications International, in a hostile bid, offered $55 billion and acquired U. S. West and Frontier Corporation, in competition with Global Crossing.

Berkshire merged with General Re for $22.3 billion and American International Group with Sun America for $17.8 billion, all insurance companies.

Lucent Technologies Inc., the world's largest phone equipment maker, agreed to acquire Ascend Communications Inc., a big supplier of computer networking gear, for $20 billion in stocks. Such deals reflect the extensive influence of the Internet on telecommunications. Others were Northern Telecom with Bay Networks worth $9.1 billion; Time Warner with Turner Broadcasting worth $7.5 billion; Tellabs with Ciena worth $6.9 billion; Westinghouse with CBS worth $5.4 billion; U.S. West with Time Warner Cable worth $2.5 billion; and two Microsoft deals with Comcast (worth $1 billion), and with WebTV (worth $0.4 billion). Moreover, Microsoft Corporation agreed to a $5 billion pact to use its software in AT&T's cable television systems.

Also, America Online (AOL) merged with Netscape Communications (worth $4.2 billion), creating a new firm that, in alliance with Sun Microsystems, is expected to compete forcefully with Microsoft Corporation, which is under review for antitrust violation regarding Internet operations. On the other hand, Amazon.com, Microsoft Corporation, and Barnes & Noble Inc. agreed to weave together their on-line services. Charter Communications Inc. agreed to buy Falcon Cable holdings for $3.6 billion.

In the oil industry, significant mergers include Exxon and Mobil (worth $86.4 billion), the biggest corporate merger ever of two Goliath oil companies, with operations all over the world. The low price of oil (from $23 in 1997 to around $10 now) is the main reason for such mergers, which usually lead to lower cost, primarily through labor reduction (of some 9,000 jobs or about 8 percent of payroll). However, no antitrust problems are expected in such cases, as long as exploration and drilling operations are involved. Nevertheless, if competition is reduced, mainly regarding retailing and marketing operations, antitrust regulations may block such mergers in a similar way to the John D. Rockefeller's Standard Oil trust in 1911.[6]

Also, in the early 1980s, Chevron acquired Gulf Oil for $13.2 billion and is considering a merger with Texaco Inc. for $42 billion.

British Petroleum recently acquired Amoco Corporation, worth $42.8 billion, forming BP Amoco P.L.C., which, in turn, agreed to buy Arco for $26.6 billion, as well as Atlantic Richfield Company. Other marriages of oil and other companies are expected to follow for economies of scale and international competition.

Recent M&A's, accomplished or planned, in addition to the huge deals of Exxon-Mobil, include: Boeing Company with McDonnell Douglas Corporation (1996), worth $16 billion, in order to compete more effectively with Airbus Industries, the European consortium; Tyco International, the largest provider of alarms and other security systems, and AMP Inc. worth $11.3 billion, topping a $9.7 hostile takeover by Allied Signals; International Paper and Union Camp, worth $5 billion; Provident and UNUM, both disability insurers, worth $4.8 billion. Many other M&A's occur almost every week, nationally and internationally.

Excess capacity, affecting computer makers, banks, retailers, and many industries producing paper, steel, chemicals, and a host of other commodities, is one of the main reasons of mergers. This is what happened a century ago, when prices declined, as many goods were chasing too few consumers, and mergers turned 1,800 companies into 150. However, consolidations are not always good for the shareholders as most mergers have negative effects on stocks.[7]

Measures to Encourage Competition

Because of the disadvantages of monopolies and the benefits of competition to the consumers, many countries introduced antimonopoly laws, whereas the European Commission used the EU anti-trust regulations to break up a joint distribution firm owned by three American movie companies, Viacom Inc.; MCA, owned by Seagram Company; and Metro-Goldwyn-Mayer-United Artists.

In the United States, the Federal Trade Commission blocked a number of planned mergers, including the combination of Staples and Office Depot, two large office supply companies worth $4 billion, as well as four large drug wholesalers. However, it approved the acquisition of McDonnell Douglas by Boeing for $14 billion and other big mergers, such as the acquisition of Getty by Texaco, the two large oil firms.

Moreover, efforts are being made by the U.S. Department of Justice to stop the monopolization of computer software by the Microsoft Corporation, but, as mentioned earlier, the planned takeover of the Netscape Communications Corporation by America Online would create a serious competitor and palliate the antitrust case against Microsoft. However, it is difficult to enforce an old antitrust system, dating back to the railway barons, on our modern, high-technology economy.

Global competition and technology make combinations of giant companies in telecommunications, financial services, energy, automobiles, and other industries practical and even necessary. Efficiency improvement and cost reduction can be achieved through capital concentration and mass production techniques, in which case, it is more likely that average or per unit cost of production would be reduced and the long-run average cost curve would be down-sloping. That is why antitrust regulators are cautious and reluctant to implement related legislation. However, it is questionable if giant monopolies would pass low-cost benefits to consumers, through price reduction, instead of increasing profits. Thus, Hoffmann-LaRoche Ltd. and BASF A.G. of Germany paid $500 million and $250 million, respectively, to U.S. federal prosecutors for their global conspiracy to fix prices and production quotas for vitamin ingredients.

Nevertheless, other countries encourage mergers in order to increase the size of enterprises and improve management for global competition. For example, the Chinese government supports formation of conglomerates in order to compete in international markets. Although the government participates in the management of such conglomerates, accountability and market responsiveness are expected to change the nature of such large enterprises.

EFFECTS OF PRIVATIZATIONS

The waves of denationalizations or privatizations on a global scale present new problems from the standpoint of investment and international finance. In many cases, governments sell a percentage of a state-owned enterprise through domestic or foreign stock exchange markets or all the assets of such an enterprise through auction or otherwise to the private sector.

Almost all countries around the world sell such inefficient firms, usually with high deficits, which are subsidized by the budgets of the central governments. Normally, politicians or other people in power employ more people than needed and keep low prices of the products and primarily services of those state-owned firms for social reasons. The result is higher costs than revenues, large deficits, and heavy domestic and foreign debts. Some of the most important privatizations, related to international investment and finance, are presented next.

In their efforts to reform their economies from communism into the market system, Eastern European countries and Russia and other re-publics of the former Soviet Union are under extensive programs of privatization of state-owned enterprises.

Poland announced the privatization of Telekomunikacja Polska SA (TPSA), one of the biggest companies of Poland and one of the largest privatizations in Central Europe, starting from an initial public offering (IPO) of 20 percent. The Credit Suisse Group and Deutsche Morgan Grenfell, among others, are in competition to offer their advice regard-ing the most profitable sale of the company, which is worth over $10 billion. About two thirds of the total issue of shares will be offered to international buyers, but at least 51 percent ownership will remain under the control of the state, which will receive half of the proceeds of privatization. Similar arrangements take place in the telecoms of other countries as well.

The Czech Republic is in the process of selling three big banks, thereby opening the banking sector to foreign investment. Komercni Banka, the largest bank in central Europe, Ceska Sporitelna, a big retail bank, and Ceskoslovenska Obchodni Banka, a foreign trade bank, are to be privatized soon. Goldman Sachs, Merrill Lynch, and Schroders, in competition with some twenty-three other investment banks (including Lehman Brothers and J.P. Morgan), were assigned to advise the privatization of these banks, respectively. It is expected that the state will not keep a stake in these privatized banks, which will be sold to the private sector in about two years.

Following the example of former communist countries, Hungary is privatizing a number of state-owned enterprises, including five of the country's six electricity firms. Also, the Hungarian government is sell-ing its remaining 5.4 percent stake in Matav, the dominant telecom firm.

With the help of the World Bank and the IMF, Ghana privatized about 200 out of a total of 300 state-owned enterprises since 1988, including Ashanti Goldfields Company, which recently bought Freda Rebecca,

Zimbabwe's largest gold mine, as well as Tropical Glass, producing beer bottles, Tema Steel Company, and West Africa Mills Company, a cocoa butter–producing firm that was saved from imminent collapse by German buyers. Ashanti, which was privatized in 1994, is now listed also on the New York, London, Sydney, Toronto, and Harare Stock Exchanges.

The French government is in the process of privatizing France Telecom S.A., the third-largest phone company in Europe. Recently it sold to the public shares worth $10.5 billion (FF60 billion), in addition to the initial public offering of $7 billion in October 1997. About 3 million people signed up for twice the number of shares offered; institutional investors requested more than three times their allotment. The remaining state's stake in the company is about 62 percent.[8] Moreover, Air France is under partial privatization, in which pilots are allowed to acquire shares in return for a wage cut, as are other state-owned companies not only in France but in many other European and emerging nations. Furthermore, AXA S.A. and Assurances Generales de France, large French insurers, spun off real estate assets to raise capital and lift share prices.

Following a European-wide trend, Italy is selling state-owned firms to private shareholders for better efficiency and competition in the EU with a common currency. Among the Italian enterprises under privatization or spin-off process are Telecom Italia, the national phone carrier; Enel, a utility company; and Banca Nazionale del Lavoro, a state-owned commercial bank, for which the government achieved good results from the standpoint of revenue. Other firms that spin off property holdings include Banca Intesa S.p.A., one of the largest banks of Italy; Instituto Nazionale delle Assicurazioni, or I.N.A., a big insurer, which spun off 85 percent of its property; and Unione Immobiliare, or Unim, which owns and manages properties mainly in Milan and Rome.

Moreover, SE Banken, the largest bank of Sweden, spun off Diligentia, a company with assets more than $2 billion. Also, a group of state banks and insurance firms of Finland parked assets in a firm named Sfonda.

The government of New Zealand, in its effort to privatize more state firms, decided to sell to the public Contact Energy, an electricity generator, for $1.1 billion (NZ$2 billion).

EFFECTS OF ANTIMONOPOLY MEASURES

To discourage monopolization of the market, special laws and regulations have already been introduced in many nations. For example, in the United States such laws include the Sherman Act (1890), prohibiting activities that restrain trade and monopolize the market;

the Clayton Act (1914), forbidding price discrimination and elimination of competition between corporations through interlocking directorates and other devices; the Trade Commission Act (1914), prohibiting unfair methods of competition; the Robinson-Patman Act (1936), making it illegal to try to eliminate smaller rivals by charging unreasonably low prices and using other supply discrimination techniques; the Cellar-Kefauver Anti-Merger Act (1950); and other laws and regulations enacted later to achieve these goals—that is, to restrict monopoly and maintain competition. Such pieces of legislation extended the powers of the government in order to protect the public from unfair practices by monopolies and trusts. Similar laws prevail in many developed and developing countries.

In many countries, public regulations and public enterprises have appeared as an alternative to the shortcomings of the antitrust legislation. The responsibility of public utility regulations is mostly entrusted to state and local agencies. However, federal or central government commissions have also been introduced to reinforce local and state controls, mainly during and after the Great Depression. In the United States, they include the Federal Power Commission (FPC), regulating gas and electricity; the Securities and Exchange Commission (SEC), regulating stock and security markets; the Federal Communications Commission (FCC), controlling telephone and telegram as well as radio and television services; the Interstate Commerce Commission (ICC), regulating interstate and foreign trade movements; the Federal Aviation Agency (FAA) and the Civil Aeronautics Board (CAB), responsible for enforcing airlines safety rules and economic aviation regulations, respectively. However, the CAB was abolished, and the Department of Transportation assumed some of its remaining functions.

In spite of all these regulations and controls, some commissions, especially the FCC, proved on many occasions to be helpless or indifferent. Two or more regulated industries may compete through offering services that can be substituted for each other. Such measures can reduce the budget deficits, stabilize the economy, and restore financial confidence for the survival of the system. However, to avoid environmental deterioration and prevent monopolization of the market and the charging of unjustifiably high prices, more so on a global scale, some controls are needed.

In recent years worldwide expansion of trade and investment as well as the introduction of floating currency rates has necessitated a new consideration of antitrust laws. Up to now, the main purpose of the antitrust laws has been to promote primarily domestic competition. The increasing importance of global competition, though, suggests a change in antitrust treatment and regulatory developments. Thus, the U.S. Justice Department and the Federal Trade Commission (FTC) look favorably on joint international ventures. Also, because of strong competition from Europe and Japan, a new look at the steel and car industries has been taken by the antitrust regulatory authorities in order to effect investment and technological development.

Deregulation in air transportation, financial markets, and communications, oil prices, and stock exchange brokerage has intensified price competition and spurred efficiency in those industries. Moreover, proposals for regulatory reforms have been made by many countries for further deregulation in banking and natural gas prices, deposit insurance and private pensions, and environmental restrictions. In some cases, however, deregulation has led to overlapping markets, turbulent entry of new firms, and maneuvers toward price discrimination.

Regarding U.S. foreign trade deregulations, restrictions on color television sets and nonrubber footwear, mainly from South Korea, Taiwan, and Brazil, were lifted and quotas on copper were not imposed in spite of the cries of domestic industries for protection. For a number of products such as steel, cars, and cloth, voluntary quotas or other limitations were introduced to reduce imports. Such quotas, though, may be considered detrimental to international competition and universal free trade. They seem to be worse than tariffs because they make it difficult for foreign competitors to increase sales and reduce prices.

Supporters of legislative intervention argue that in order to ease the imbalance and reverse the trend of U.S. companies that move their facilities overseas and export jobs, the government should adopt protective measures and take steps to direct trade with other countries. This is so especially for manufacturing products such as textiles and shoes (three fourths of which are imported). To avoid further self-inflicting wounds, they suggest that the U.S. government set a fixed ratio between exports and imports, particularly on nations with a history of excessive trade surpluses. Also, limitations on the percentages of import-increases are considered, mainly by other countries with large trade deficits.

NATURAL MONOPOLIES AND SUBSIDIES

In almost all countries, the public sector operates some public utility and other enterprises involved in the provision of marketable goods, primarily in the field of electricity, water, telephones, and transportation. This takes place because the private sector may not provide the optimal amount of goods or services, or for the protection of consumers. There are industries that are natural monopolies because it is difficult or impossible to have a large number of firms competing in the market. By nature, you cannot have many firms providing electricity or telephones or water in the same house and yet compete in prices and quantity.

Such monopolies can set prices above marginal cost, producing less than optimum output. When such firms exhibit increasing returns to scale and realize declining marginal cost, however, average cost is more than marginal cost by the amount of average fixed cost. In such cases, setting a price at the point where average revenue (the demand curve) equals marginal cost would result in losses for the firm, which may be covered by government tax revenue (that is, a subsidy). To break even, the firm must charge a price equal to average cost.

In many instances, the government uses regulations to restrict the pricing policy of natural monopoly firms to that which covers average cost or else sets up its own public enterprises or nationalizes monopolistic industries.

From the standpoint of efficiency, it is difficult for the state to decide whether it is better to establish a public enterprise or to rely on a regulated private natural monopoly.

In the first case, larger outputs and lower prices (equal to marginal costs) would be the outcome, but it should be desirable by society to pay for the losses incurred. In the second case of the regulated monopoly, the prevailing principle of profit maximization or cost minimization would increase efficiency compared to public enterprises, which usually run with less efficiency, but prices would be set at the point where the price is equal to average cost. Moreover, the existence of significant external benefits may be another reason for establishing public enterprises.

If the capacity limit of a public or a regulated enterprise is fixed, then part or the whole amount of output may be rationed or bought by a public institution at a determined price, while storing any remaining output for sale at a later period. However, the capacity may be expanded in discrete steps, or it may fluctuate. When the capacity is fully used, we have peak periods. When it is not, the capacity is at off-peak periods. Therefore, investment decisions of public or regulated enterprises should consider the problem of capacity related to demand for the products in question.

Usually, public enterprises have deficits that are covered by government subsidies. Ceteris paribus, this leads to inflation and eventually to currency depreciation or devaluation, particularly in emerging nations.

INTERNAL AND EXTERNAL BALANCE

The gradual globalization of the economy affects fiscal and monetary policies toward internal and external balances. Policies to combat inflation or unemployment should consider the effects of international trade and capital inflows and outflows. Here an attempt would be made to integrate domestic and external equilibrium policies.

Figure 9.1 shows the derivation of the investment-saving (IS) curve, which relates interest rates and income (Y). The lower-level curve shows the relationship of saving and investment to national income. The equality of savings (S) and investments (I) determines point a in the IS curve at certain income (Y1) and interest rate, whereas the new equilibrium of saving and investment at point b relates a higher income (Y2) and a lower interest rate, and so on.

Likewise, the left part of Figure 9.2 shows the derivation of the loans-money (LM) equilibrium curve, which relates interest rates and

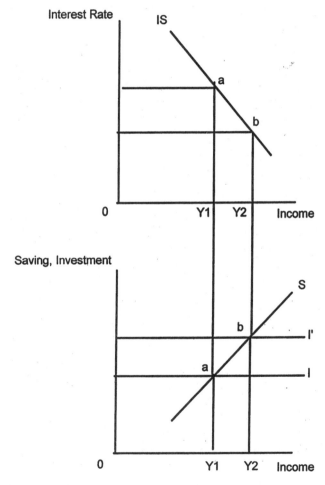

Figure 9.1. Derivation of the IS curve

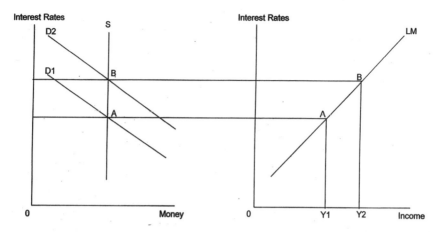

Figure 9.2. Derivation of LM curve

income. The quantity of money supply (fixed by the central bank), line (S), and the demand for money (D1), determine point (A) in the LM curve at a certain interest rate and income. The new equilibrium of fixed supply (S) and a higher demand (D2) for money determines another point (B) in the LM curve at a higher interest rate and higher income (Y2), and so on.

As Figure 9.3 indicates, different interest rates are associated with different income levels. At equilibrium point b, there is a shift in the IS curve to a new position IS'. This is so mainly because of expansionary fiscal policies that lead to higher interest rates and higher income, compared to the equilibrium at point a. Ceteris paribus, this leads to more employment and less unemployment but higher inflation. This is shown in the Okun's law curve, which relates income or production and unemployment, on the one hand, and the Phillips curve, which relates unemployment with inflation, on the other hand. However, a monetary easing would shift the LM curve outward, keeping interests rates down, thereby stimulating investment and increasing income and employment.

FISCAL AND MONETARY POLICIES UNDER FIXED AND FLOATING EXCHANGE RATES

Figure 9.4 shows the result of expansionary fiscal policy, through government expenditures or tax cuts, with fixed exchange rates; such as a policy would shift the IS curve to IS' and the equilibrium point from a to c at higher interest rates and higher income. However, the higher

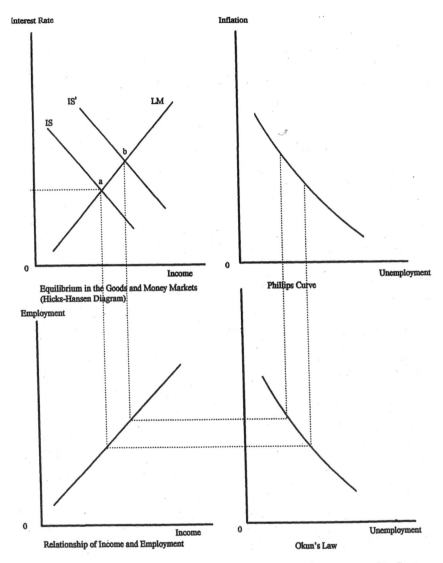

Figure 9.3. The relationship of interest, income, unemployment, and inflation

interest rate would increase the inflow of capital from abroad, thereby increasing the money supply (via exchanging foreign for domestic currency) and shifting the LM curve to LM'. This shift establishes a new equilibrium at a' in the horizontal balance of payment (BP) line at the interest rate that is the same as that prevailing on the international markets. In the case of free exchange rates, the inflow of capital from abroad would appreciate the domestic currency, thereby increasing

Interest Rates

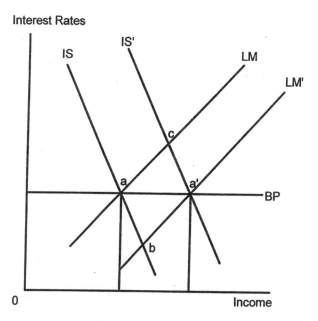

Figure 9.4. Monetary and fiscal expansion with fixed and floating exchange rates

imports and reducing exports, shifting the IS curve back to the initial point a, making fiscal policy ineffective.

Under fixed exchange rates, in which case the monetary authorities are free to exercise monetary policy, the domestic interest rate would be the same as that prevailing in foreign markets and the balance of payments would be at equilibrium. This is so, because if the domestic interest rate is higher, then capital inflows would force it downward and vice versa. Under floating exchange rates, an expansionary monetary policy would shift the LM to the LM' curve, establishing a new equilibrium in money and goods markets at point b. However, the lower domestic than foreign interest rate would result in capital outflow, restoring equilibrium through currency depreciation, which would increase exports. This would shift the IS curve to IS', establishing a new equilibrium at point a' with higher income and the same domestic and foreign interest rates at the BP line.

Social and National Aspects of Globalization

GLOBALIZATION, AUTOMATION, AND INDIVIDUAL FREEDOM

Economic progress is, to a large extent, the result of the division of labor. Division of labor means splitting up the process of production into small and simple processes, which leads to higher productivity and growth because the workers and the machines become more efficient through specialization. Specialization, in turn, leads to professional interdependence in the various stages of production and distribution. Every person may perform an isolated small function, say, turning a screw in an assembly line or opening buttonholes in a dress shop, for a number of years. For a complete product, ready to be used by the consumers, a great number of independent small actions may be involved. The mutual interdependence of labor and the other cooperating factors in the production process, therefore, is obvious, not only domestically but internationally as well.

The lack of complementary resources or the improper factor proportions lead to structural unemployment. In many countries, the lack of natural resources, capital, and know-how is primarily responsible for the structural unemployment of labor. Capital-intensive methods of production, employed by many emerging nations in some impressive projects, use more machines and less labor or even displace labor already at work. This is part of the problem of automation or mechanization, which may lead to regional or local unemployment in the short run. In the long run, however, mass production techniques introduced into the entire economy by automation, followed by social policies, may lead to higher levels of productivity and job-creating innovations. Automation, which expands with globalization, therefore, may be considered as a curse by unemployed workers but a blessing for long-term development and progress of society as a whole. In addition to the replacement of manual work, machines can perform calculation, keep records, and accomplish data-processing operations far faster than humans can. Even management and control of large factories and other enterprises may be performed by high-speed machines (cybernetics).

Historically, innovations and advancements were associated with labor-saving techniques and, therefore, with reduction in employment for individual firms. From an aggregate or macroeconomic and global point of view, however, total employment did not fall. Instead, it kept growing most of the time.

Productivity is associated with indirect effects that increase employment. Employment increase in one industry or a country creates additional income and therefore demand for output produced by other industries or countries. This means additional demand for workers, which usually more than offsets the adverse effects of labor-saving mechanization. Proper policies of adjustment, relocation, training, and job information can improve the employment market and reduce the unsocial impacts of automation and mechanization stemming mainly from globalization.

Economic globalization intensifies the quest for savings, promotes individualism, and encourages the movement of villagers into the cities. However, the concept of saving and economizing stimulates the spirit of materialism at the expense of other ethical and traditional values; individualism isolates the person from society, making him think and care for himself more than his family or the community; the concentration of peasants in industrial and commercial centers creates slums and intensifies isolationism. Furthermore, development and growth require more industrialization and the subordination of individuals to the operations of machines and factories. People must rush to be at work at a fixed time. The soulless machine, the factory, the mining-cellar, or the office awaits them. They have to stay at work for seven or more hours per day. That is their company for most of their lifetime. Higher rates of growth require more intensive operation of the machines and more physical and psychological pressure upon individuals, who become slaves to both the clock and the machine.

Machines are getting bigger and noisier, whereas individuals are getting smaller and less important. Individuals worship the machine, the creature, to the neglect of themselves, the creators. They even strive to be machines themselves as they try to catch up and compete with them. Such a gradual effort to imitate the soulless machine and focus attention on technical rather than cultural values may result in the mechanization of life, social isolation, nervous fatigue, heart trouble, and mental disturbances.

Technological innovations, promoted by globalization, introduce new transportation and communications media, such as automobiles, televisions, computers, radios, telephones, and other impersonal devices, which alienate people from each other. The television and the mechanization of life, both products of economic development and globalization, isolate individuals and deprive them of the benefits of direct contact and friendship.

Nevertheless, the human rights movement, the freedom of minorities, the quest for a more equitable distribution of income, the increase in welfarism and women's economic and social activities, which have grown rapidly in parliamentary democracies, along with the increase in intervention in the market, may lead to the gradual replacement of economic laissez-faire by social laissez-faire. Ecological problems and resource conservation impose controls and threaten to bring free markets into discredit. In some countries, inflation has also produced a general crisis of the free enterprise system, more so in emerging nations. It is argued that free enterprise has no moral charms and that it is very unimportant as such. What must be protected is the freedom of individuals, not the freedom of enterprises.

It seems that we should not be frightened of controls altogether. Some selective controls might be necessary. Extensive controls on demand and prices, however, may be ineffective and retard development. History provides many examples of such ineffectiveness of detailed price controls.[1] Depending on the degree of competition and, in cases, on the atmosphere of patriotic and social euphoria, as in periods of wartime for example, some degree of controls might be workable, but not for all firms for long periods. Extensive deviations from the principle of supply and demand cannot survive for a long time, regardless of the system of controls.

The concept of liberty is related to the belief in the dignity of the individual and his freedom to make his own choices as long as this does not interfere with the freedom of other individuals. Given that anyone has an equal right to freedom, the question is: What are the limits of free choice, if any, as one individual may want to do different things with his freedom that might interfere with the free choice of others? The crux of the matter is how to determine the area of freedom of each individual and avoid overlapping and conflicts in the process of exercising it. The main function of society's laws and regulations is how to achieve this delicate balance of individual freedoms. But the laws themselves may be the products of economic and political group power—a phenomenon that is frequent in developing countries. In any case, individuals want to substitute compulsory with voluntary action and disapprove of oppression in favor of freedom. Even though this trend is as ancient as the appearance of human beings on earth, recently more emphasis has been placed on such values. The wonders of Plato and Euripides and the Aristotelian exercise of logic, regarding personal values, freedom, women's status, and the social and political role of the individual, have become important again in recent years, through education, intellectual stimulation, and globalization in general.

As a result of economic development and growth, production and distribution enterprises are enlarged into huge multinational oligopolies. This trend creates problems of a social and moral nature. People are suspicious of large-scale corporations and regard bureaucratic organizations as malignant institutions because of the fear of oppression and social alienation. In the pursuit of profit maximization, big corporations sometimes behave in an antisocial or amoral fashion. In practice, they propagate their technological and economic growth, neglecting or ignoring the growth of public goods and the potential environmental damages. Suspicions and fears are spread, primarily between middle-class individuals, who see globalism as an authoritarian institution that downgrades them to little men attached to unimportant little jobs. The whole economy, organized in corporation pyramids, is composed of a federation of international firms with a highly skewed size distribution. Under such a corporate structure the individual is subordinated to the invisible power of a large enterprise and feels some form of authoritarian pressure.[2]

Bureaucratization and personal subordination increase with higher economic concentration and the increase in the size of the firms. Even managers and other corporate officials might be replaceable by computers and robots, which would predict patterns of consumption and command optimal allocation of resources. Under such conditions, entrepreneurial flexibility, creativity, and managerial incentives would be reduced while bureaucracy would be increased, in a similar fashion as in command economies.

The quest for high rates of economic growth and increase in social welfare may lead to more government and centralism. And the question is: How can a balance be maintained between governmental authority and personal liberties? Historically, liberty and freedom are associated with limitation of governmental power. The wider the role of government or the central authority in economic activities, the narrower the area for individual freedoms. The acceptance of the notion that an expanding central authority or a supergovernment, in developing as well as developed countries, can stimulate growth and guide the economy to its proper goals means the acceptance of more regimentation, more controls, and extensive intervention. Concentration of power frequently results in police states, corruption, and full-scale dictatorship. With bugging devices, computers, the Internet, and other sophisticated means of surveillance in the hands of an administrative czar or a central authority, the dangers to individual freedom and social justice are obvious. Such communication and surveillance devices may be able even to read human minds and thoughts. In such a case the human being, full of fears and suspicions and intimidation, would be forced to act and behave like a mechanical robot at the will of a dictator or group of dictators who are in possession of these devices and related police files.

Lately, in a number of emerging nations, there seems to be a harmonious cooperation between the economically powerful elite and the army so that they can preserve their economic and political power through open or covert military dictatorships. There is mutual support between these two groups; they work together in a way that one hand washes the other and both wash the face. In their effort to preserve their advantages, and in cases cooperating with foreign interests, they use modern sophisticated military technology to abolish existing democratic institutions and resort to secret police terrorism to oppress the will of the majority of the people. The argument that some degree of political oppression is required during the early stages of development, because large segments of the population are uneducated and do not respect democratic rules, is unfounded. Oppression usually feeds instability and backwardness and deprives the free and anxious mind of new inventions, innovations, and the desire to improve.

Everywhere in the developing nations, colonial servitude, a remnant of the past, is regarded as the chief obstacle to social rights and economic development. In the distrustful minds of developing people the thinking is that by keeping the levers of economic domination, metropolitan powers will exercise a great influence in emerging nations and that their supposed independent governments are puppets of foreign powers. Rival ideologies influence local aspirations and affect developing nations. The Great Powers maneuver, through globalization, to maintain and extend their dominion. Poor nations are, in many instances, pawns in the bigger game, and as it is said, "When the elephants fight, it is the grass that suffers." They are scared and search for neutrality. However, neutrality may not provide more security and safety than alliance with big powers. But turning to one side or the other to get help is equally dangerous because by riding the tiger you may end up inside.

The main goal of multinational corporations, moving around the globe, is to maximize profits. This is determined by the point where marginal cost (MC) is equal to marginal revenue (MR). As Figure 10.1 shows, at this point, price is P1 and quantity Q1. However, the firm may want to conquer more markets by maximizing sales, producing a higher quantity Q2 with a lower price P2. This price is equal to unit cost. At this break-even point, average cost (AC) is equal to average revenue

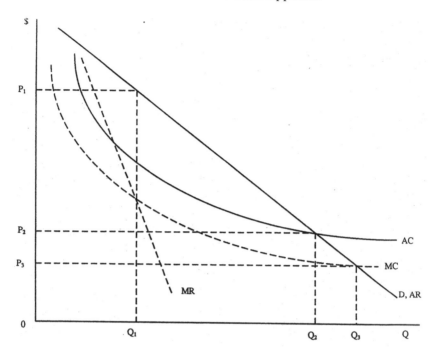

Figure 10.1. Social allocation with declining costs

(AR)—that is, AC = AR—and there are no profits and no losses either. Moreover, production can take place at a further larger quantity Q3 at an even lower price P3, but the public sector should subsidize the loss if it is desirable to produce at Q3, which loss is equal to the difference between MC and AC at this point.

With this form of globalized capitalism, many firms issue additional shares, which may be given to the employees or sold to investors of different countries in which they operate, thereby spreading shareholder capitalism all over the world.

GLOBALIZATION AND INCOME INEQUALITIES

Measurement of Inequality

The problem of global inequalities in the distribution of income and wealth is of major importance not only from ethical and economic points of view but, more importantly, from social and political points of view. Distribution of income means who gets what; wealth means who has what. Extensive inequality in income and wealth is a source of social unrest and instability. It creates feelings of inferiority and generates self-hate, anger, and violence. People hardly starve quietly. Even pollution is more concentrated in poor neighborhoods, whereas the wealthy people can always get away and enjoy fresh air and other amenities.

Differences in incomes generate differences in education, consumption, health, shelter, recreation, and even length of life. People living under poverty conditions are subject to more diseases than people living under prosperous conditions. They do not have easy access to doctors, hospitals, and medicine; they lack warm and modern houses; and they do not have the proper food to eat for their subsistence. A low level of education is associated with low productivity and low level of income which, in turn, is responsible for low level of education, as poor people cannot afford to go to school to acquire the needed skills. This is one segment of the vicious circle of poverty in many countries.

Figure 10.2 relates the percentages of population to percentages of income received. Thus, 80 percent of the population receives 60 percent of the national income in country A and only 30 percent in country B. The ratio of the area between the equality line and the income distribution (Lorenze) curve to the entire area below the equality line (Gini ratio) measures the degree of inequality. Country B, for example, with the entire Lorenz curve at a greater distance from the equality line, has greater inequality (Gini ratio) than country A. If the two curves cross, the Gini ratio may be lower for parts of B and vice versa.

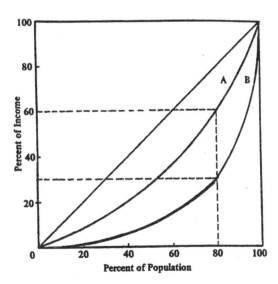

Figure 10.2. Inequality of income distribution

Empirical research reveals that in nonindustrial economies, with small subsistence farms and small factories, income inequality is not high. But in economies where landlordism, surplus labor, discrimination among cultural or ethnic groups, and inheritance laws favorable to wealth concentration prevail, income inequality is high. At low levels of development, economic growth increases the inequality of income distribution, especially between the urban and the rural sectors. Farm workers move into the cities, where they enjoy higher incomes; and professional classes, earning comparatively high income, rise.

Table 10.1 shows the share in income of the lowest 20 percent, as well as the highest 10 percent, of population in a number of selected countries. Also, it shows the Gini index, that is, the area between the hypothetical line of absolute equality and the Lorenz curve of income distribution, expressed as a percentage of the maximum area under the straight equality line. Not only emerging nations, such as Brazil, Chile, Colombia, Kenya, Mexico, South Africa, Venezuela, and Zimbabwe, but rich countries such as Australia and the United States have a high Gini index and high income inequality. Sweden, Norway, and Germany have the lowest Gini index and therefore the lowest inequality.

At high levels of development, where per capita income is relatively high, inequality is reduced. However, in many countries, including the United States, the poorest 20 percent of the population receives less than 5 percent of total income, while the top 10 percent of population in some poor countries receives more than 40 percent of income.

The position of the poorest population worsens with development as does that of the middle 20 percent, but that of the top 5 percent improves significantly.[3] This is so not only because of the regional and technological concentration but also because of the low elasticity of international demand for agricultural products and the accumulation of assets in the hands of a few global owners of modern enterprises.

Other poor developing countries with low per capita income of the poorest 20 percent of the population include India, Pakistan, Ceylon, Tanzania, Nigeria, Honduras, Gabon, Mexico, Panama, Tunisia, Turkey, and almost all other developing countries with large, underemployed, rural populations. The high income groups are primarily commercial farmers, landlords, and people living mainly in urban centers.

Globalization itself is a cause of rural-urban inequality through the transformation of resources and talented and educated people from the backward agricultural to the modern industrial and services sectors. Income redistribution, in such cases, may be associated with an adverse development process by placing more emphasis on the rural sector where average per capita income in low. This may lead to lower rates of overall economic growth, especially if redistribution is associated with lower rates of saving and investment. The dilemma, therefore, is

Table 10.1   Percentage Share of Income in Selected Countries and the Gini Index (most recent years)

Country	Lowest 20%	Highest 10%	Gini Index
Australia	7.0	24.8	33.7
Bolivia	5.6	31.7	42.0
Brazil	2.5	47.9	60.1
Bulgaria	8.3	24.7	30.8
Canada	7.5	23.8	31.5
Chile	3.5	46.1	56.5
China	5.5	30.9	41.5
Colombia	3.1	46.9	57.2
Egypt	8.7	26.7	32.0
France	7.2	24.9	32.7
Germany	9.0	22.6	28.1
India	9.2	25.0	29.7
Indonesia	8.4	28.3	34.2
Israel	6.9	26.9	35.5
Italy	7.6	23.7	31.2
Kenya	3.4	47.7	57.5
Malaysia	4.6	37.9	48.4
Mexico	4.1	39.2	50.3
Norway	10.0	21.2	25.2
Pakistan	8.4	25.2	31.2
Peru	4.9	34.3	44.9
Poland	9.3	22.1	27.2
Russian Fed.	7.4	22.2	31.0
South Africa	3.3	47.3	58.4
Spain	7.5	25.2	32.5
Sweden	9.6	20.1	25.0
Tanzania	6.9	30.2	38.1
Thailand	5.6	37.1	46.2
United Kingdom	7.1	24.7	32.6
United States	4.8	28.5	40.1
Venezuela	4.3	35.6	46.8
Zimbabwe	4.0	46.9	56.8

Source: World Bank, *World Development Report,* 1999/2000, 238–239.

how to correct the extensive inequalities or mitigate poverty and human misery in poor countries and regions without reducing the growth rate of their economies.

Inequalities of income are common to not only poor but rich countries as well. In the United States, for example, the total income of the richest one fifth of American families (absorbing 45.2 percent of income) was far more than that received by the lowest three fifths (31.3 percent) in 1997; while the top one fifth of Americans owned more than 75 percent of personal wealth, that is, three times more than the total wealth of the bottom 80 percent. Also, the wealthiest 1 percent of the population owns 70 percent of the corporate stocks, even though the number of stock investors increased from 9 million in 1956 to 31 million in 1970 and 79 million in October 1999.

Although the strong U.S. economy uplifted many families, there are still 46 million Americans or 17 percent of the population below the poverty line, determined at $19,000 by the Census Bureau. Up to September 1999, the poverty line was determined at $16,600, below which was 12.7 percent of the U.S. population. Also, 44.3 million Americans are without health insurance.

Even in centrally planned economies, which are based on the Marxist doctrine of equality, there are differences in wages and salaries. Managers in state enterprises, scientists, or military officers get more than average factory workers. The welfare Scandinavian countries, and primarily Sweden, have not much income inequality. But most of the developing countries of Africa, Asia, and Latin America have great inequalities.

At high levels of development, globalization may promote income equality, but at low levels of development it may hurt rather than help poor people, unless it includes guarantees of social justice. The frightening implication of empirical findings is that economic growth promotes social injustice and makes things worse in many emerging nations. It increases the wealth and power of existing and newly created elite classes at the sacrifice of the poorest segments of the population. Such elite classes, mainly in developing nations, are primarily small expatriate groups, descendants of aliens or conquerors and tribal chieftains, or culturally and economically distinct indigenous oligarchies.

Inequality and Growth

From the viewpoint of total consumer or social satisfaction, it is argued by the supporters of income equality that a dollar taken away from a rich person and given to a poor person would increase total social utility. Critics of income equality, on the other hand, argue that inequality provides work and creative incentives as well as greater amounts of saving and investment. According to them, under a completely egalitarian system, society would be dull and stagnant. However, great disparities in living standards and material welfare breed tensions between the political principles of democracy and the economic principles of capitalism.

Even though statistical data are not provided by many countries, it is safe to say that the extremes of poverty and wealth are far greater in most developing countries than in developed countries; and unless Herculean efforts are made in the economic and social fields, the despair will continue and things might get worse. Social mobility and advancement is not easy. Changes in social stratification, wealth, minority and sex discrimination, power, and status quo are difficult. Great aspirations and strong desires for advancement exist in all emerging nations, but the execution of actual development projects and the improvement in the standards of living of large parts of the population meet serious barriers.

Many people (more than 50 percent) in the Third World countries do not live as well as the stray cats and dogs in the Western world. Because of globalization and communications, people everywhere know the differences between their standard of living and that of other people. They hardly accept the idea that their poverty is the will of any other supernatural power. They no longer listen to such shortsighted and manipulating prophecies. Instead, they demand economic improvement and social justice. The pressure for replacing superstitions, taboos, and magic convictions with material progress is widespread. The demand for land reforms, industrialization, employment, freedom, and better health and education continues to be high, no matter how heavy the political and dictatorial oppression in some cases. People demand these changes not only for their own individual improvement but, in many cases, for the development and the increase of the power of their nations, although globalization is liquidating such concepts. Even though such nationalistic feelings have proven to be detrimental to social welfare, because they occasionally lead to conflicts and wars, many people want their country to be powerful, respected, and, in some cases, feared by others.

The main pressure on poor countries, at the present time, comes from starvation or the lack of the means of subsistence. For many individuals the situation is bleak. Poverty and squalor surround the majority of people in these countries. In some cases, as in Calcutta, for example, some people have no shelter at all and sleep in the streets. In other cases a number of families are crowded into a single room. Fire and police protection, schools, and other public services are limited, if they exist at all; furniture and household appliances rarely exist. Basic food is limited. High-quality consumer goods are a dream for many people.

Even a few meat meals per year, say at two or three important holidays, may be considered an achievement.

People living under poverty conditions are predominantly the aged, female heads of family, minorities, and peasant farmers. There seems to be a positive correlation between large families and low incomes. Perhaps the major deficiency on the part of the poor is their irrational propensity to proliferate, as Malthus suggested, which perpetuates their poverty.[4]

There are arguments that poor children nurtured in the bracing school of poverty become geniuses, epoch-makers, and leaders in every branch of human action. According to these arguments, such children always have marched straight to the front, advancing the world to greatness and goodness; whereas rich children, who are exposed to the temptations of wealth and position, contribute little, if anything, to the advancement of the human race.[5] Such arguments might have some application in the past when entrepreneurial and other personal talents were important in economic and social leadership. Modern times, however, require advanced skills and extensive education and training that hardly can be provided by the bracing school of poverty.

Various schemes and programs have been suggested in different countries to mitigate the problem of income inequalities, resulting from savage capitalism and globalization. The most important program of reducing inequality is that of "welfare" prevailing in a number of countries. In such a program the government or the city will guarantee an income to every family according to its size. Any person unable to work, either because of sickness and age or because of nonavailability of a job, will receive a basic income sufficient to maintain his or her family at a determined standard of living. An administratively efficient welfare scheme is that of negative taxation, according to which each individual reporting an annual income below a fixed income floor will receive a supplementary payment up to this amount in monthly checks. The main dilemma, however, in such welfare schemes is how to guarantee an income to anybody without destroying the incentive to work and creating a Solomonic bureaucracy.

To avoid severe disincentives to work, individuals covered by the scheme can earn up to a certain amount, without facing reduction in the guarantee-level. For higher earnings the guaranted income can be reduced, up to a certain amount, again. An alternative scheme would be to establish a progressively negative income tax on earnings per hour. The higher the hourly earnings, the lower the supplementary income from the government, until it becomes zero. Such welfare schemes, however, require sufficient government revenues and efficient administrative mechanisms, which do not exist in most emerging nations.

Certain forces, though, such as the attainment of independence from colonialism and imperialism, better education (especially elementary and practical), pressures exerted by social groups with higher expectations, and sociopolitical revolutions, work to reduce income inequality. Also, introduction of innovations that generate higher overall and per capita income through the interaction of the multiplier and the accelerator may improve income distribution, if they are not followed by disemployment of labor. Innovations generating reemployment from the rural to the urban sector are expected to reduce inequality of the poorest farming workers, as their income will increase in the cities, and their rural families will be left with more food to eat. Within the agricultural sector, however, innovations leading to mechanization and other improvements may increase inequality through the disemployment of the peasants remaining in this sector, unless they introduce multicropping processes and increase the demand for labor. Furthermore, a rapid rural population growth will increase the population below working age and intensify income inequality.

Depending on the political climate, the administrative capability, certain governmental measures such as direct employment in rural public works, land reforms or socialization of large enterprises (mainly public utilities), elimination of subsidies and artificial price support, and proper taxation can reduce income inequality. The main problem with the tax systems in many emerging nations though is that they have not generally been effective in redistributing income. Progressive income tax legislation is difficult to enact because of the strong political influence of wealthy groups; indirect taxes are regressive because they are shifted primarily to low-income consumers. Other development strategies, stressing promotion of human resources, diversification of manufacturing, credit facilities to indigenous small entrepreneurs, reduction of rural-urban dualism, political participation, and institutional reforms may palliate extensive inequalities in developing countries.

GLOBALIZATION AND MULTINATIONAL CORPORATIONS

Foreign investment by multinational firms remains the main financial source for emerging nations. In order to have the flow of foreign investment continue, favorable conditions must prevail. Such conditions include socioeconomic stability, profitable investment opportunities, guarantees against administrative controls, tax discrimination, and nationalization.

There may be short-run disadvantages in the capital exporting country, from the viewpoint of the balance of payments and domestic employment, but in the long run the continuous inflow of profits, interest, and dividends will enhance the welfare of the creditor country. From a sectoral point of view, investment in petroleum and mining was the most profitable during the postwar years, followed by manufacturing, tourism, and information and financial services.

In spite of the high profits in developing countries, Western Europe and Canada absorbed the largest amounts of, primarily American, investment, mainly because of their socioeconomic stability, available skills, and the existence of favorable business institutions.

The creation or improvement of capital markets in emerging nations can solve the problem of financing development projects by attracting excess reserves, mainly from developed and some oil-producing countries.

Modern communications and transportation have shrunk the world, and large corporations, with global investment and market strategies, are contributing to a new emerging global economy. These multinational corporations provide capital, organize production, equalize factor prices, and transfer technology, as they move from country to country, searching for resources and new markets. With their awesome size and power, however, they can exercise considerable economic and political control upon other countries, particularly the less developed ones. In their effort to maximize returns to their corporate assets, they may ignore or even act against the interests of the host countries, from the viewpoint of employment, managerial and technical training, and infrastructural and industrial development.

Governments and politicians around the world have raised questions as to whether this expansion is a form of neocolonialism and imperialism. They have fears that the economic and political life of their countries will soon be dominated by these giant corporations. To limit preemptive foreign control, they have begun to formulate policies toward self-reliance and to enact protective legislation regarding ownership, profit sharing, and employment of personnel. Such restrictive tendencies have been intensified as a result of rising tides of nationalism, and gradually mitigated because of the advantages of foreign investment and globalization.

Notwithstanding criticisms and suspicions, multinational corporations are invited by almost all the economies to invest and create employment and income. In many cases, tax reductions and other benefits are offered to attract investment by foreign firms.

Global expansion of multinationals leads, at times, to regional integration between nation states and multinational labor unions, acting as a countervailing power to corporate giants.

Under different schemes and agreements of cooperation and joint ventures, multinational companies enter not only the countries with market economies but also countries with planned economies. Such movements create the required bridges between the two systems of capitalism and socialism and speed up the process of convergence of ideologies to the benefit of global shareholder capitalism.

Advantages

The most important advantage of any corporation, including the multinational, is its unlimited life. The corporation continues its operations in spite of the fact that the persons in charge of its management may resign or die. It is a legal person independent of the life of the physical persons managing it. This advantage of unlimited life is vital for economic stability and perpetual growth. The enterprise is not resolved or split after the death or the resignation of the corporation executives. It continues to exist. Only new managers and executives replace the old ones. The corporation continues and may further expand its operations. Production continues to take place, and employment is provided. From that point of view, the existence and expansion of the private or public corporation is of vital importance to modern economic life. It is a vehicle of economic development and globalization.

Another advantage of the corporate form of enterprise is its feature of limited liability. The stockholders or owners of the corporation are held financially responsible only up to the amount of capital they invested in the corporation. They are not responsible beyond this amount. Creditors of the corporation cannot put their hands on the owner's personal or other property. The corporation, as an independent entity, has its own rights and obligations, its own property to pay its debts. In the event that its property is not enough to pay for its accumulated debts, the corporation would be forced to go into bankruptcy and the creditors would have to be satisfied with the existing property. They do not have any right to direct their claims or part of them against the personal property of the owners or stockholders, no matter what their nationality. This advantage supports global corporate expansion and shareholder capitalism.

Transferability of shares is another advantage of the corporation. The stockholder can sell or otherwise transfer the shares anywhere and at anytime. Well-organized stock markets can facilitate the transfer of shares between individuals or nations and increase the willingness of more and more people to participate in such ventures. This process liquidates or eliminates oligarchy, reduces polarization between "haves" and "have-nots," and strengthens the democratic way of life, as more and more people become owners of the means of production and the economic system tends toward what Joseph Schumpeter called

people's capitalism. All the aforementioned corporate advantages—
that is, unlimited life, limited liability, and share-transferability—help
attract savings and bring in large sums of money, which in turn can be
used for the application of modern technology, industrial expansion,
extensive research, and specialized management, so desperately
needed in emerging nations.

Multinational firms, or simply multinationals, promote international
cooperation and improvement in living standards as they enlarge markets and exploit new processes, new ideas, and new resources. They
dominate much of the world's production, distribution, and financial
affairs. Foreign resources and markets may receive attention equal to
that of the domestic, and management authority can be distributed
among different regions and countries. Modern communications and
transportation have shrunk the world, and multinational corporations
are contributing, in a dynamic fashion, to the new emerging world
economy.

Such large corporations provide capital for other countries, organize
production, introduce new techniques and skills, and increase the
search for new resources and new markets.[6] They move to various
countries, similar to bees among flowers, helping to introduce technological and economic progress. The taxes and royalties they pay provide
a source of capital formation for the countries in which they operate.

Although there may be short-run trauma in domestic jobs, the overall
economy of the home country benefits in the long run. Multinationals
export components to factories abroad, provide high-paying jobs in
management and research, and contribute to improvement in the balance of payments.[7]

There is no doubt that additional capital and technology are needed
for economic development of low-income countries. There are wide
differences of opinion, however, as to the economic and social role
foreign private companies should play in the development of these
countries. Whereas some writers see these companies and their investment as the main vehicle for transfer of technology, improvement in
skills, industrialization, additional employment, and social betterment,
others see them as imperialistic instruments of political infiltration and
economic exploitation. The main economic argument against such foreign investment by multinationals is the high cost of servicing the debt
they create relative to the benefits they bring to the host countries.

Disadvantages

It is argued that multinational corporations should consider their
social responsibilities in broader terms, instead of pursuing only maximization of economic results. Managers of world business should look

at their obligations from the point of view of human accomplishments, instead of reverting to anachronistic, mercantilist policies of economic, military, and political domination. They must be agents of technological change and economic progress, instead of being agents of social unrest and national conflicts, which are used as tools of foreign policy outside the channels of normal diplomacy.

The growth of corporate "beasts," as they are called at times, threatens national sovereignty and stirs up natives who are afraid of the uncontrolled economic and political power that have come to characterize these enterprises in recent years. These corporations may not be accountable to or regulated by any parliament or institution, and they may form their own economic and, in many cases, political power in different countries, undermining or overthrowing governments that are not favorable to them.

The inherent conflict between multinational firms and nationalism stems from the fact that most of these firms regard their program of research, production, and distribution in terms of values related to the parent country. Their economic policy, therefore, is largely influenced by the foreign policy of the parent country. The larger and richer country in which management resides will exert the greatest pressure on the corporation, making it an instrument of national goals. Such national bias in decision-making can partially be eliminated if the corporation is owned and managed by nationals of different countries, transcending, thereby, national identity and avoiding regional friction and isolation. Cross-country mergers and acquisitions, which grow rapidly in our day, may help to achieve these goals.

The globalization of trade and industry creates problems not only of coordination and managerial importance but of social and environmental importance as well. The main decision-makers of the company living in one country, say the United States, Europe, or Japan, cannot be expected to concern themselves too much with fiscal or ecological problems of other distant countries.

To the arguments that multinationals provide managerial expertise and additional revenue from taxes, transfer technology, finance capital investment, increase exports, and provide employment, the critics argue:

1. They overvalue imports to subsidiaries in foreign poor countries and undervalue exports from them. It is estimated that overpricing of imports in developing countries ranges from 30 percent to as much as or more than 1,000 percent, whereas underpricing of their exports ranges from 40 to 60 percent.
2. The technology transferred from rich countries is not only overvalued but is mostly capital-intensive and thus intensifies the

problem of unemployment and income inequalities, especially in poor countries of Latin America. The total labor force of all subsidiaries of transnational enterprises in all developing countries is not much, perhaps less than 6 million people.

3. Because of the high degree of loan security and guarantees multinationals provide, they can borrow large amounts of local funds. Actually, 80 percent of the operations of U.S. companies in Latin America were financed with local capital or reinvested earnings, preempting thereby local scarce resources instead of providing new capital. Such multinationals prefer local debt funds to hedge against host country pressure.

From a sociopolitical standpoint, global economic concentration leads to gradual transfer of political powers from elected governments to big corporations, which are managed by persons with large amounts of shares. They care mainly about profit maximization and wealth accumulation, with not much interest in environmental protection and income distribution. Important decisions are made by the boards of directors of huge companies and not much by the people of each country through democratic rules.

National governments, to a large extent, do not control such corporate giants, but they are controlled by them, whereas the citizens are transformed from participants in the production process to mere observers. Although they support the reduction of the role of government, at the same time they support a certain degree of governmental power, enough to support the maintenance of their economico-political domination, regardless of the growing inequalities. According to the United Nations, the gap between the top 20 percent rich and the lowest 20 percent poor in the world increased by 50 percent after 1960.[8]

Notes

CHAPTER 1

1. For external direct and portfolio investment in emerging markets, see International Monetary Fund (IMF), *International Capital Markets* (Washington, D.C.: IMF, September 1999), 52–53.

2. "Foreign Stock Indexes, " *New York Times*, December 18, 1999, C4; and December 20, 1999, C29, C30. Also, *Imerisia*, Athens, December 10, 1999, 51; and *Financial Times*, December 15, 1999, 43.

3. Richard A. Grasso, Chairman, New York Stock Exchange, "Globalization of the Equity Markets," *Fordham International Law Journal* 20, no. 4 (1997).

4. More details in Nicholas V. Gianaris, *The European Community, Eastern Europe, and Russia: Economic and Political Changes* (Westport, Conn.: Praeger, 1994), Chapter 1; and his "Helping Eastern Europe Helps the West," *New York Times*, February 8, 1990, A28.

5. More on regional inequalities in Nicholas V. Gianaris, *Economic Development: Thought and Problems* (Hanover, Mass.: Christopher Publishing House, 1978), Chapter 4. Translated into French and Spanish by the IMF and used for its seminars on Financial Analysis and Policy.

6. For the support of the argument against protectionism, see the related letter to the U.S. president by 240 economists in different universities in the *New York Times*, June 8, 1999, C5. Also, Alison Butler, "Environmental Protection and Free Trade: Are They Mutually Exclusive?," in Jeffry A. Frieden and David A. Lake, *International Political Economy*, 4th edition (Boston: Bedford/St. Martin's, 2000), Chapter 29.

7. Robert D. Kaplan, "Could This Be the New World?" *New York Times*, December 27, 1999, A23. Also, Fred Maslin, "Globalism in 2100," *New York Times*, December 28, 1999, A24. For the arguments that greater inequality in developing countries, and decentralization in favor of local authorities, will take place in the future, see John Kenneth Galbraith, "Issues for the New Millennium," *Finance and Development* 36, no. 4 (December 1999): 2–5.

CHAPTER 2

1. John M. Goddard, "Kayaks down the Nile," *National Geographic Magazine* 107, no. 5 (May 1955): 713–714; and Walter W. Haines, *Money, Prices, and Policy* (New York: McGraw-Hill, 1961), 34.

2. More details in Aris N. Poulianos, *Anthropos* (Athens: A.E.E. Publishers, 1977), 16–61. Also, Kon. B. Kourtouvelis, *I Anthropologisi tis Proistorias* (The Human Pre-history) (Athens: Davlos, 1998), Chapter 1; *Epsilon,* Athens, October 10, 1995; *Apogevmatini*, February 17, 1994; and *Ethnos*, February 17, 1994. For the crossing of the Atlantic by Odysseus, around 1200 B.C., to Nova Scotia of Canada and down the U.S. seashores to the straits of Cuba and Haiti, where he faced the Sirens, and back to Ithaca (Greece), as well as the crossing of the Argonauts, before, to the area of the Amazon river in Latin America, see Henriette Mertz (the American archeologist), *The Wine Dark Sea: Homer's Heroic Epic of the North Atlantic* (Chicago: H. Mertz, 1964), Chapters 12–14; and *Kampana*, New York, August 10, 1999, 2–3.

3. Norman Angell, *The Story of Money* (New York: Frederick A. Stokes Company, 1929), Chapter 5.

4. Plato, *Laws*, Book V, 313.

5. More details in Terrot Glover, *The Challenge of the Greeks and Other Essays* (New York: Macmillan, 1942), Chapters 1–3. Also, C. Stanley, *Roots of the Tree* (London: Oxford University Press, 1936), 24. For the existence of bankers in the Greek cities and of the circulation of bills of exchange, see Thorold Rogers, *The Economic Interpretation of History* (London: 1888), 184, 206.

6. A. R. Burns, *Money and Monetary Policy in Early Times* (London: 1927), 365; and Norman Angell, *The Story of Money*, 104.

7. Walter W. Haines, *Money, Prices, and Policy* (New York: McGraw-Hill, 1961), 42.

8. David Ricardo, *Principles of Political Economy and Taxation* (London: 1817), 341. More on gold and liberalism in Joseph A. Schumpeter, *History of Economic Analysis*, with a new introduction by Mark Perlman (New York: Oxford University Press, 1994), 1074–1079.

9. More details on the functions and structure of the Fed in the Board of Governors, *The Federal Reserve System: Purposes and Functions* (Washington, D.C.: Federal Reserve Bank, 1963), 1–29. Also, Clifton H. Kreps, Jr., *Money, Banking and Monetary Policy* (New York: Ronald Press, 1962), Chapter 27. For the support of controls by the central bank, see John M. Keynes, *A Treatise on Money*, Vol. 1, Book 3 (London: 1930), Chapter 9.

10. William N. Gianaris, "Weighted Voting in the International Monetary Fund and the World Bank," *Fordham International Law Journal* 14, no. 4 (1990–1991): 910–945.

11. Robert Triffin, *Gold and the Dollar Crisis* (New Haven: Yale University Press, 1961), 89.

12. For IMF's criticism, see George P. Shultz, William E. Simon, and Walter B. Wriston, "Who Needs the IMF?" *Wall Street Journal*, February 3, 1998, A22.

13. Ibrahim F. Shihata, "The World Bank in the 1990s," in Dilip K. Das, ed., *International Finance: Contemporary Issues* (New York: Routledge, 1993), 72, 84.

14. Richard T. Baillie and William P. Osterberg, "Why Do Central Banks Intervene?," *Journal of International Money and Finance* 16, no. 6 (December 1997): 909–919.

15. For credit creation, see Joseph A. Schumpeter, *History of Economic Analysis*, with a new Introduction by Mark Perlman (New York: Oxford University Press, 1994), 1110–1117; and Walter Bagehot, *Lombard Street: A Description of the Money Market* (London: 1873).

16. Robert M. Morgenthau, "On the Trail of Global Capital," *New York Times*, November 9, 1998, A25.

17. Joseph Kahn, "Thailand Nationalizes Three Faltering Private Banks," *New York Times*, February 7, 1998, D1, D3.

18. Anthony DePalma, "Bank Merger Fever Spreads to Canada," *New York Times*, April 18, 1998, D1 and D2.

CHAPTER 3

1. David Ricardo, *The Principles of Political Economy and Taxation* (Homewood, Ill.: Irwin, 1963), Chapter 7; and Bella Balassa, "An Empirical Demonstration of Classical Comparative Cost Theory," *Review of Economics and Statistics* (August 1963): 231–38.

2. Dominick Salvatore, *International Economics* (Englewood Cliffs, N.J.: Prentice Hall, 1998), Chapter 13; and Peter B. Kenen, *The International Economy* (New York: Cambridge University Press, 1994), Chapter 14.

3. For a comparison with the Renaissance, see Thomas L. Friedman, *The Lexus and the Olive Tree* (New York: Farrar, Straus and Giroux, 1999), Chapter 1.

4. Further discussion in John Gray, *False Dawn: The Delusions of Globalism* (New York: The New Press, 1999).

5. Nicholas V. Gianaris, *Contemporary Public Finance* (Westport, Conn.: Greenwood, 1989), Chapter 3. For the social benefits of gasoline taxes, see Nicholas V. Gianaris, "A Tax on Gasoline? Better Get Used to It," *New York Times*, February 17, 1993, A18; and his "Making It Progressive," *New York Times*, April 29, 1993, A22.

6. David E. Sanger, "The Shipwreck in Seattle," *New York Times*, December 5, 1999, A26.

7. For trade and investment liberalization, see C. P. Rao, ed., *Globalization, Privatization, and Free Market Economy* (Westport, Conn.: Greenwood, 1998).

8. Socioeconomic outcomes of tariffs in Michael H. Lane, *Customs Modernization and the International Trade Superhighway* (Westport, Conn.: Greenwood, 1998).

9. "Banana Wars," *New York Times*, December 23, 1998, A30.

10. Ricky W. Griffin and Michael W. Pustay, *International Business: A Managerial Approach* (New York: Addison-Wesley, 1999), Chapter 3.

CHAPTER 4

1. For empirical findings, see Peter Isard, "How Far Can We Push the Law of One Price," *American Economic Review* (December 1977), 942–948; and N. Abuaf and P. Jorion, "Purchasing Power Parity in the Long Run," *Journal of Finance* (March 1990), 157–174.

2. Jane Martinson, "Amvescap Aims for Full Listing on NYSE," *Financial Times*, 3 November 1997, 19.

3. Paul Betts, "Italian Stock Exchange Set to Simplify Rules," *Financial Times*, 5 November 1997, 15.

4. Edward Wyatt, "Mutual Fund Lesson: How It Feels to Lose," *New York Times*, April 6, 1997, F1.

5. David Barboza, "Value of Seats on the Major Exchanges Decline," *New York Times*, June 12, 1998, D1.

6. The Bank of New York, *The Complete Depository Receipt Directory* (New York: The Bank of New York, 1996), 20–67.

7. Richard A. Grasso, "Globalization of the Equity Markets," *Fordham International Law Journal* 20, no. 4 (New York: Fordham International Law Journal, 1997), 11.

8. More in Thomas K. Grose, "U.S. Shares Cross Border via Internet," *USA Today*, June 1, 1999, 1B.

9. More details in Maximo V. Eng, Francis A. Lees, and Laurence J. Mauer, *Global Finance*, 2nd edition (New York: Addison-Wesley, 1998), 541–546.

10. International Monetary Fund, *International Capital Markets* (Washington, D.C.: International Monetary Fund, 1997), 10.

11. More details in Michael Melvin, *International Money and Finance*, 5th edition (New York: Addison-Wesley, 1996), Chapter 4; Dennis E. Logue, ed, *The WG&L Handbook of International Finance* (Cincinnati, Ohio: South-Western, 1995), Chapter 3; and James R. Lothian and Mark P. Taylor, "Real Exchange Rate Behavior," *Journal of International Money and Finance* 16, no. 6 (December 1997), 945–954.

12. Further analysis in Robert M. Gardiner, *The Dean Witter Guide to Personal Investing*, Revised edition (New York: Penguin Group, 1997), Chapter 9; and Gregory M. Martinez, "Extracting Market Views from the Price of Options and Futures," *Journal of Futures and Markets* 18, no. 1 (February 1998).

13. See F. Black and M. Scholes, "The Pricing of Options and Corporate Liabilities," *Journal of Political Economy* 81 (May-June 1973): 673–654; Myron S. Scholes, "Derivatives in a Dynamic Environment," *American Economic Review* 88, no. 3 (June 1998): 350–370; and R. C. Mexton, "Theory of Rational Option Pricing," *Bell Journal of Economics and Management Science* 4 (Spring 1973): 141–183. Also, Edward Tenner, "The Icarus Complex," *New York Times*, 13 October 1998, A19.

14. Burton G. Malkiel and J. P. Mei, "Hedge Funds: The New Barbarians at the Gate,"*Wall Street Journal*, September 29, 1998, A22.

CHAPTER 5

1. More details in Pedro Aspe, *Economic Transformation the Mexican Way* (Cambridge: MIT Press, 1993); Bradford De Long et al., "The Case for Mexico's Rescue," *Foreign Affairs* 25, 3 (May–June 1996): 8–14.

2. For privatizations in Canada, see Janet Smith, "Canada's Privatization Programme," in *Privatization and Deregulation in Canada and Britain*, ed. Jeremy Richardson (Aldershot, U.K.: Dartmouth, 1990), Chapter 3.

3. "France to Open to Investors Merged Aerospace Firm," *Wall Street Journal*, January 9, 1997, A8.

4. More in Nicholas V. Gianaris, *Modern Capitalism: Privatization, Employee Ownership, and Industrial Democracy* (Westport, Conn.: Praeger, 1996), Chapter 9. Also, Joseph Schumpeter, *Can Capitalism Survive* (New York: Harper and Row, 1978).

5. "Continent of Shareholders," *Financial Times*, 15 October 1997, 15. For the proportions of American households owning stock, see Edward Wyatt, "Share of Wealth in Stock Holdings Hits 50-Year High," *New York Times*, February 11, 1998, A1 and D4, and "A Snapshot of Stock Owners," *New York Times*, October 22, 1999, C10.

6. Anne Tergesen, "Making the Most of Your Stock Options," *Business Week*, May 31, 1999, 178–180.

7. Adam Bryant, "Feeding the New Work Ethic," *New York Times*, April 19, 1998, 1 and 4 week. John S. Reed, who expressed his desire for Citicorp expansion in his lecture in a seminar on foreign investment given by the author of this book at Fordham University, added $67 million in profit in a single day to his holdings of Citicorp's stock after the merger with Travelers was announced. Also, Sanford I. Weill, the chairman of Travelers, added $248 million for the same reason.

8. James Surowiecki, "Instant Gratification," *New York Times Magazine*, June 7, 1998, 94–98.

9. More in Joseph B. Treaster, "A $12 Billion Carrot for Prudential Policyholders," *New York Times*, 13 February 1998, A1, D3; and Leslie Scism, "Prudential's Plan to Go Public Reflects Industry Trend," *Wall Street Journal*, 18 February 1998, B4.

10. David Rynecki, "Internet IPOs: What Follows the Ballyhoo?" *USA Today*, May 28, 1999, 3B. For more, see www.IPO-fund.com.

11. Jacob Weisberg, "United Shareholders of America," *New York Times Magazine*, 25 January 1998, 29–32. Also, Rob Walker, "The IPO Boomers," *New York Times Magazine*, June 20, 1999, 15.

12. For assets shifting to stocks, see Edward Wyatt, "Share of Wealth in Stock Holdings Hits 50-Year High," *New York Times*, February 9, 1998, 1 and D4.

13. For Aristotle's aspect of labor, see James B. Murphy, *The Moral Economy of Labor: Aristotelian Theories on Economic Theory* (New Haven: Yale University Press, 1993).

14. For the share economic system see Nicholas V. Gianaris, *Contemporary Economic Systems: A Regional and Country Approach* (Westport, Conn.: Praeger, 1993), Chapter 7. Also, Jeffrey R. Bernstein, "Japanese Capitalism," in Thomas K. McCraw ed., *Creating Modern Capitalism* (Cambridge, Mass.: Oxford University Press, 1997), Chapter 12.

15. For the use of Keynesian theory to avoid depression, see Paul Krugman, *The Return of Depression Economics* (New York: W.W. Norton, 1999).

16. Paul Lews, "World Bank Says Poverty Is Increasing," *New York Times*, June 3, 1999, C7.

17. Nicholas V. Gianaris, *I Ellada kai I Evropaiki Enosi* (Greece and the European Union) (Athens: Estia, 1997), Chapter 4; and his "Aftodiahirizomena Panepistimia" (Self-Managed Universities), *Oikonomikos*, August 6, 1998, 101–102.

18. Manolis Kefalogiannis, "Dimosio Chreos: Elliniki Iconomia se Krisi" (Public Debt: The Greek Economy in Crisis), *Banking & Leasing* 2 (February 1998): 25–26; and George Kalamotousakis, "Dimosio Chreos: Exelixi, Chrimatodotisi, Epiptosis" (Public Debt: Evolution, Financing, Effects), *Banking & Leasing* 2 (February 1998) 18–19.

19. More on debt in Ian H. Giddy, *Global Financial Markets* (Lexington, Mass.: D.C. Heath and Company, 1993), Chapter 16. Also, Ronald I. McKinnon, "EMU as a Device for Collective Fiscal Retrenchment," *American Economic Review: Papers and Proceedings*, May 1997, 227–229.

20. "Kolibai Sta Hrei to Turkiko Kratos" (The Turkish Government Swims in Debt), *Proini*, New York, June 10, 1999, 12.

21. For the role of IMF, see Ephraim Clark, Michael Levasseur, and Patrick Rousseau, *International Finance* (London: Charman & Hall, 1993), Chapter 4.

CHAPTER 6

1. Further information in J. Jay Choi and John A. Doukas, ed., *Emerging Capital Markets* (Westport, Conn.: Quorum, 1998); and "Emerging Markets," *Financial Times*, November 17, 1998, 23.

2. More details in Bruno Solnik, *International Investments*, 3rd edition (New York: Addison-Wesley, 1996), Chapter 9.

3. More in Nicholas D. Kristof, "Asians Worry That U.S. Aid Is a New Colonialism," *New York Times*, 17 February 1998, A4. For innovations and growth in China, see Yuko Arayama and Panos Mourdoukoutas, *China against Herself: Innovation or Imitation in Global Business?* (Westport, Conn.: Quorum, 1999). For the United States–China trade agreement, see Steven Butler, "The Great Trade Wall," *U.S. News and World Report*, November 29, 1999, 51–52.

4. For recent reforms in Russia, see Rose Brady, *Kapitalizm: Russia's Struggle to Free Its Economy* (New Haven, Conn.: Yale University Press, 1999). Also, Yegor Gaidar, "Lessons of the Russian Crisis for Transition Economies," *Finance and Development*, June 1996; and Jeffry Bown, "Russia Keeps Up Momentum," *Financial Times*, 20 October 1997, 26.

5. For similar trends in Eastern Europe, see Demetreus S. Iatridis, *Privatization in Central and Eastern Europe* (Westport, Conn.: Quorum, 1998).

6. Christopher Bobinski and Vincent Boland, "Schroders to Advise Poland on Phone Float," *Financial Times*, February 4, 1998, 16.

7. For the Balkan stock markets, see Ionian Bank, *The Financial Services Market in the Balkans* (Athens: Haemus S.A., 1998), 7–142.

8. Alex Sarrigeorgiou, "Ta Ellinika Amivea pro tou 2000" (The Greek Mutual Funds before 2000), *Kathimerini*, February 1, 1998, 52.

9. Rudiger Dornbush, "Brazil's Incomplete Stabilization and Reform," in *Brookings Papers on Economic Activity* (Washington, D.C.: Brookings Institution, 1997), 367–394.

10. For inflationary rates in Venezuela, see IMF, *International Financial Statistics*, various issues.

CHAPTER 7

1. In the United States, for example, overseas private investment in developing countries is insured against three types of risk: war, expropriation, and inconvertibility of currency.

2. During the postwar period, most of the developing countries had high rates of return on total investment (domestic and foreign).

3. Majority-owned foreign affiliates of U.S. companies use, on the average, about 30 percent foreign funds, 15 percent U.S. funds, and 50 percent internal funds. See U.S. Government, *Survey of Current Business*, various issues.

4. There may be fears, though, that the trend of import substitution might lead to protectionism.

5. Foreign direct investment (FDI) outflow was $424 billion in 1997. FDI growth during 1980–1997 was 13 percent per year. Further information at www.IMF.org.

6. For example, IT&T has operations in about 70 countries and Citigroup in more than 100 countries.

7. In Canada, where many U.S. companies operate, people feel that economically they sleep in the same bed with an elephant (the United States).

8. For example, Japanese firms, such as Namura, Mitsubishi, and Mitsui, establish operations around the world, from Korea to Iran, Spain, and the United States, as do German and other firms.

9. Many European firms are moving lately into the emerging markets of Latin America to compete with similar American firms.

10. Cathy Newman, "Reed in $1.65 bn Deal to Buy Times Mirror Units," *Financial Times*, April 28, 1998, 1.

11. Claudia H. Deutsch, "Ciba Is Set for a Merger with Clariant," *New York Times*, November 10, 1998, C1.

12. Robert Thomson, "GE Capital Target Collapsed LTCB Unit," *Financial Times*, November 30, 1998, 19.

13. "VW Wins Fight to Buy Rolls-Royce," *Wall Street Journal*, June 8, 1998, A16.

14. Ken Warn, "Asian Cloud over Buenos Aires," *Financial Times*, February 2, 1998, 24.

CHAPTER 8

1. Nicholas V. Gianaris, *Economic Development: Thought and Problems* (Hanover, Mass.: Christopher Publishing House, 1978), Chapter 5.

2. For further analysis, see Jacob Viner, *The Customs Union Issue* (New York: Carnegie Endowment for International Peace, 1950), 43; and Peter B. Kenen, *The International Economy* (New York: Cambridge University Press, 1994), Chapter 11.

3. Jane Martinson, "Euro 'Will Be Stronger Currency than the Dollar and the Yen,'" *Financial Times*, December 16, 1998, 3.

4. For EU expansion, see Nicholas V. Gianaris, *The European Community, Eastern Europe and Russia* (Westport, Conn.: Praeger, 1993), Chapter 2; and his *The European Community and the United States: Economic Relations* (Westport, Conn.: Praeger, 1991), Chapter 9. Also, Erik Jones, ed., *Joining Europe's Monetary Club: The Challenges for Smaller States* (New York: St. Martin's Press, 1998).

5. Regarding the stability and the usefulness of the capital / output ratio, see Nicholas V. Gianaris, "International Differences in Capital Output Ratios," *American Economic Review* 67 (June 1970): 465-477.

6. Athanasios Kanellopoulos (Euvoulos), "I Evropi kai o Horos tou Mellontos mas" (Europe and the Place of Our Future), *To Vima*, Athens, July 5, 1992, A14.

7. "European Union Looks Outwards," *Financial Times*, November 10, 1998, 3.

8. For related statistics, see *International Financial Statistics Yearbook*, 1998, 893, 897.

9. More on NAFTA in Nicholas V. Gianaris, *The North American Free Trade Agreement and the European Union* (Westport, Conn.: Praeger, 1998), Chapter 2.

10. For the trade effects of the euro upon the economies of Latin America and the Caribbean, see Dorte Verner, "The Euro and Latin America," *Finance and Development*, June 1999, 43-45.

CHAPTER 9

1. "Around the World in Brackets," *New York Times*, April 13, 1997, F10. For the U.S. simplification of tax brackets, see Nicholas V. Gianaris, "Greeks Had a Word for Regan Tax Plan," *New York Times*, January 1, 1985, A26.

2. Maximo V. Eng, Francis A. Lees, and Lawrence J. Mauer, *Global Finance*, 2nd edition (New York: Addison-Wesley, 1998), 442.

3. Thomas K. McCraw, "American Capitalism," in Thomas K. McCraw, ed., *Creating Modern Capitalism* (Cambridge, Mass.: Harvard University Press, 1997), Chapter 9.

4. More in "Dial M for Merger," *New York Times*, July 28, 1998, D6. Also, Richard Waters, "U.S. Telecoms Industry Set for Another Mega-Merger," *Financial Times*, May 17, 1999, 1, 17.

5. Christopher Parkes, "Comcast to Buy MediaOne for $60 bn," *Financial Times*, March 23, 1999, 1. Also, David Bank, "Comcast Mulls Role for Microsoft, AOL," *Wall Street Journal*, April 27, 1999, A3.

6. William L. Randol, "Rockefeller's Revenge," *New York Times*, December 3, 1998, A31.

7. Mark L. Sirower, *Synergy Trap: How Companies Lose the Acquisition Game* (New York: Simon & Schuster, 1997), Chapter 1.

8. David Owen, "France Completes Telecom Sale," *Financial Times*, November 30, 1998, 24.

CHAPTER 10

1. Thus, strict price controls, imposed in Athens during the fourth century B.C., in Rome in the Edict of Diocletian in A.D. 301, in England in the twelfth century, in India in 1770, in France during the French Revolution, in America in 1788, and in many countries during World War II, have always been a miserable failure.

2. A distinction can be made between the corporate economy (a market system with a large number of big corporations, as that of the Western countries) and the corporate state (a single hierarchical economic structure, as that of mainland China and the former Soviet Union and Eastern European countries).

3. More data in World Bank, *World Development Report* (Washington, D.C.: Oxford University Press, 1999), 198, 199.

4. There seems to be a subjective element in defining poverty. All of us are poor compared to a big shipowner, and all of us are rich compared to the starving peasant of India, for example. Although there is some degree of arbitrariness in the determination of income below which poverty exists, the level of nutrition and other basic requirements of life can be used for such a determination.

5. See, for example, Andrew Carnegie, *The Gospel of Wealth and Other Essays*, 1901.

6. They may even bring home new technology. Thus, Grace's Davidson Chemical joined the Laporte Industries of London to introduce new catalysts for synthetic gas. Also, Uniroyal's French subsidiary developed the steel-belted radial tire.

7. It is estimated that multinationals sell about three fourths of their manufacturing exports to their own subsidiaries.

8. Judith Miller, "Globalization Widens Rich-Poor Gap, U.N. Report Says," *New York Times*, July 13, 1999, A8.

Selected Bibliography

Angell, Norman. *The Story of Money*. New York: Frederick A. Stokes Company, 1929.

Arayama, Yuko and Panos Mourdoukoutas. *China against Herself: Innovation or Imitation in Global Business?* Westport, Conn.: Quorum, 1999.

Bagehot, Walter. *Lombard Street: A Description of the Money Market*. London: 1873.

Baillie, Richard T. and William P. Osterberg. "Why Do Central Banks Intervene?" *Journal of International Money and Finance* 16, 6 (1997).

Ballassa, Bella. "An Empirical Demonstration of Classical Comparative Cost Theory." *Review of Economics and Statistics* (August 1963).

Black, F. and M. Scholes. "The Pricing of Options and Corporate Liabilities." *Journal of Political Economy* 81 (May-June 1973).

Brady, Rose. *Kapitalizm: Russia's Struggle to Free Its Economy*. New Haven, Conn.: Yale University Press, 1999.

Burns, A. R. *Money and Monetary Policy in Early Times*. London, 1927.

Butler, Steven. "The Great Trade Wall." *U.S. News and World Report* (29 November 1999): 51–52.

Choi, J. and John A. Doukas, ed. *Emerging Capital Markets*. Westport, Conn.: Quorum, 1998.

Clark, Ephraim, Michael Levasseur, and Patrick Rousseau. *International Finance*. London: Charman & Hall, 1993.

Dornbush, Rudiger. "Brazil's Incomplete Stabilization and Reform" In *Brookings Papers on Economic Activity*. Washington, D.C.: Brookings Institution, 1997.

Eng, Maximo, Francis A. Lees, and Laurence J. Mauer. *Global Finance*. New York: Addison-Wesley, 1998.

Galbraith, John Kenneth. "Issues for the Millennium," *Finance and Development* 36, 4 (1999): 2–5.

Gianaris, Nicholas V. *Contemporary Economic Systems: A Regional and Country Approach*. Westport, Conn.: Praeger, 1993.

——. *The European Community, Eastern Europe and Russia*. Westport, Conn.: Praeger 1993.

——. *The European Community and the United States: Economic Relations*. Westport, Conn.: Praeger, 1991.

——. *Geopolitical and Economic Changes in the Balkan Countries*. Westport, Conn.: Praeger, 1996.

——. "Helping Eastern Europe Helps the West." *New York Times* (6 February 1990): A28.

——. "International Differences in Capital Output Ratios." *American Economic Review* 67 (June 1970): 465–477.

——. "Making It Progressive." *New York Times* (29 April 1993): A22.

——. *Modern Capitalism: Privatization, Employee Ownership, and Industrial Democracy*. Westport, Conn.: Praeger, 1996.

——. *The North American Free Trade Agreement and the European Union*. Westport, Conn.: Praeger, 1998.

Gianaris, William N. "Weighted Voting in the International Monetary Fund and the World Bank." *Fordham International Law Journal* 14, 4 (1990–1991).

Giddy, Ian H. *Global Financial Markets*. Lexington, Mass.: D.C. Heath and Company, 1993.

Glover, Terrot. *The Challenge of the Greeks and Other Essays*. New York: Macmillan, 1942.

Grasso, Richard A. "Globalization of the Equity Market," *Fordham International Law Journal* 20, 4 (1997).

Gray, John. *False Dawn: The Delusions of Globalism*. New York: The New Press, 1999.

Grose, Thomas K. "U.S. Shares Cross Border via Internet." *USA Today* (1 June 1999): 1B.

Haines, Walter W. *Money, Prices and Policy*. New York: McGraw-Hill, 1961.

Iatrides, Demetreus S. *Privatization in Central and Eastern Europe*. Westport, Conn.: Quorum, 1998.

International Monetary Fund (IMF) *International Capital Markets*. Washington, D.C.: IMF, 1999.

Isard, Peter. "How Far We Can Push the Law of One Price." *American Economic Review* (1977).

Kaplan, Robert D. "Could This Be the New World?" *New York Times* (27 December 1999): A23.

Kenen, Peter. *The International Economy*. New York: Cambridge University Press, 1994.

Keynes, John M. *A Treatise on Money*. London: 1930.

Krugman, Paul. *The Return to Depression Economics*. New York: W.W. Norton, 1999.

Lews, Paul. "World Bank Says Poverty Is Increasing." *New York Times* (3 June 1999): C7.

Logue, Dennis E., ed. *The WG&L Handbook of International Finance*. Cincinnati, Ohio: South-Western, 1995.

Malkiel, Burton G. and J. P. Mei. "Hedge Funds: The New Barbarians at the Gate." *Wall Street Journal* (29 September 1998): A22.

Martinez, Gregory M. "Extracting Market Views from the Price of Options and Futures." *Journal of Futures and Markets* 18, 1 (1998).

Martinson, Jane. "Amvescap Aims for Full Listing on NYSE." *Financial Times* (3 November 1997): 19.

Maslin, Fred. "Globalism in 2100," *New York Times* (28 December 1999): A24.

Melvin, Michael. *International Money and Finance*. New York: Addison-Wesley, 1996.

Miller, Judith. "Globalization Widens Rich-Poor Gap, U.N. Report Says." *New York Times* (13 July 1999): A8.

Morgenthau, Robert M. "On the Trail of Global Capital," *New York Times* (9 November 1998): A25.

Murphy, James B. *The Moral Economy of Labor: Aristotelian Theories on Economic Theory*. New Haven: Yale University Press, 1993.

Plato, *Laws*. In *The Dialogs of Plato*, trans. B. Jowett. New York, 1876.

Poulianos, Aris N. *Anthropos*. Athens: A.E.E. Publishers, 1977.

Rao, C. P., ed. *Globalization, Privatization, and Free Market Economy*. Westport, Conn.: Greenwood, 1998.

Ricardo, David. *The Principles of Political Economy and Taxation*. 1817.

Rynecki, David. "Internet IPOs: What Follows the Ballyhoo." *USA Today* (28 May 1999): 3B.

Salvatore, Dominick. *International Economics*. Englewood Clffs, N.J.: Prentice Hall, 1998.

Sanger, David E. "The Shipwreck in Seattle." *New York Times* (5 December 1999): A26.

Scholes, Myron S. "Derivatives in a Dynamic Environment." *American Economic Review* 88, 3 (June 1998): 350–370.

Schumpeter, Joseph A. *Capitalism, Socialism and Democracy*, 2d edition. New York: Harper and Brothers, 1947.

Shultz, George, William E. Simon, and Walter B. Wriston. "Who Needs the IMF?" *Wall Street Journal* (3 February 1998): A22.

Sirower, Mark L. *Synergy Trap: How Companies Lose the Acquisition Game*. New York: Simon & Schuster, 1997.

Smith, Janet. "Canada's Privatization Programme." In *Privatization and Deregulation in Canada and Britain*, ed. Jeremy Richardson. Aldershot, U.K.: Darmouth, 1990.

Solnik, Bruno. *International Investment*, 3rd edition. New York: Addison-Wesley, 1996.

Stanley, C. *Roots of the Tree*. London: Oxford University Press, 1936.

Tenner, Edward. "The Icarus Complex." *New York Times* (13 October 1998): A19.

Tergesen, Anne. "Making the Most of Your Stock Options." *Business Week* (31 May 1999): 178–180.

Triffin, Robert. *Gold and the Dollar Crisis*. New Haven: Yale University Press, 1961.

Verner, Dorte. "The Euro and Latin America." *Finance and Development* (June 1999): 43–45.

Viner, Jacob. *The Customs Union Issue*. New York: Carnegie Endowment for International Peace, 1950.

World Bank. *World Development Report*. Washington, D.C.: Oxford University Press, 1999.

www. IMF.org.

www.IPO-fund.com.

Wyatt, Edward. "Share of Wealth in Stock Holdings Hits 50-Year High." *New York Times* (11 February 1998): A1.

Index

Offshore banks, 26
Option markets, 83
Organization for Economic Coopera-
tion and Development (OECD),
28, 78, 197
Organization of Petroleum Exporting
Countries (OPEC), 174

Pareto's optimum, 56
People's capitalism, 92
Peru, 112, 117–122, 141, 166, 193
Plato, 13, 65, 102, 224
Poland, 34, 112, 129, 212
Poverty conditions, 232
Protectionism, 55
Purchasing power parity (PPP), 63–65

Repurchase agreements (repos), 90,
143
Ricardo, David, 103
Roman Empire, 14
Romania, 60, 128–130, 156, 170–171,
188
Russia, 4–5, 16, 21, 55, 67, 89, 113,
117–120, 125, 128, 132, 144, 147,
156, 199, 212

Schumpeter, Joseph, 3, 92, 235
Shareholder capitalism, 48, 226
Smith, Adam, 3, 16, 58, 103

Spain, 14, 21, 87, 140, 169, 180, 199
Sparta, ancient, 13, 202
Structural inflation, 52

Tariffs, 58–60
Tax rates, 198
Terms of trade, 42–46
Thatcherism, 47
Thucydides, 3, 165
Trade creation, 174–176
Trade diversion, 174–176
Turkey, 104, 112, 117–124, 159, 170–
171, 188, 195, 228

United Nations Relief and Rehabilita-
tion Administration (UNRA), 173
Uruguay, 142, 165
Uruguay Round, 57

Venezuela, 21, 76, 79, 117–122, 133–
142, 166, 174, 191, 193, 199, 228

World Bank, 4–5, 10, 18–19, 21, 23,
120, 130, 151–152, 174, 203
World Trade Organization (WTO), 4–
5, 10, 18, 57–58, 61, 124, 174
World War I, 17
World War II, 19, 39, 38, 149

Yugoslavia, 128, 130, 156, 165, 188

ABOUT THE AUTHOR

NICHOLAS V. GIANARIS is Professor of Economics at Fordham University. Dr. Gianaris is the author of several books, including, most recently, *The North American Free Trade Agreement and the European Union* (Praeger, 1998); *Modern Capitalism, Privatization, Employee Ownership, and Industrial Democracy* (Praeger, 1996); *Geopolitical and Economic Changes in the Balkan Countries* (Praeger, 1996); *Modern Capitalism* (Praeger, 1995); and *The European Community, Eastern Europe, and Russia* (Praeger, 1994).